MW00780801

Wordless Books

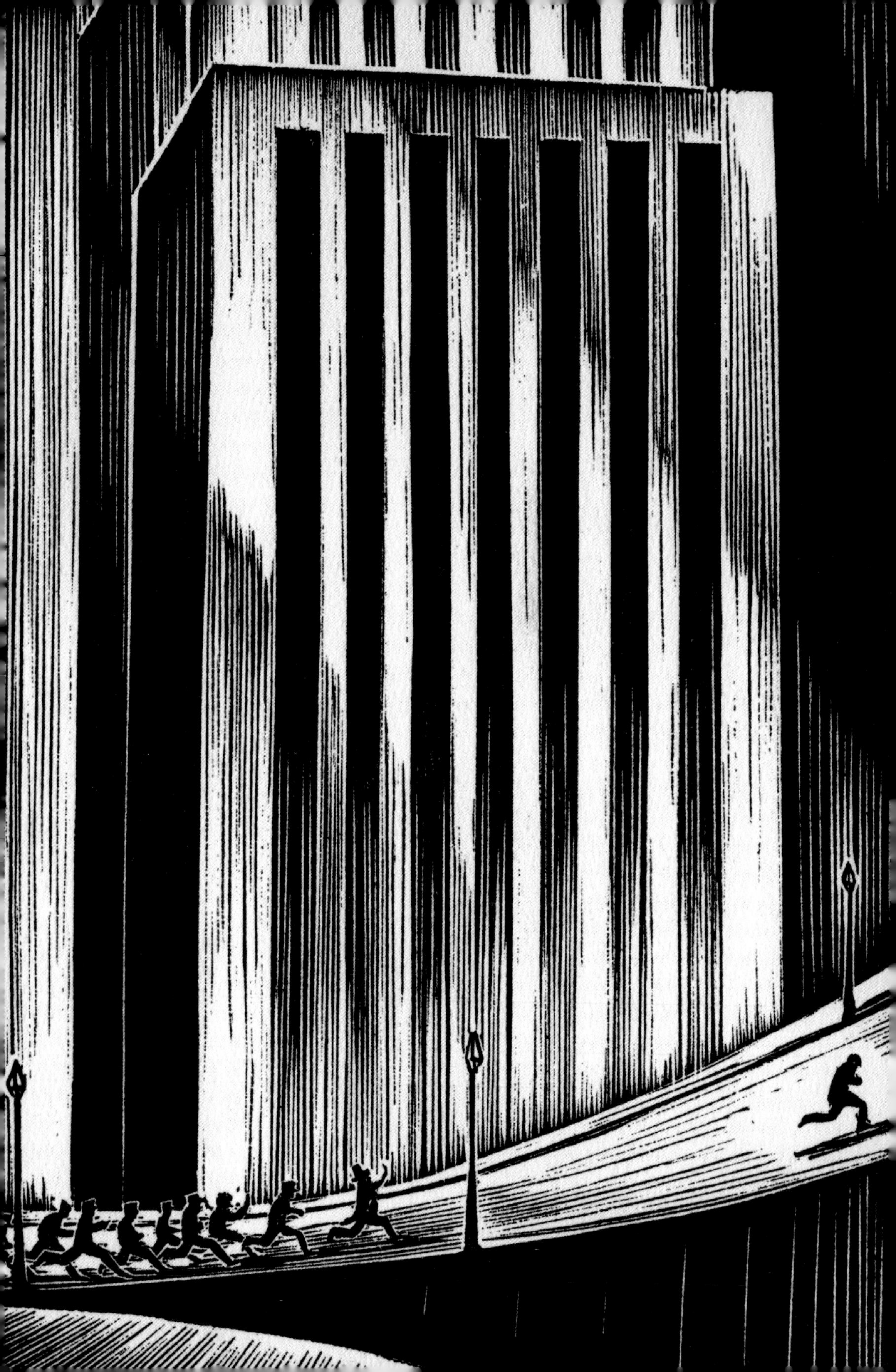

Wordless Books

The Original Graphic Novels

David A. Beronä

Introduction by
Peter Kuper

Abrams, New York

TO ROSE, WHO MAKES IT ALL SO MUCH EASIER

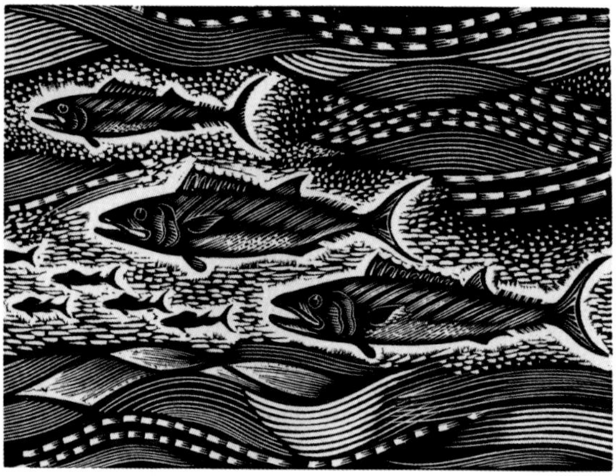

Author's Note

Although this book represents the major woodcut novels and wordless books from 1918 to 1951, there are some titles that I have not included. These include lesser-known works by Frans Masereel, who published more than fifty wordless books before his death in 1972, biblical works related to the life of Christ, biographical works, and some anomalies.

The biblical works are *The Life of Christ in Woodcuts* (1930) by James Reid, *Die Passion* (1936) by Otto Pankok, and *Kristus* (1944) by Helena Bochořáková-Dittrichová.

The biographical works are by Charles Turzak, and they are *Abraham Lincoln: A Biography in Woodcuts* (1933) and *Benjamin Franklin: A Biography in Woodcuts* (1935).

The anomalies are *Mitsou Quarante Images par Baltusz* (1921) by thirteen-year-old Balthus; a sailor's journal, *Das Logbuch* (1929), by Hans Alexander Müller; a short work, *Gottlose* (1932) by Willy Fries; print albums by Clément Moreau (Carl Meffert); *Horse and Rider* (1930) and *The Road of Suffering: A History of the Jews in 13 Woodcuts* (1933) by P. K. Hoenich, which were self-published works with reprinted editions; and *Scottsboro Alabama: A Story in Linoleum Cuts* (1935) by Lin Shi Khan and Tony Perez, which was reprinted in 2002 from the only known copy.

Contents

Speechless

Introduction by Peter Kuper

It may seem a little contrary to write about a wordless art form, but a blank sheet of paper doesn't carry much in the way of insight, so bear with me.

In the biblical story of the Tower of Babel, humanity has developed one unifying language and comes together to build a stairway to heaven. God, as was His wont, destroys the structure and as an added bonus undoes people's ability to communicate through a single language for all time.

Apparently He overlooked Lynd Ward's picture story *Gods' Man*.

Ward, like Frans Masereel, Otto Nückel, and the other artists included in this collection, discovered a way to sidestep our language barriers and create complex, political, emotional, and humorous stories that can be universally understood.

We humans have been using drawings to tell stories as far back as when our ancestors called caves home. Pictures were used to describe their actions—say hunting a wooly mammoth—and the very traces of human existence remain thanks to the artists who scrawled on those cavernous walls.

Throughout human history, image functioned as language—including the Sumerians' cuneiform pictograms carved in clay tablets, the expressive symbols painted on the tombs in Egypt, and Chinese scrolls with silent illustrated epics that unrolled before readers' eyes.

Wordless picture stories have a unique and especially intimate relationship to their reader. In order to follow the narrative, these works ask the viewer to decipher what has taken place, then connect the dots from one image to the next. Though these stories can be quickly scanned and comprehended, what they offer grows with repeated viewing. The more you scrutinize each image, the more information unfolds. The process is a rewarding one as details, unnoticed at first glance, gain significance and express a world of meaning. The effective use of symbols by these artists is a reminder of the symbols' power. Just as a simple ring can represent a couple's lifelong commitment to each other, a flower can suggest all that is innocent and chaste.

Looking for similarities among these artists you find that many share a contrasting use of black and white, dark and light, with a dash of yin and yang. Most also share a connection through choice of materials. From wood engraving to leadcut to linoleum printing, these artists have chosen a medium with a process beyond the immediacy achieved by putting pen to paper. There is a unique quality to these print images that is arresting and iconic. It's as though the art were announcing a rally and needed to be read as easily on a lamp post as seen in a book. But a greater connection comes through in the choice of content. These artists were interested in illuminating the darkest corners of the human experience—not surprising given the times they lived through. From a couple of world wars to the Great Depression to the nuclear age, the artists were motivated by a fire they saw burning just outside their windows as well as in their hearts. They were acutely aware that this inferno could as easily immolate their world as it could their souls, and they wanted to share this vision.

Though these tales are from another era and could be regarded as mere relics of the past, they are as current as our daily newspaper headlines. They capture the horror, humor, and challenges of our modern times, much as Franz Kafka and Charlie Chaplin have, and transcend the date of their creation. They have also gone on to influence a legion of artists, including comics master Will Eisner, who coined the term "graphic novel," and was clearly inspired by Lynd Ward's monumental cityscapes and pantomime storytelling.

Looking through this diverse collection of work you'll discover that David A. Beronä has excavated a treasure trove. In these pages you'll experience nothing less than *Childhood*, *Passionate Journey*, and *Destiny*. You will laughingly see *He Done Her Wrong*, and encounter the lyrical underbelly of *Song Without Words*. From one chapter to the next, the vibrant storytellers included here provide us with the opportunity to simultaneously have an intimate conversation with history, while shaking hands with our future.

Peter Kuper is an accomplished illustrator and writer whose work appears regularly in *Time, The Nation,* and *The New York Times*. His wordless picture stories include *The System, Eye of the Beholder, Mind's Eye, Speechless,* and *Sticks and Stones,* which won the 2004 Society of Illustrators' Gold Medal. Kuper has done adaptations of *Franz Kafka's Metamorphosis* and *Upton Sinclair's The Jungle,* as well as numerous other graphic novels, including his most recent, *Stop Forgetting to Remember.* He also writes and draws the pantomime strip "Spy vs. Spy" for *MAD* Magazine every month.

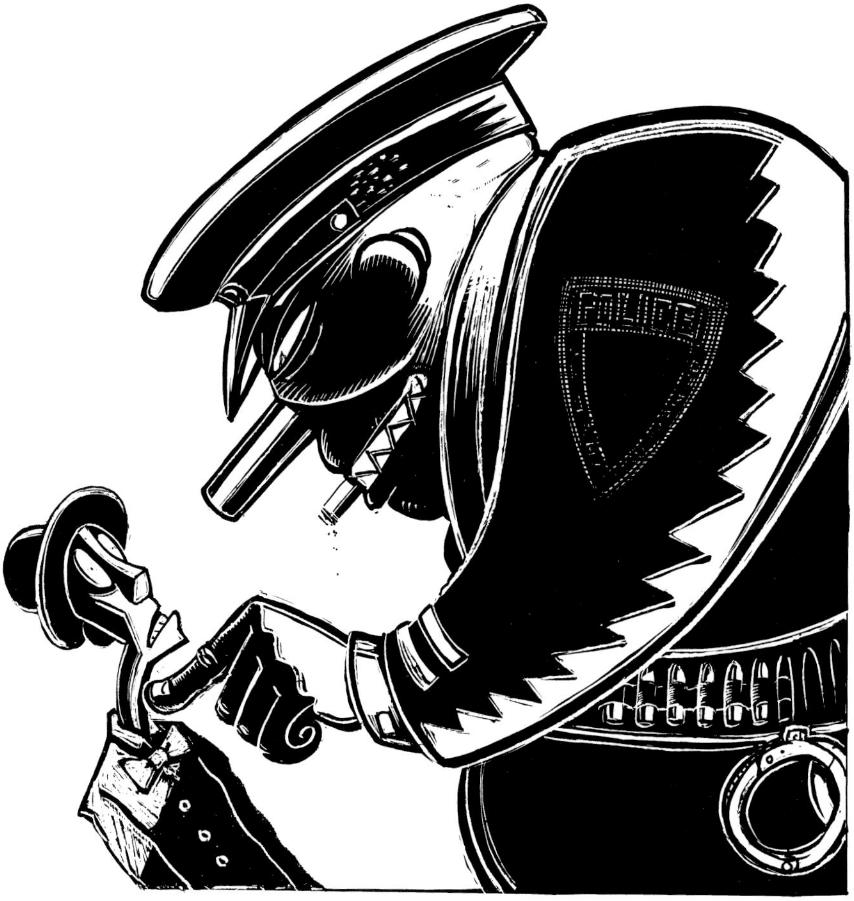
POLICE

Chapter One
Historical Background

When Thomas Mann, winner of the Nobel Prize for Literature in 1929, was asked what movie had made the greatest impression on him, Mann replied, *"Passionate Journey."* Although Mann's reply sounds like the title of a film by D. W. Griffith, it was, in fact, a novel in woodcuts by Frans Masereel.

These unconventional wordless books are imaginative and realistic stories told in black-and-white pictures. The term "woodcut novels" refers to the medium of not only woodcuts but wood engravings, linocuts, and leadcuts. Although woodcut novels have their roots spreading back through the history of graphic arts, including block books and playing cards, it was not until the early part of the twentieth century that they were conceived and published. The genre never reached a large audience except for a few titles by the early pioneers Frans Masereel and Lynd Ward that still remain in print today. Despite their short-lived popularity, woodcut novels had an important impact on the development of comics art, particularly the contemporary graphic novel with its focus on adult themes.

There were three elements in prominence at the time that Frans Masereel created his wordless books. First was the revival of the woodcut as a means of artistic expression, especially by the German Expressionists. By the end of the nineteenth century, the woodcut, with its aggressive display of black-and-white images, enjoyed a revival among Western artists, who focused on the social ills of a technological culture. Expressionism in the arts was also reflected in book illustration in Germany between 1907 and 1927, with work by recognized artists such as Oskar Kokoschka, Ernst Ludwig Kirchner, and Erich Heckel.

There are differences in thought about placing Masereel within the Expressionist movement. Roger Avermaete, who was Masereel's friend and author of one of the definitive books on Masereel, confirms that Masereel was against any type of label for his work and the natural tendency to include him in a group with other artists. It would be best to look at Masereel as affected by Expressionism with some strong links to the ideals of the movement, especially in his portrayal of the city in many of his woodcut novels, and notably in *La Ville* (*The City*), that the writer Lothar Lang, in *Expressionist Book Illustration in Germany 1907–1927,* credits persuasively as "the pictorial vocabulary of Expressionism." Despite this tenuous connection and the fact that Masereel was a Belgian, the common link with the German Expressionists and Masereel was their use of the woodcut.

DIE PASSION EINES MENSCHEN

25 HOLZSCHNITTE V. FRANS MASEREEL

BEI KURT WOLFF MUENCHEN

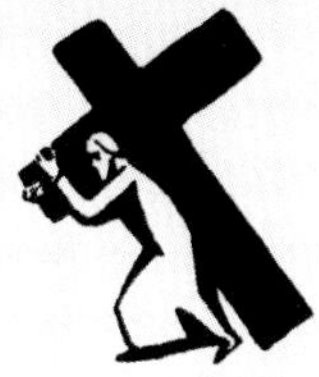

The second significant element at the time was the influence of silent cinema on the general public. Following World War I, film came into prominence with an influx of artists who left the theater for the increasing creative potential of the cinema. Examples of the visual innovations in cinema include the silent German masterpieces such as Robert Wiene's *The Cabinet of Dr. Caligari* (1920) and F. W. Murnau's *The Last Laugh* (1924). These two dynamic, *visual* films displayed thematic elements from the fantastic and realistic worlds that would be successfully repeated in the early wordless novels of Masereel. The silent cinema also had its heroes, such as the comedian Charlie Chaplin, who was able to create a distinctive character who reflected not only the humor but also the tragedy of life. This ability of the cinema to provide entertainment and strong public recognition was at the heart of the cinema's popularity. The more successful wordless novels captured these elements. For a public already familiar with black-and-white pictures that told a story, wordless books offered the public, in one sense, silent cinema in a portable book that they could "watch" at their leisure.

The third element was the medium of the cartoon in newspapers and journals, which had the ability to display a political and socially relevant idea in pictorial form. Like the cinema, comic strips also reached a pivotal development during the early years of the twentieth century. From the early work of the Swiss artist Rodolphe Töpffer (1799–1846)

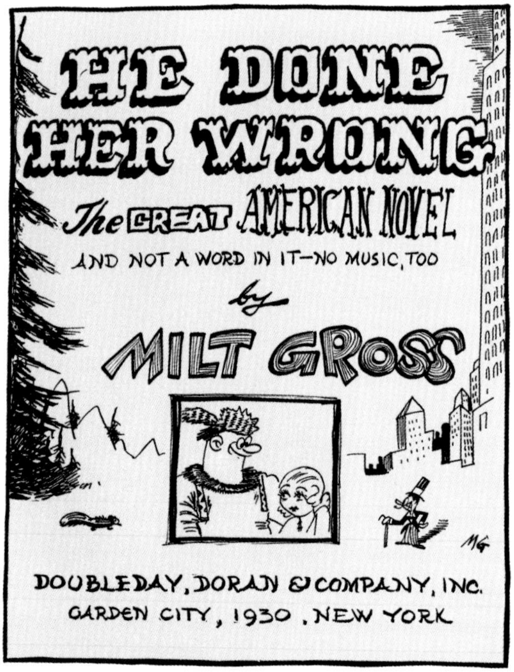
HE DONE HER WRONG
The GREAT AMERICAN NOVEL
AND NOT A WORD IN IT—NO MUSIC, TOO
by
MILT GROSS
MG
DOUBLEDAY, DORAN & COMPANY, INC.
GARDEN CITY, 1930. NEW YORK

and the publication of his *histoires en images*, or picture stories, to Richard F. Outcault's *The Yellow Kid*, published in 1895, comics grew into a powerful visual medium that entertained and satirized a growing industrialized society.

Woodcut novels developed from this growing comics culture and are recognized by comic artists and scholars today. In *Understanding Comics* (1993), artist and writer Scott McCloud refers to the woodcut novels of Masereel and Lynd Ward as "missing links" in the development of comics. Comics historian R. C. Harvey points out that Ward's woodcut novels "demonstrated the potential narrative function of body posture and facial expression." Graphic-novel pioneer Will Eisner acknowledged a great debt to Ward, who he claimed "established an historical precedent for modern graphic storytelling."

The growing use of woodcuts in book illustrations by the German Expressionists, the public's growing appetite for entertainment and information in the media of the silent cinema, and the comics and cartoons of the early part of the twentieth century were integral factors in the growing preoccupation with pictorial images. This dynamic period of artistic experimentation in Europe that followed World War I became a fertile period for the arrival of books without words. Although these three elements contributed to the arrival of the wordless book, it cannot be overstated how much debt is owed to Masereel himself.

PRELUDE
TO A MILLION YEARS

A BOOK OF WOOD
ENGRAVINGS
BY LYND WARD

EQUINOX · NEW YORK · 1933

Chapter Two

Frans Masereel

(1889–1972)

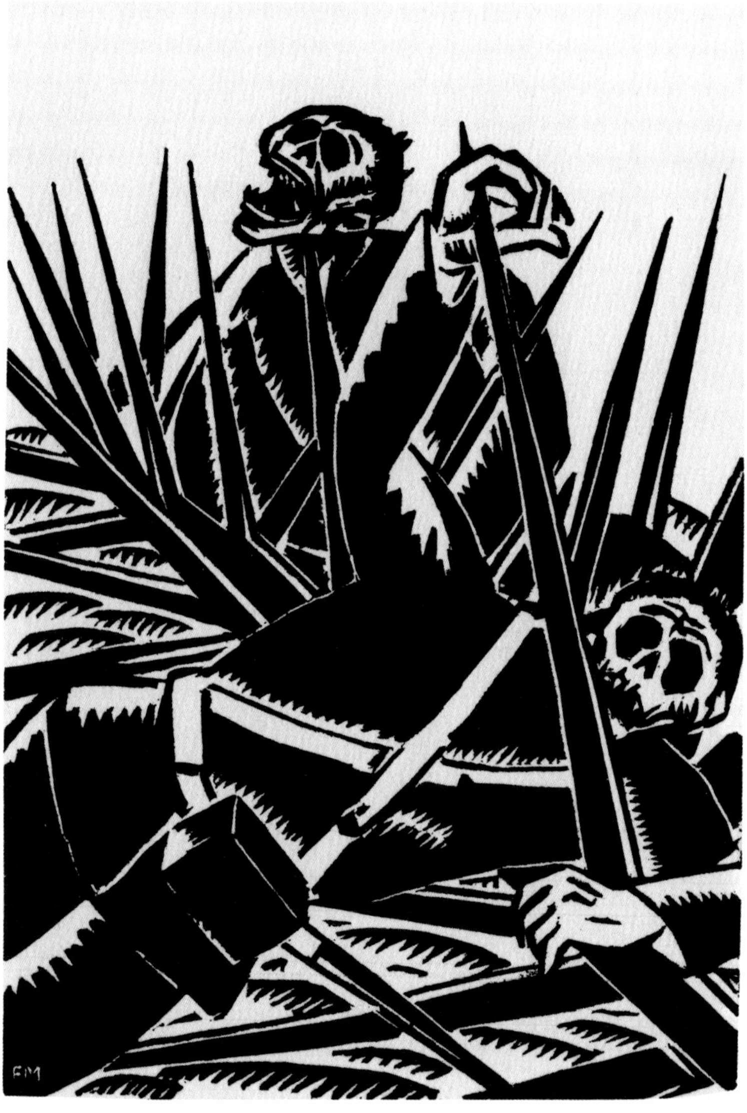
FM

Frans Masereel was born in 1889 to an upper-middle-class family in Ghent, Belgium. He showed interest in drawing at an early age and studied at the Académie des Beaux-Arts in Ghent in 1907 before traveling to Paris and Brittany. He returned to Ghent when World War I started, and moved to Geneva where he worked for the International Red Cross and the International Pacifist Movement. He then started his career as a political cartoonist, contributing drawings and woodcuts to the Swiss newspaper *La Feuille* and the periodical *Les Tablettes*. From this experience, Masereel learned to work effectively. He was given only a few hours to read the news, develop a theme, and create a drawing. It was from these early drawings that Masereel developed his style of characters wearing different coats of black and white that he would later use in his woodcut novels.

No other artist had such a lifelong love of the woodcut than Masereel. Throughout his life until his death in 1972, his predominant mode of expression was the woodcut. Both in his numerous book illustrations and over fifty wordless books, his passion, coupled with the vigor of his style, makes him a force to continually admire and study. Masereel's depiction of the Western industrial world is so complete that his friend, writer Stefan Zweig, wrote, "Should everything perish, all the books, the photographs and the documents, and we were left only with the woodcuts Masereel has created, through them alone we could reconstruct our contemporary world."

Masereel's first portfolios of woodcuts, printed in 1917, were *Debout les Morts* (*Arise Ye Dead*) (opposite) and *Les Morts Parlent* (*The Dead Speak*), which dealt with the disasters of war and presented shocking images of cruelty and death. Masereel displayed a culture that orchestrated World War I, where soldiers not only fought one another in hand-to-hand combat, but also fought machines such as tanks and airplanes. Following this military war, another war was fought—not in the trenches but in the factories, pitting human against machine. This striking picture of the battle between men and machines reflected the degree to which the industrialization of the Western world had evolved. Masereel addressed this industrial war beginning with his first woodcut novel, titled *25 Images de la Passion d'un Homme,* published in 1918.

25 Images de la Passion d'un Homme (1918)

In *25 Images de la Passion d'un Homme (Die Passion eines Menschen* in the German edition published by Kurt Wolff in 1921), Masereel provides us with a glimpse of the growing power and wealth of industrialists at the expense of a population of workers living in squalor. Masereel tells the story of a single woman who discovers she is pregnant (below), and is tossed out of her home in disgrace by her father. She has a son who is left to survive on the street alone (opposite), where he is eventually seized by the police for stealing bread and thrown into juvenile detention (page 18, top left). The boy grows up, finds a job as a laborer, works long hours (page 18, top right) and, like his fellow workers, drinks and enjoys the company of prostitutes. Eventually he grows tired of his drunken behavior and looks for other avenues of escape. To indulge his desire for knowledge, he walks in deep contemplation and reads books under a corner streetlight. He talks with the other workers about what he has learned in his books. He then shares his ideas with the factory owner, leads a revolt (page 18, bottom), and is arrested, tried by the authorities, and executed.

In this simple story, Masereel provides us with a glimpse of a young man who raises his fist in protest against the injustices endured by workers. The underclass is displayed against a backdrop of an industrialized city—constrained and unfeeling—that overshadows human beings. The lines of buildings and machines are vertical and bold, while those of the hero bend with rhythm and rise with motion. The scholar Perry Willett notes the numerous allusions to religious themes, with comparisons between the hero and Christ "suggesting that the man is a martyr for the working class." For example, at his trial, a cross that hangs on the wall behind the judges is visually centered on the hero (page 19).

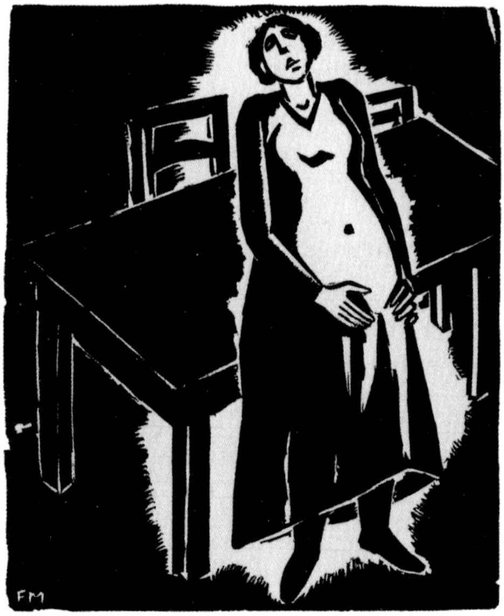
FM

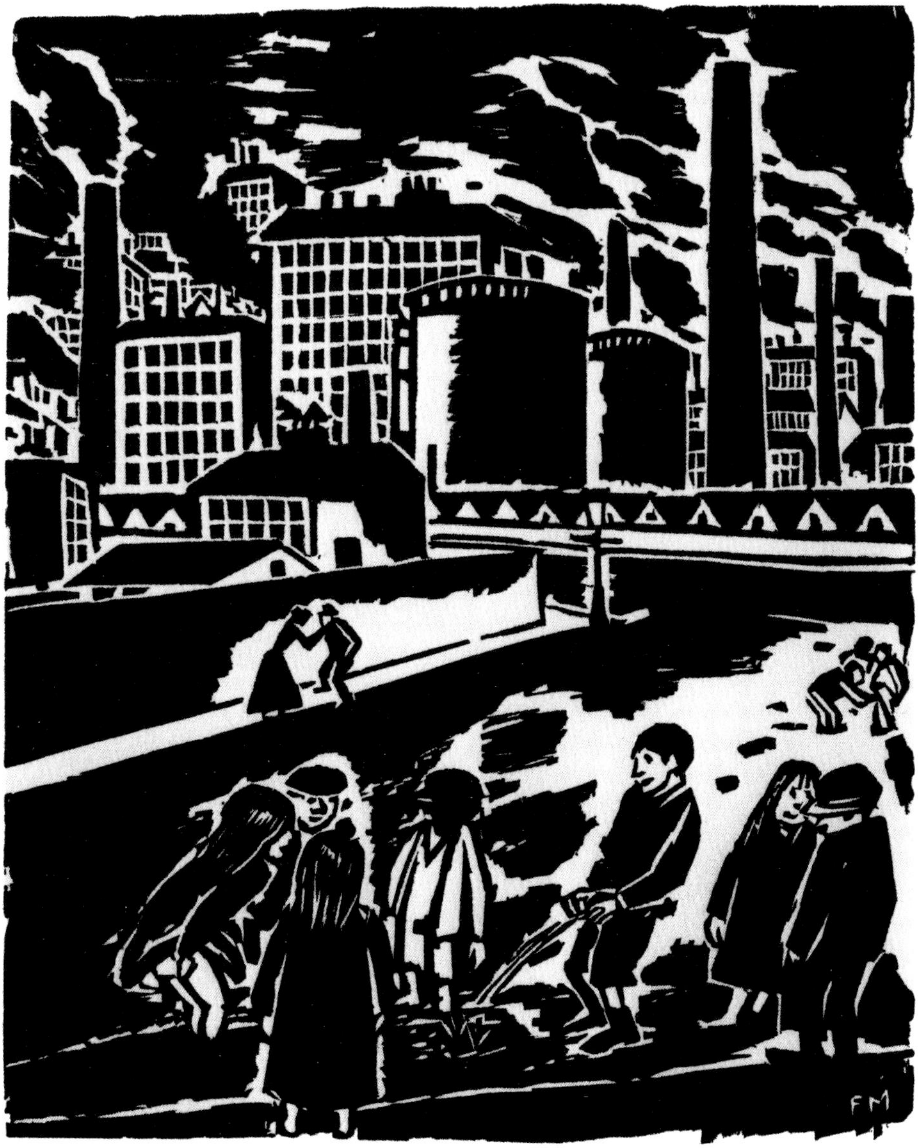
FM

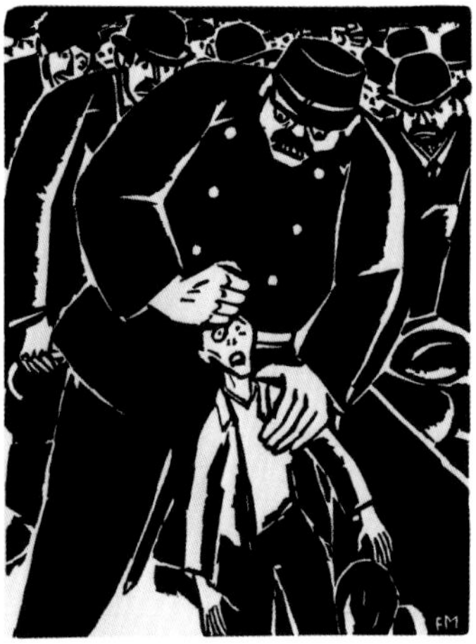
FM

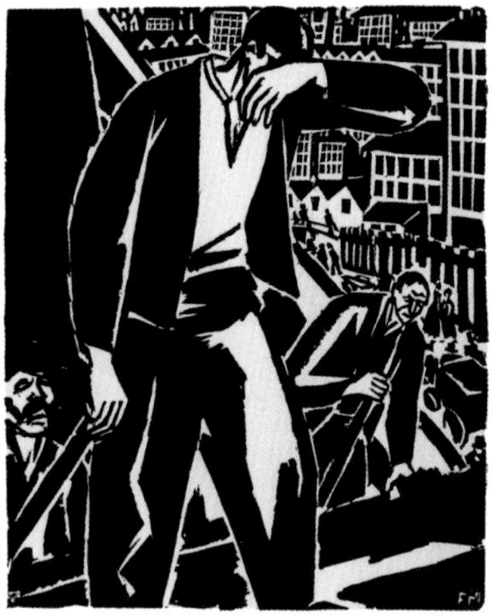
FM

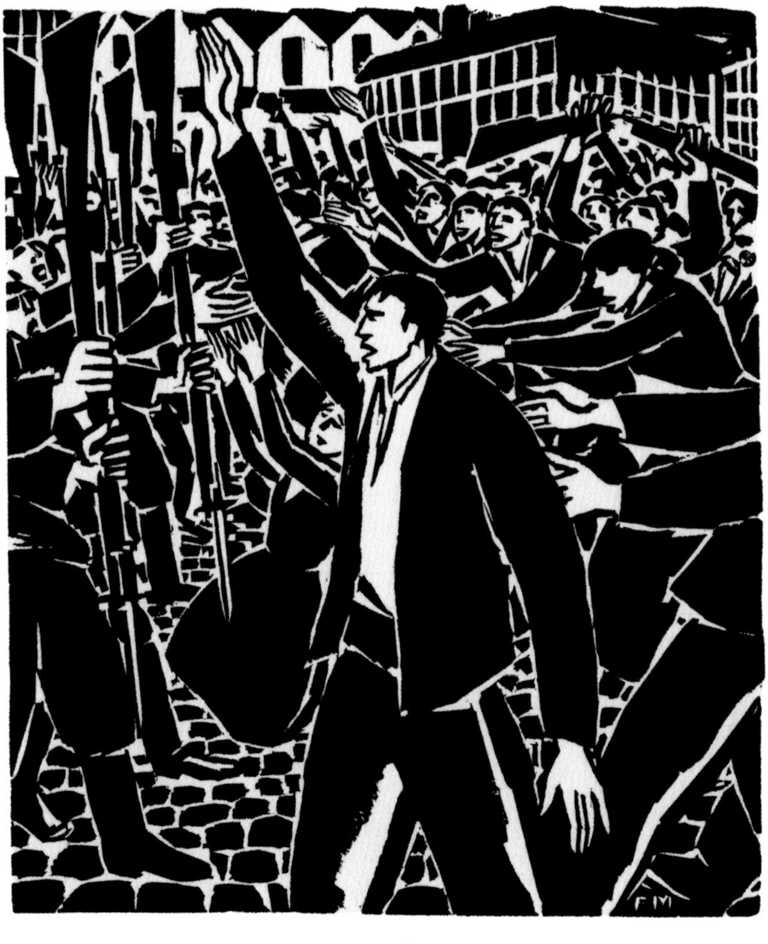
FM

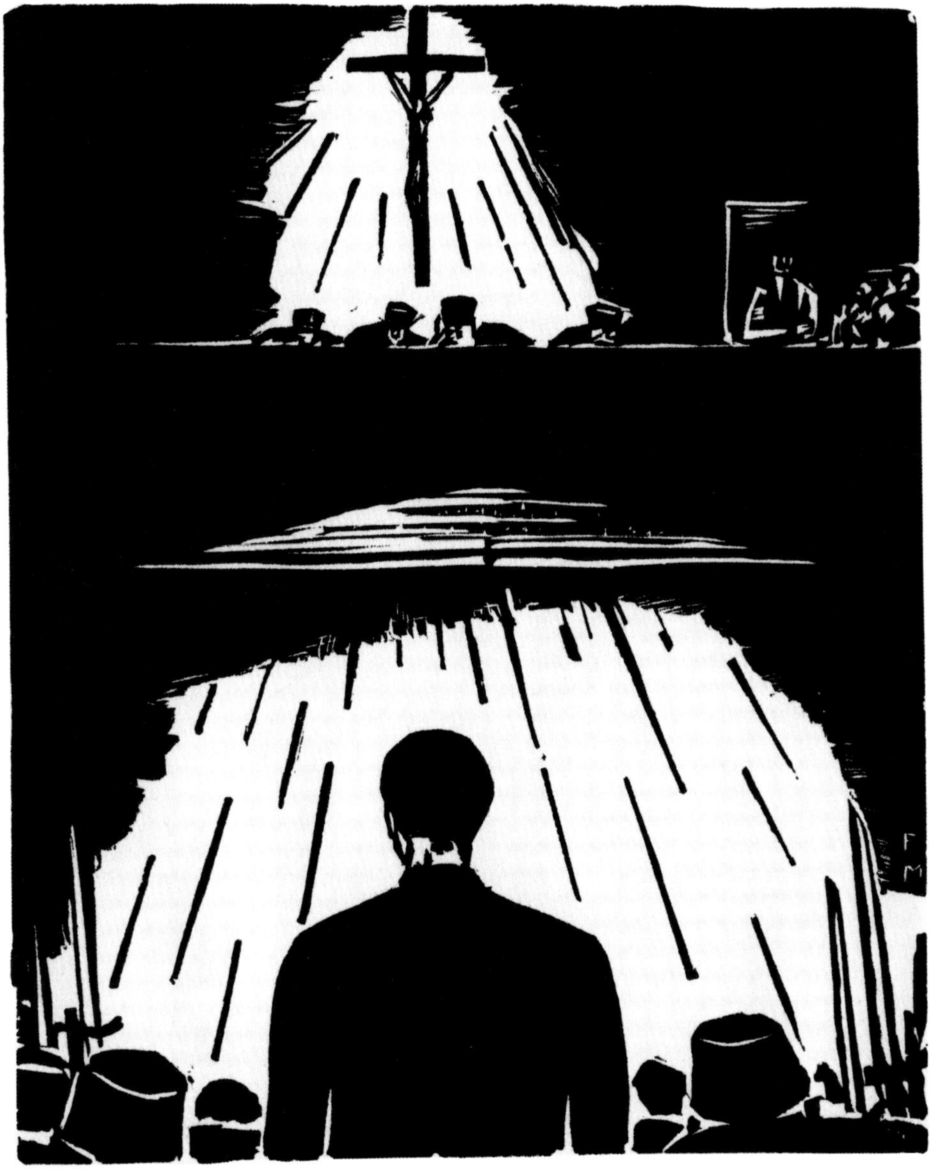

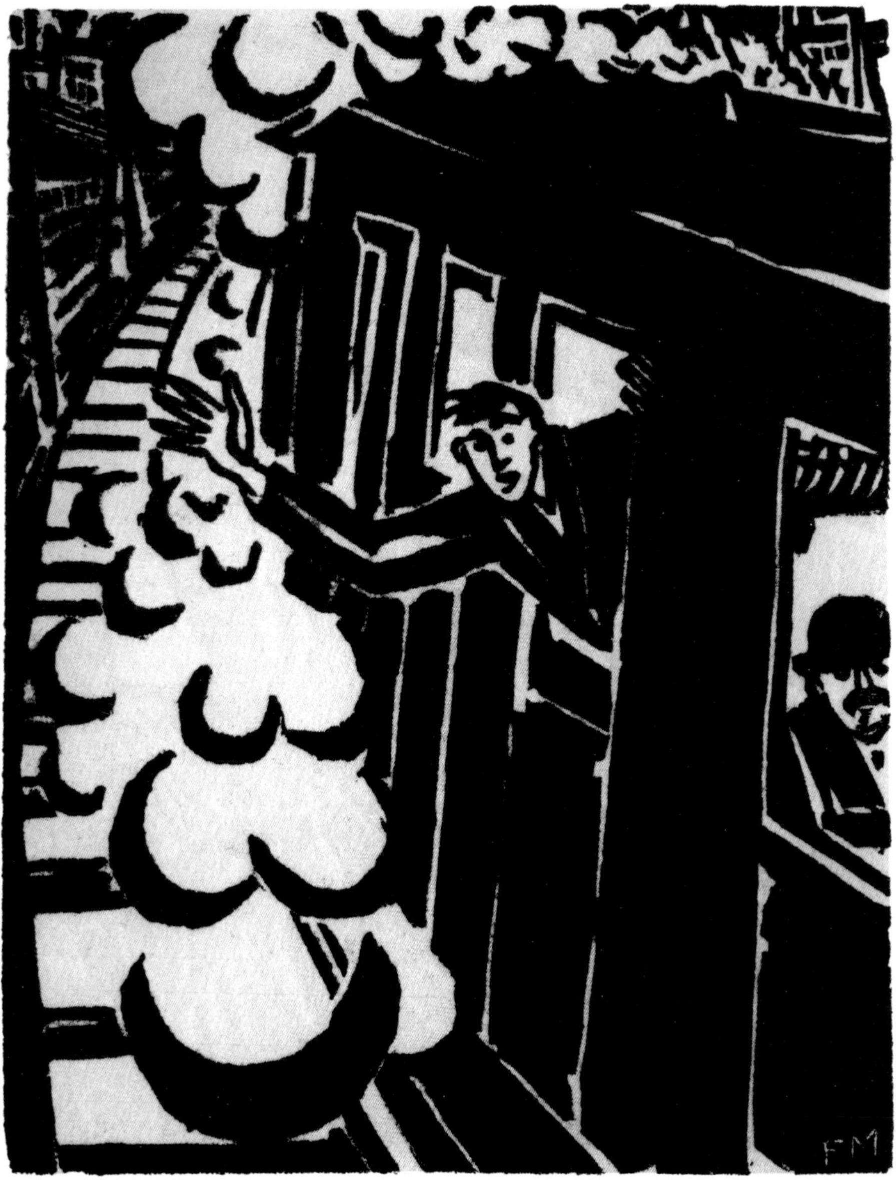
FM

Passionate Journey (1919)

A year after *25 Images de la Passion d'un Homme,* Masereel published his most successful woodcut novel, called *Mon livre d'heures: 167 images dessinées et gravées sur bois* (*Mein Stundenbuch* in German; *My Book of Hours* in English, and later known as *Passionate Journey*). The story dramatically displays the events in the life of a prototypical Western man at the turn of the century.

It is perhaps easier to get a concept of this work if one looks at Masereel's first woodcut novel as a short story and *Passionate Journey* as a novel, as far as length and plot intricacies are concerned. This woodcut novel portrays the experiences of a young man entering a city (opposite). He is a witness and, later, a participant in all the experiences that life offers, from the tragic to the comic (below and page 22).

Each page depicts an event in the hero's life, with a narrative thread running through the book. The hero is rejected by a prostitute with whom he has fallen in love (page 23), and later is left grief-stricken after the death of a woman he has cared for during her illness (page 24). In between these two relationships are numerous adventures from around the world (pages 25–27) and impetuous behavior, such as urinating from the top of a building on pedestrians on the street below (page 28, top) or farting at a passing delegation of businessmen (page 28, bottom). In both these situations, the hero's behavior is designed to snub the hypocritical and deceitful culture around him. This book reveals the enormous variety of experiences that Masereel packs into the life of his hero—a true everyman of the twentieth century.

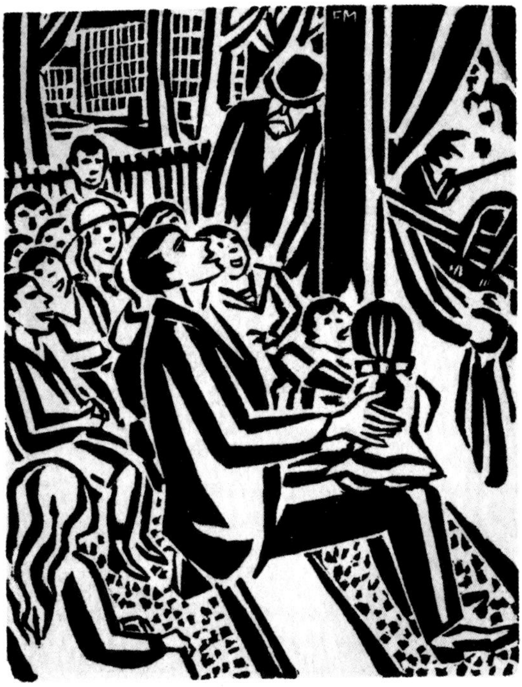
FM

Masereel weaves the emotional ties between the reader and the main character in black-and-white prints with dimensions of 3 ½ x 2 ¾ inches. The small woodcuts in this book provide an intended intimacy between the reader and Masereel. The reader is encouraged to slip this book inside his pocket, to use it as a book of prayer or meditation as well as for entertainment.

There is enough openness in the pictures to provide readers with individual interpretations and a basis for pursuing their own personal narratives, aside from Masereel's hero in the book. For example, what seems like a traditional ending to a well-spun narrative of a rather unique and unconventional individual is suddenly turned upside down in the final pages. The hero walks deep into the forest, happily raising his arms in celebration of nature, lies down to rest, and dies. His skeleton rises up with fists held high as it stomps on his heart. Without a heart, the hero skips through the universe, and in the final picture waves at the reader (page 29). The ending asks of us: After our death, is the human heart left behind on earth while the spirit is free to roam for eternity? In a sense, these silent narratives offer readers a dual reward—the author's narrative and, more closely, the reader's own unique interpretation. The artist and writer Chris Lanier observed that Masereel "does not proselytize—rather, he gives us a story as a device through which we can examine ourselves."

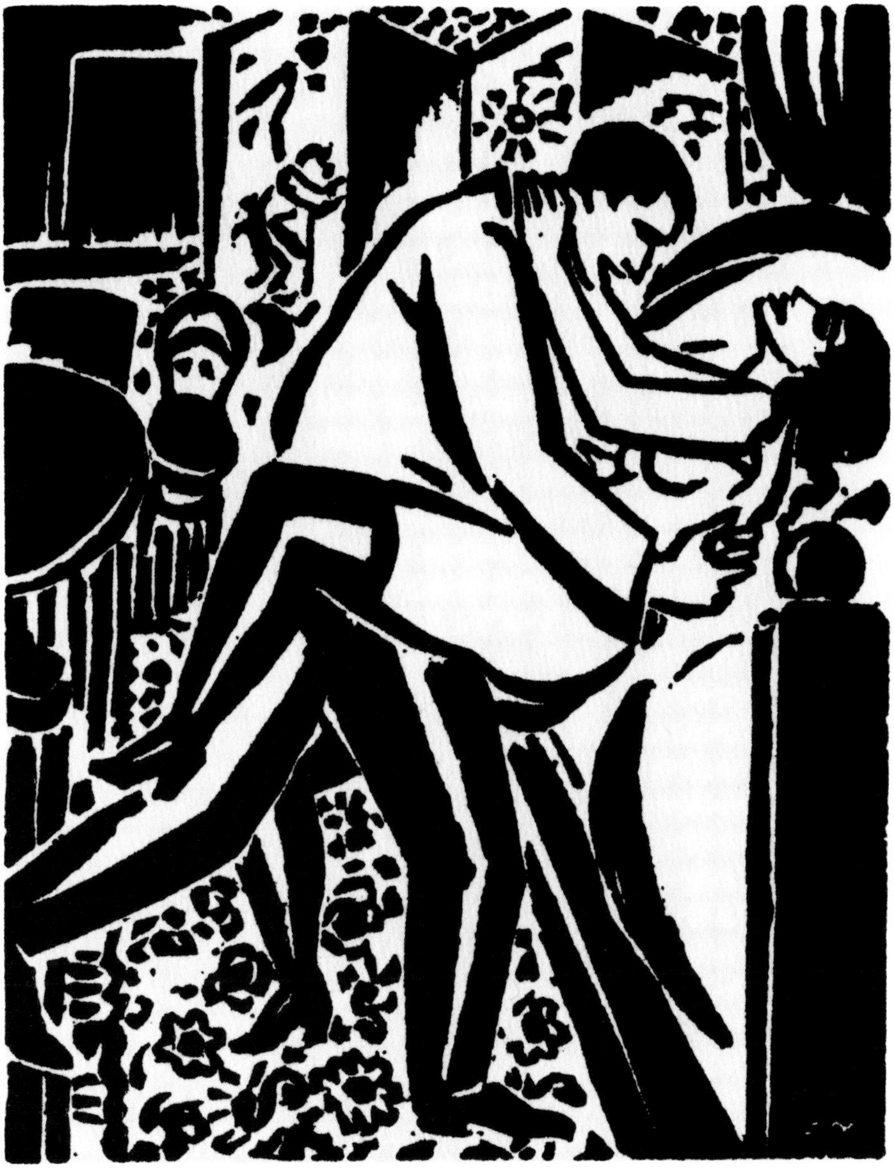

In the German edition and many subsequent editions, Thomas Mann wrote an exciting introduction that gives the best advice to readers of this and any wordless book and includes a comparison to motion pictures.

> Darken the room! Sit down with this book next to your reading lamp and concentrate on its pictures as you turn page after page. Don't deliberate too long! It is no tragedy if you fail to grasp every picture at once, just as it does not matter if you miss one or two shots in a movie. Look at these powerful black-and-white figures, their features etched in light and shadow. You will be captivated from beginning to end: from the first picture showing the train plunging through dense smoke and bearing the hero toward life, to the very last picture showing the skeleton-faced figure wandering among the stars. And where are you? Has not this passionate journey had an incomparably deeper and purer impact on you than you have ever felt before?

This book, Masereel's most famous wordless work, has been reprinted in many languages and editions throughout the world and remains in print today—perhaps the most seminal work in the genre.

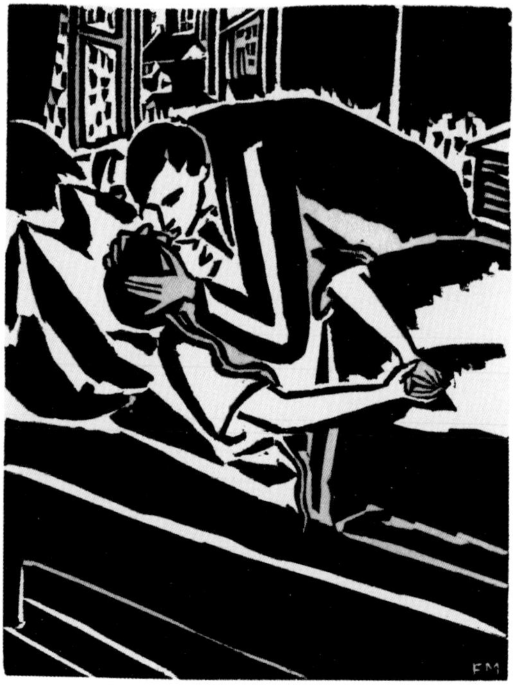
FM

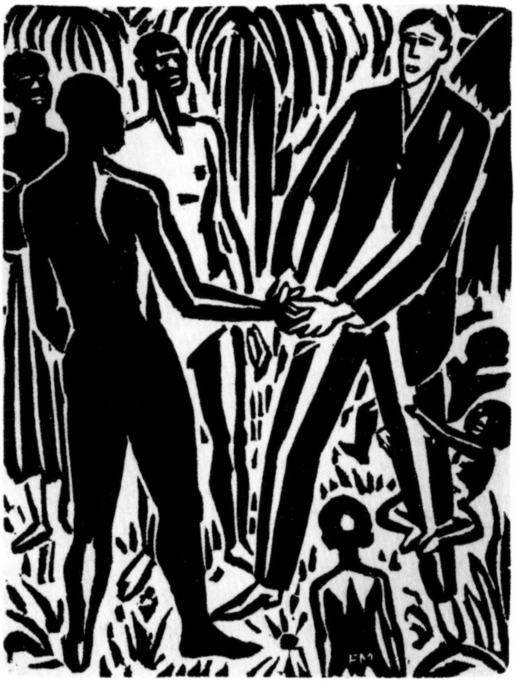
FM

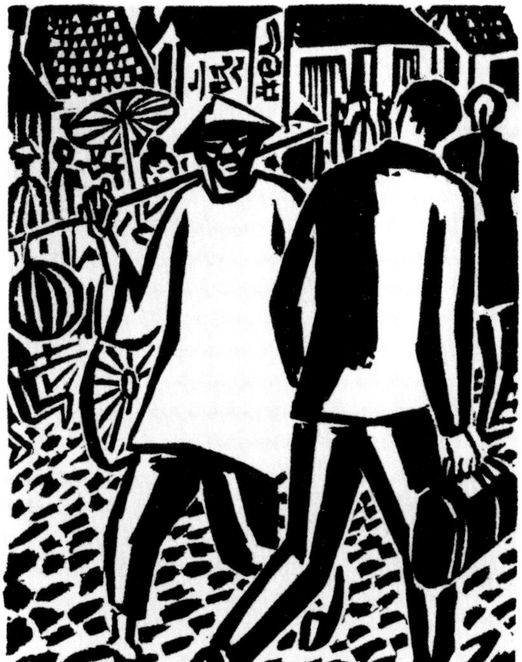
FM

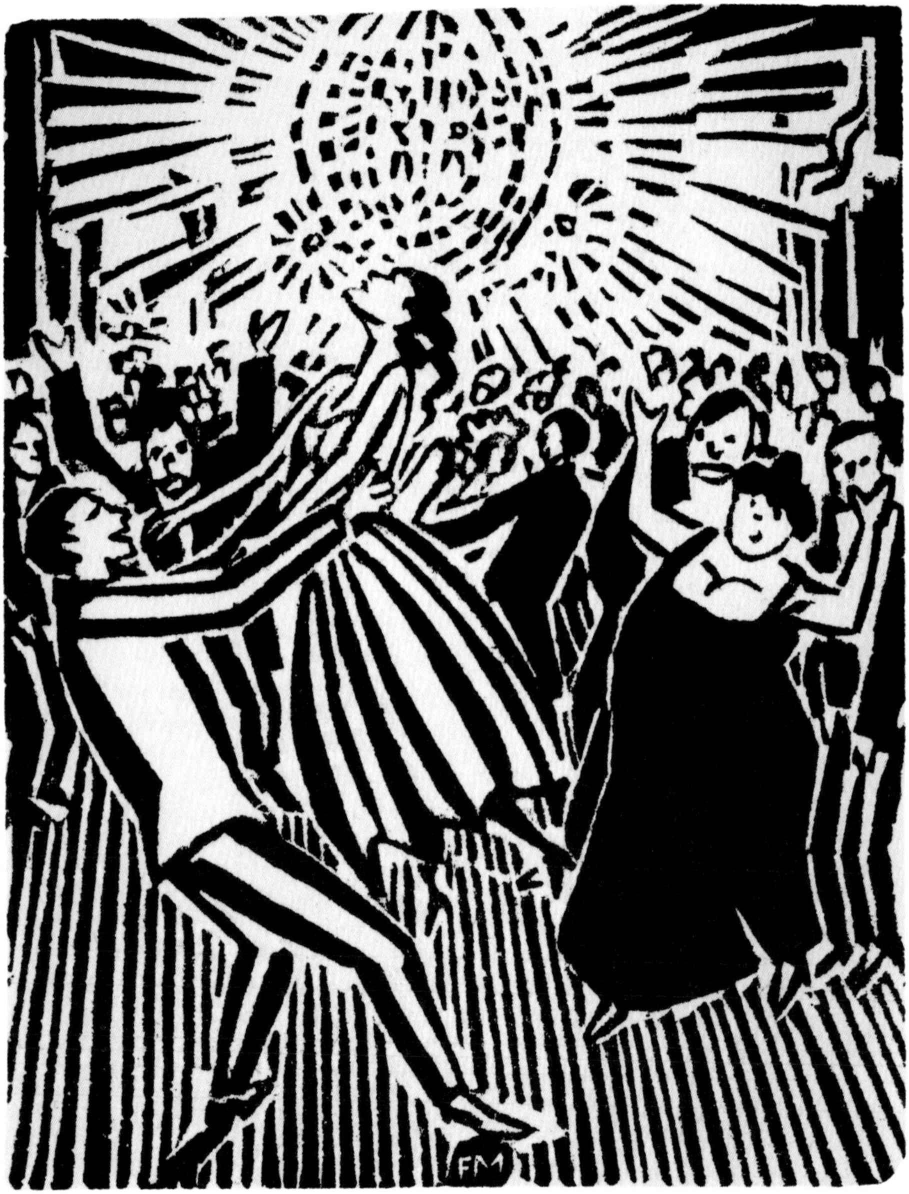
FM

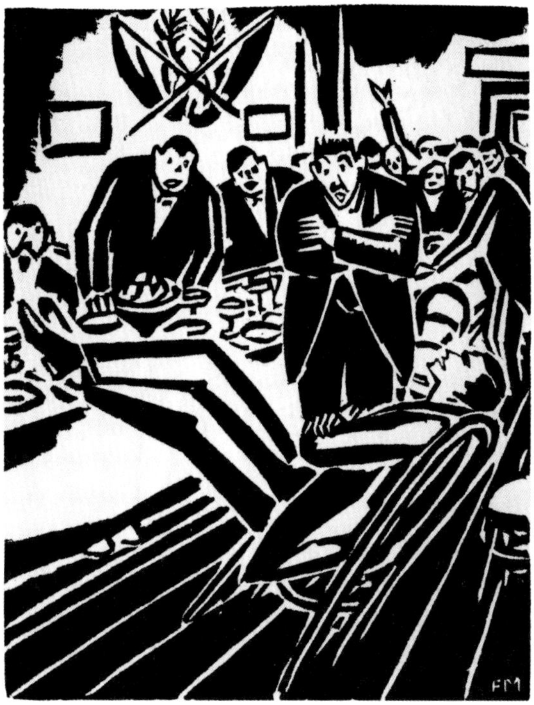
FM

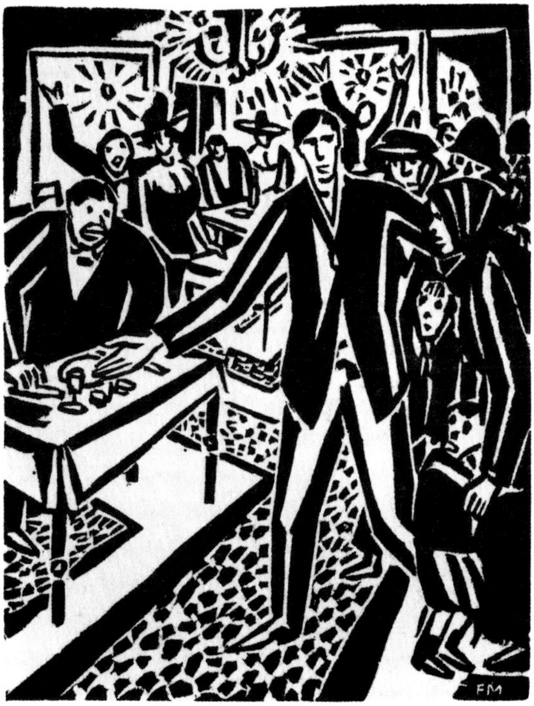
FM

The Sun (1919)

During a time of personal introspection and in reaction to the injustices around him, Masereel began a series of highly imaginative works. These are entertaining adult picture stories that allowed Masereel to share his own pondering on myths and humanistic ideas that have puzzled men and women for centuries.

The Sun is an allegory told in sixty-three woodcuts. An artist, who resembles Masereel in appearance, sits in a room and stares at the blazing sun. He lays his head down to rest, and a male figure steps out of his head and jumps out the window (below). The figure is helped to his feet by a crowd and then begins an obsessive pursuit to reach the sun. With every attempt to reach it, he is brought down by a crowd and given diversions such as alcohol and prostitutes to occupy his mind. But the hero is determined to reach the sun like a modern-day Icarus.

The hero climbs to the top of a building, chimney, tree (opposite), church steeple, ship mast, and crane in his quest. He finally races directly up a staircase of clouds and is scorched by the sun. He descends, burning, to the ground, and falls upon the desk of Masereel, who is startled from his daydream. Masereel taps his head and with a smile seems to say, "Wasn't that a pretty crazy daydream?" In the story he aligns himself with the reader by introducing himself in the beginning and by including a direct interaction with the reader at the conclusion. By using the myth of Icarus in a modern setting, he encourages the human spirit of inquiry and the passion for seeking the unattainable.

The character seeking the sun is displayed in various settings that are complex and busy with action and characters. In some cases the character seems lost in the crowd and has to be visibly discovered by the reader. Unlike the character in *Passionate Journey* who is consistently in the foreground, the character in *The Sun* is one among the crowd. This stylistic decision makes the character's obsession seem a part of us—a universal feeling of inquiry that we all share.

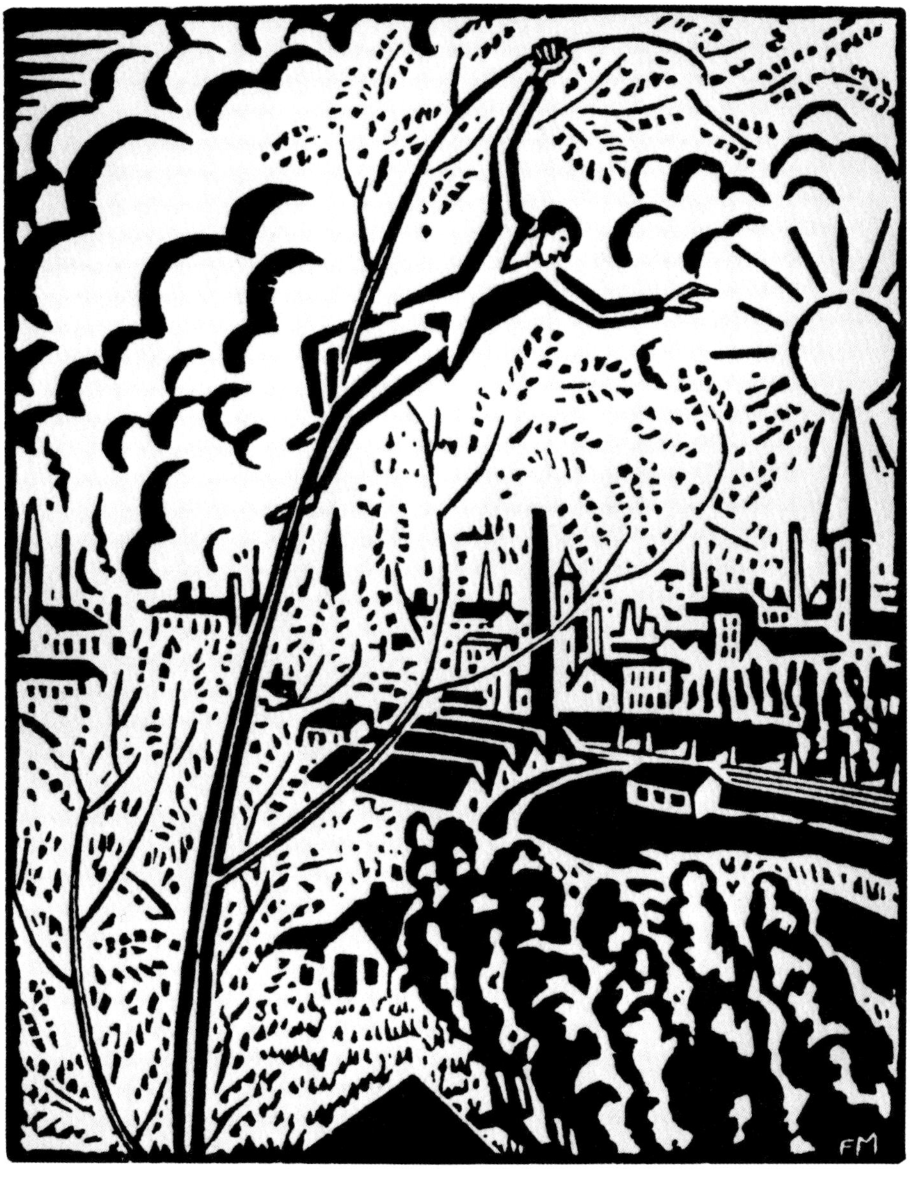
FM

Story Without Words (1920)

Story Without Words, another allegory told in sixty woodcuts, is about a man who tries to win the love of a woman. In a unique manner of display, the male shows an array of physical expressions to persuade the female of his love for her. When he seems to have exhausted every means of persuasion and threatens to kill himself, she sexually submits to him. She then becomes attached to the man, who pulls away from her after their lovemaking, leaving her sad and alone.

The effectiveness of this allegory rests on the design of the narrative. In the foreground, Masereel displays the couple. The woman is always on the left side of the panel except for the final image when she is alone, kneeling in grief. Her facial expressions display her reactions to the male's actions and behavior. The male is placed on the right side of the panel. His antics are accompanied by an intricate background that reflects his intentions. For example, when he shows her his strength, he flexes his right arm and squeezes his bicep in a show of prowess (below). In the background, Masereel constructed the interior of a circus with weight lifters in the center ring to add to the motif. The facial expression of the female shows amazement. In another example, the male sings a song of love. In the background is a forest, but instead of a songbird Masereel displays a crow in a tree and a rooster on the ground—birds that do not sing a melodious song (opposite). Given this background and the irritated facial expression on the female as she holds one hand up to her ear, we deduce that despite his song of love, the male cannot carry a tune.

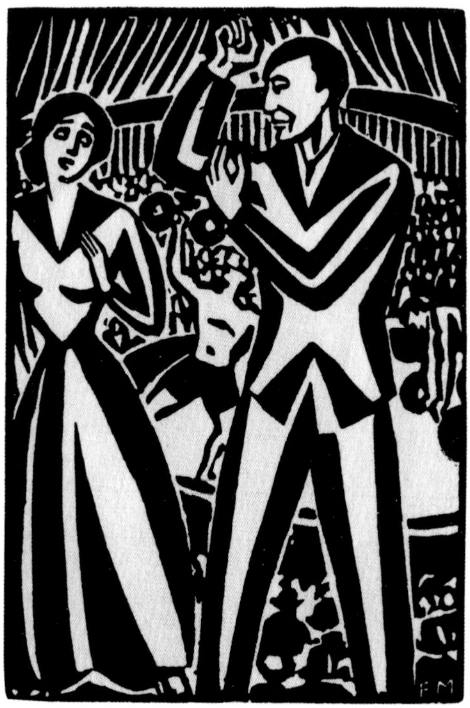
FM

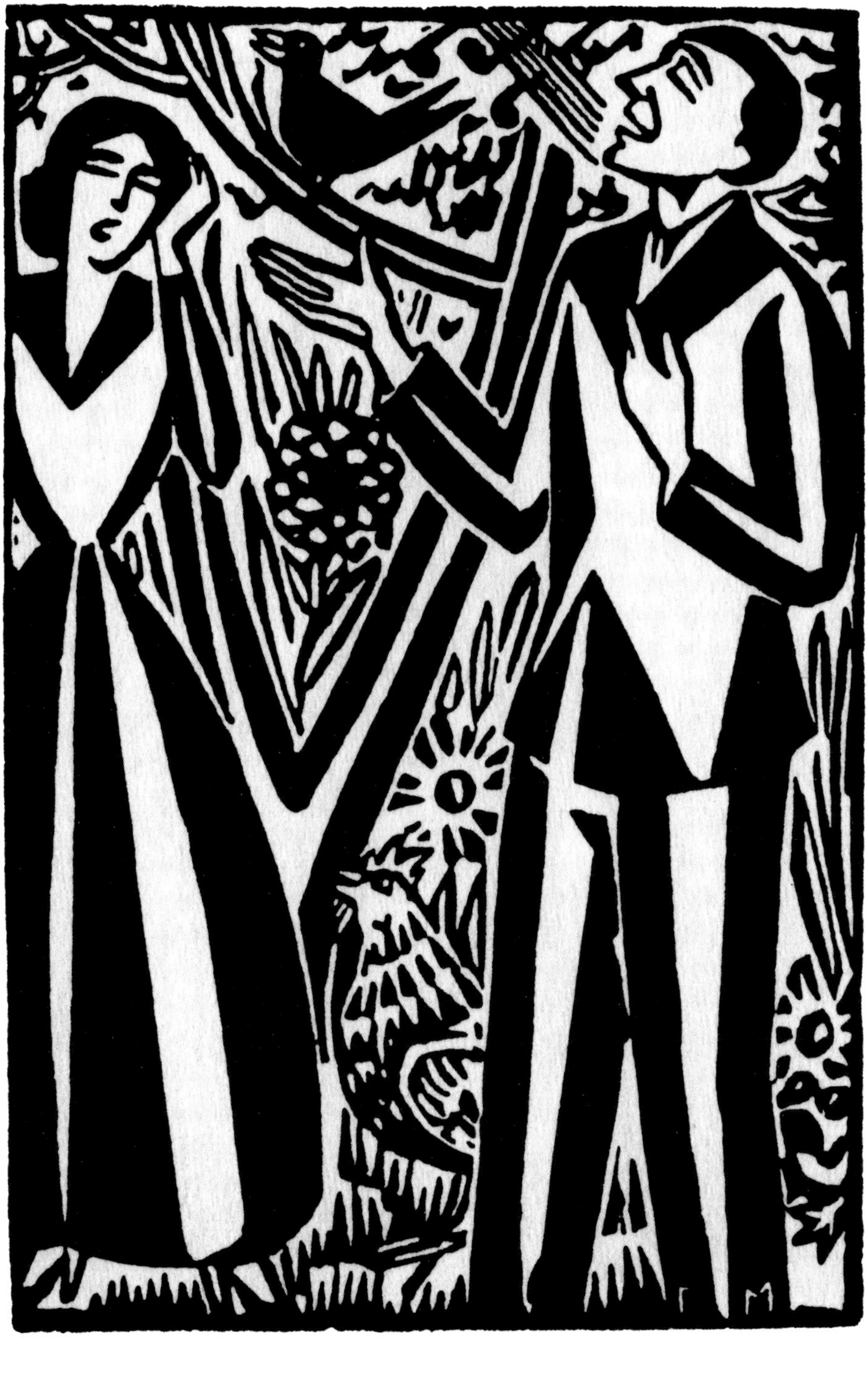

The Idea (1920)

In the same year as *Story Without Words,* Masereel continued his telling of allegorical tales with *The Idea.* This novel, consisting of eighty-three woodcuts, concerns an idea that springs from an artist who, again as in *The Sun,* resembles Masereel.

The early pages display Masereel waiting for a creative idea. His arms are crossed and his head lowered with a pout, waiting for inspiration. A spider's web in the background indicates his creative block. A bolt of inspiration strikes his room, and an idea, in the form of a naked woman with long black hair, steps out of his head. The artist slips her into an envelope, which he delivers to a curious public. The authorities, disturbed by her naked figure, chase her around the city (below). They cover her with clothes, but she flaunts her nudity by lifting her shirt and exposing herself to a public that finds her nakedness obscene. One man, however, is not repelled by her nakedness. He takes her into his arms and, with her at his side, fights against the injustice around him. He is, as in the case of the hero in Masereel's first woodcut novel, eventually tried and executed (opposite). The "idea" tries to circulate herself in print, but the authorities burn all the books with her image. It is only when she discovers the avenue of mass media in radio, telephone, film, and photography that her nudity disrupts the traditional social order. When the culture has been ruffled, she returns to the artist who

holds a new idea—a naked woman with white hair. The artist places his old idea, the one with black hair, inside a frame and hangs her on his wall. He then takes his second idea, slips her into an envelope, and sends her out into the public.

On one level the idea is seen literally as something new and shocking that is repudiated by traditional norms. Another interpretation of this tale concerns the manner in which women are perceived within Western culture. Masereel provides enough evidence to show how men manipulate the female image to fit their fantasies, and how they are threatened by women who express their individuality and independence.

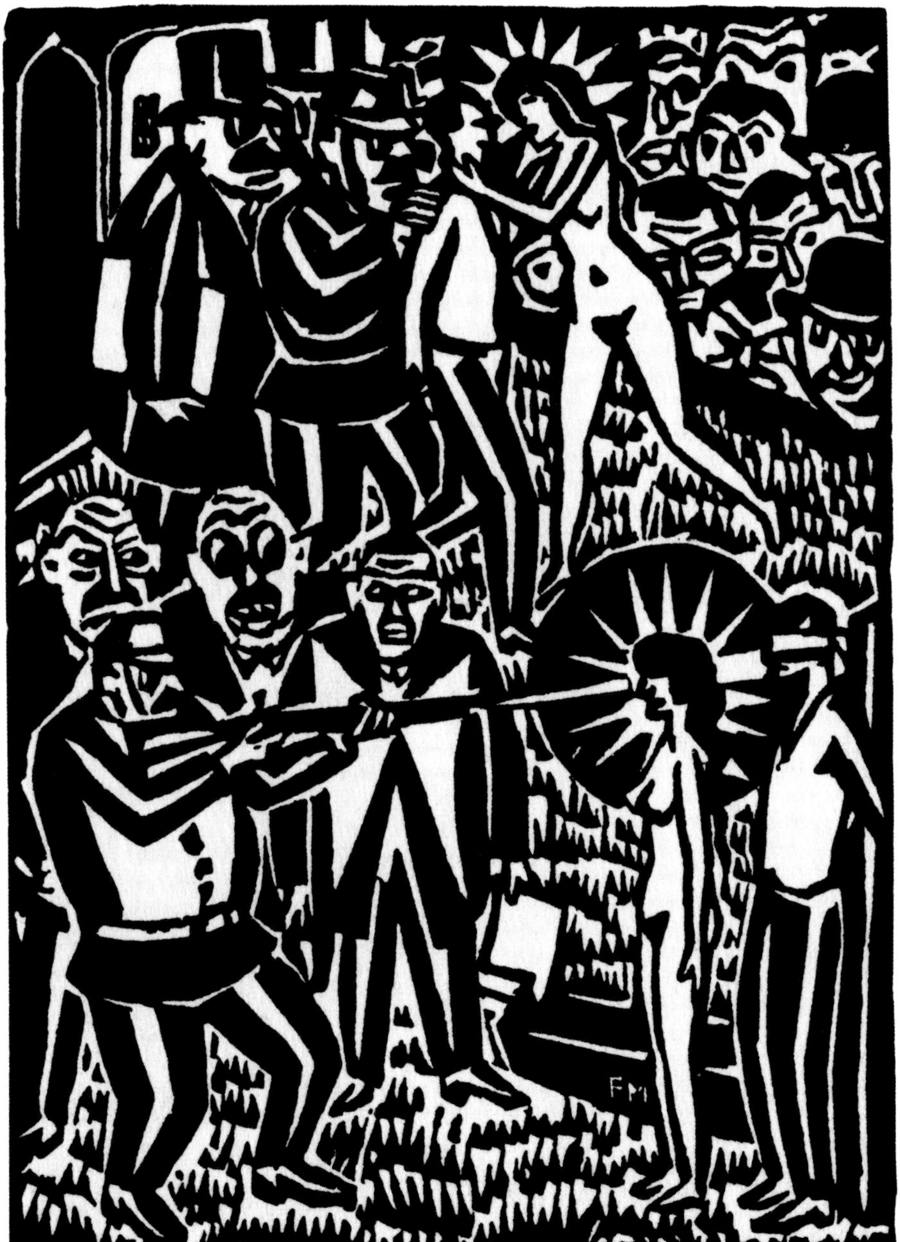
FM

The City (1925)

In addition to his wordless novels of protest and fantasy, Masereel developed a number of woodcut novels, beginning with *The City* (1925), that focused not on plot or character but on a sense of place and man's relationship to the world.

In *The City,* Masereel provides his impressions of a modern metropolis. Like the photographer Eugene Atget, Masereel shows us the nightmare behind the storefronts, as well as sentimental portrayals of men and women, that he ultimately merges into a testament for his unshakable faith in the human spirit.

It is no coincidence that Masereel begins this book with a quote from the American poet Walt Whitman: "This is the city and I am one of the citizens, / Whatever interest the rest interests me . . ." Masereel captures the pedestrian activity seen in any large city at the turn of the century. He scans the crowded streets and discovers distinct people and events such as a funeral procession of a dignitary. The procession has brought out a large crowd of onlookers that includes a pickpocket, a photographer standing on a ladder, and a pair of lovers (below). From common, everyday events, Masereel takes us behind the tourist scenes into more private displays, such as the room of a dying man in a hospital, a squalid dwelling of an impoverished family, and a drowned woman pulled from a canal. He displays events inside court rooms, factories, and houses of prostitution; cultural events like the cabaret, theater, orchestra, and dance halls; and the contrast of public occasions like an execution and the private decadence of an orgy (opposite). This cacophony of scenes comes to an abrupt halt in the last woodcut, which displays a woman with an expression of wonder and contemplation on her face as she sits in an attic room staring up into the dark sky filled with stars.

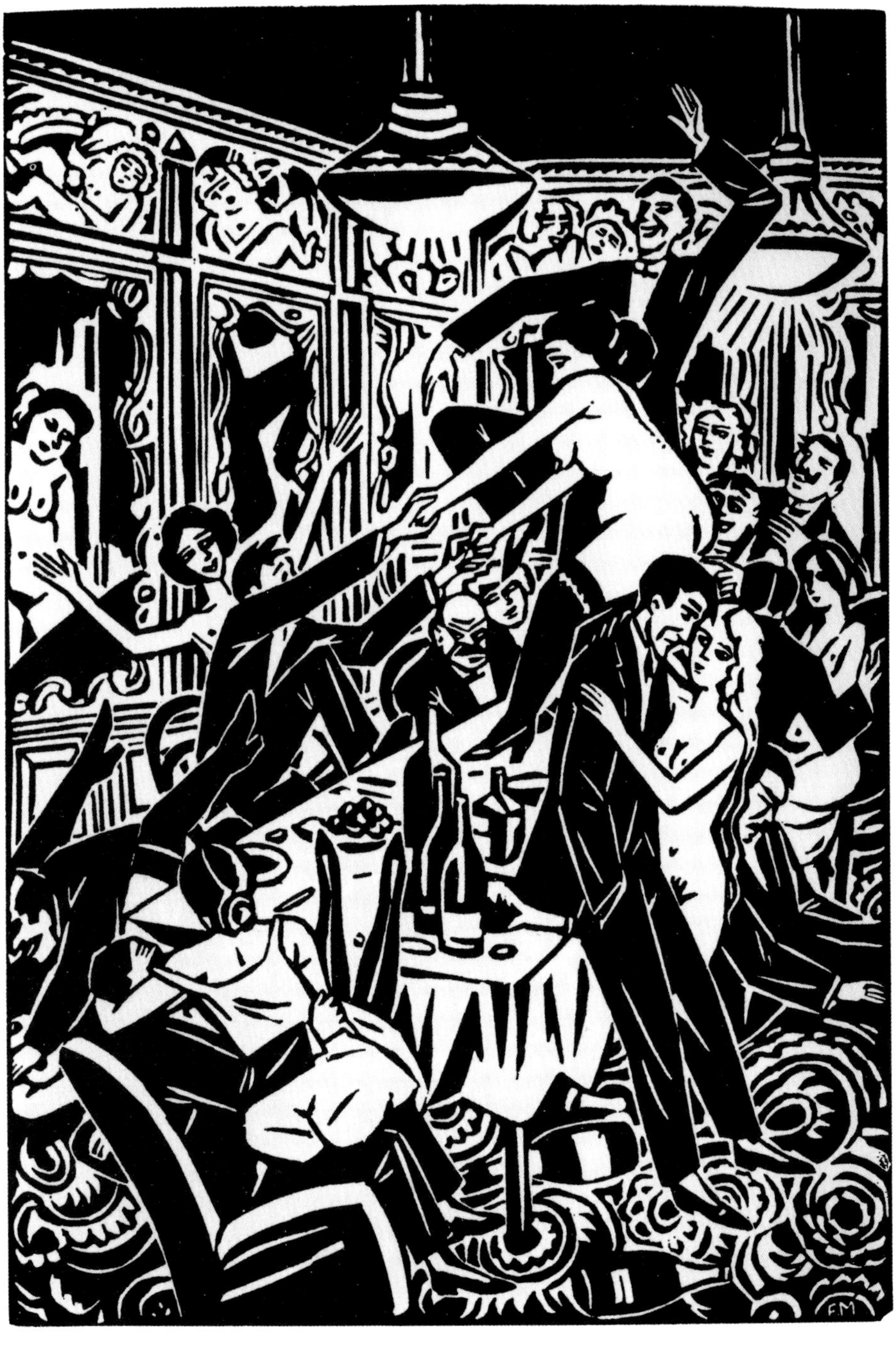

Das Werk (1928)

As with *The Idea,* in *Das Werk* (*The Work*) Masereel explores the themes of an artist's work and his attempt to fit into society. A sculptor is faced with the task of creating art from a huge stone. He hammers out a giant figure of a man who comes to life after the sculptor is asleep and crashes through the walls of his studio. This giant goes into a city and playfully observes its people, including a naked woman inside her room (below) who closes her shutters when he gets too close. The giant drinks vats of alcohol and passes out in the center of town. When he awakens, he discovers that the human population has surrounded him as if to imprison him, and he begins to destroy the city (opposite). As the buildings begin to burn, he has a change of heart and saves the population by stretching his body like a bridge over the river and out of the burning city. He gathers up people and tosses them like seeds, one by one, into the country. He is fond of one female, whom he keeps for himself and plays with like a pet until his caresses kill her. In his frustration over her death, the giant pulls God from Heaven and Satan from Hell. He tosses them together, and they fight to the giant's amusement. The giant finally climbs the mountain of stars and planets in the universe until he finds a planet where he seems to find comfort. Then he wraps himself around the planet and appears content as an infant nursing at his mother's breast.

The popularity of Masereel is entirely credited to the German publisher Kurt Wolff, who published cheap editions of Masereel's distinctive books for the general public. Wolff published five woodcut novels with introductions by popular writers like Thomas Mann and Hermann Hesse. These editions sold thousands of copies and established Masereel's name and the wordless novel—a form that became popular for an audience of readers without regard for language or literacy.

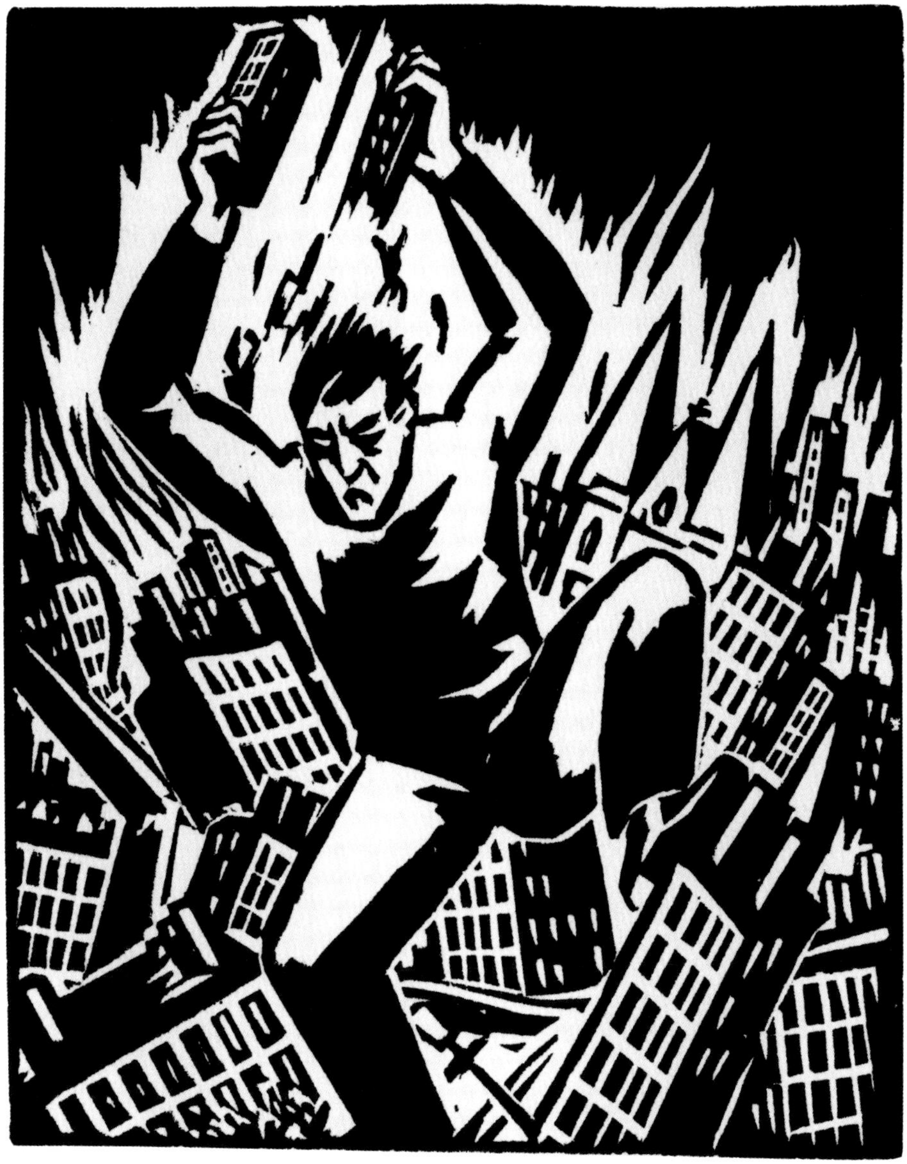

Chapter Three
Lynd Ward
(1905–1985)

Lynd Kendall Ward was the second of three children of Daisy Kendall Ward and Dr. Harry F. Ward, a Methodist minister who became a writer, an outspoken promoter of social activism, and the first board chairman of the American Civil Liberties Union. Ward inherited Harry's love of nature and his concern for social injustice, both of which he displayed so readily in his wordless books.

After graduating from Columbia University in New York in 1926, Ward married a fellow student, May McNeer, and on the day of their marriage they left for Germany, where Ward studied wood engraving under Hans Mueller in Leipzig at the National Academy for Graphic Arts. Ward discovered the woodcut novels of Frans Masereel during this year, specifically *The Sun*, and was drawn to the idea of a novel told entirely in black-and-white pictures. Ward's medium of choice was wood engraving rather than the woodcut that Masereel preferred. (Woodcuts are made from blocks of wood cut horizontally *with* the grain, running parallel to the surface. Wood engravings use blocks cut *across* the grain.)

In addition to Ward's career as a pioneer in wordless novels, he was highly regarded in the United States as a book illustrator for George Macy's Limited Editions Club, Heritage Press, and a prolific children's book artist who illustrated over a hundred books for Landmark Books, Illustrated Junior Library, and other works including several books written by his wife, May McNeer. Ward illustrated Elizabeth Coatsworth's *Cat Who Went to Heaven* (1931) and Ester Forbes's *Johnny Tremain* (1943), which each won Newbery Medals, and was awarded the Caldecott Medal in 1953 for *The Biggest Bear*, which he illustrated as well as wrote. Ward died of Alzheimer's disease in 1985.

Gods' Man (1929)

After Lynd Ward returned to the United States from Leipzig, he published his first woodcut novel, *Gods' Man,* in 1929. Frans Masereel's woodcut novels were not distributed widely in the United States and as a result, upon publication Ward's "wordless book" *Gods' Man* became an overnight success, selling 20,000 copies in six printings over four years.

Gods' Man, composed of 139 wood engravings, tells the Faustian story of an artist arriving in a city (opposite) who signs a contract with a masked figure in exchange for fame and fortune. He gains success (page 43) but soon becomes disillusioned when he discovers the extent to which money, in the guise of his mistress, has corrupted every facet of society (page 44). When he assaults her, he is thrown into jail (page 45). He eventually escapes, is chased from the city by an angry mob, and jumps into an abyss to avoid his captors. A woman, living alone in the woods, discovers his body and nurses him back to health. The artist discovers happiness in her simple country life.

The woman gives birth to their child, and they seem totally content (page 46) until a masked figure appears (page 51, top) and commands the artist to follow him to the summit of a cliff. When the figure removes his mask, revealing himself as the embodiment of Death, the artist recoils and falls off the edge of the cliff to his death.

What immediately becomes evident in this novel of wood engravings is not only the obvious lack of text, but that as the pages are turned, the narrative relationship between each print transpires almost magically. Ward's aim was to present the necessary amount of visual information, which would flow evenly on each page so that the reader's imagination could follow the pictures and weave the various aspects of plot, theme, and personal interpretation into a cohesive whole.

In *Storyteller Without Words: The Wood Engravings of Lynd Ward*, Ward describes his commitment to the integrity of his narrative and the standards that are now central in today's graphic novels.

> The first visual units immediately establish character and setting. Each succeeding unit must relate to what has been established and, by focusing on a slightly later point in the developing action, move the story that much further along. The difficulty, of course, lies in determining how much of an interval between units will be effective. If it is too great, you lose the reader because he cannot make that leap with the information you have given him. On the other hand, if the interval is too slight, the new unit will seem repetitious and the reader's interest will flag.

Ward used pictorial composition to intensify the impact of his narrative. Looking at a few of these compositions will reveal a technique of pictorial arrangement that he continued to develop in his future novels.

The first element of Ward's composition involves the black-and-white print. Working in black and white allowed Ward to take advantage of the association of darkness and light. For example, in the city, the characters are outlined only in the most minimal terms by gaslight and candles. When the artist seeks comfort in the church (page 47) his meek figure kneels in the darkness below the looming arches of the columns, suggesting a prison rather than a sanctuary. He later discovers that money has corrupted even the clergy. Ward takes us into the darkness of a prison cell as we gaze through the artist's eyes (page 48). Even in the daylight, the looming buildings block the sunlight. The sterile buildings overshadow the humans that scurry around like ants (page 2). It is noteworthy that in poet Allen Ginsberg's annotations to his masterpiece *Howl*, Ginsberg referenced these powerful images of the city and jailhouse by Ward.

In *Gods' Man,* the darkness creates a feeling that one is not safe on the streets and that danger exists around every corner (page 241). In contrast to the element of

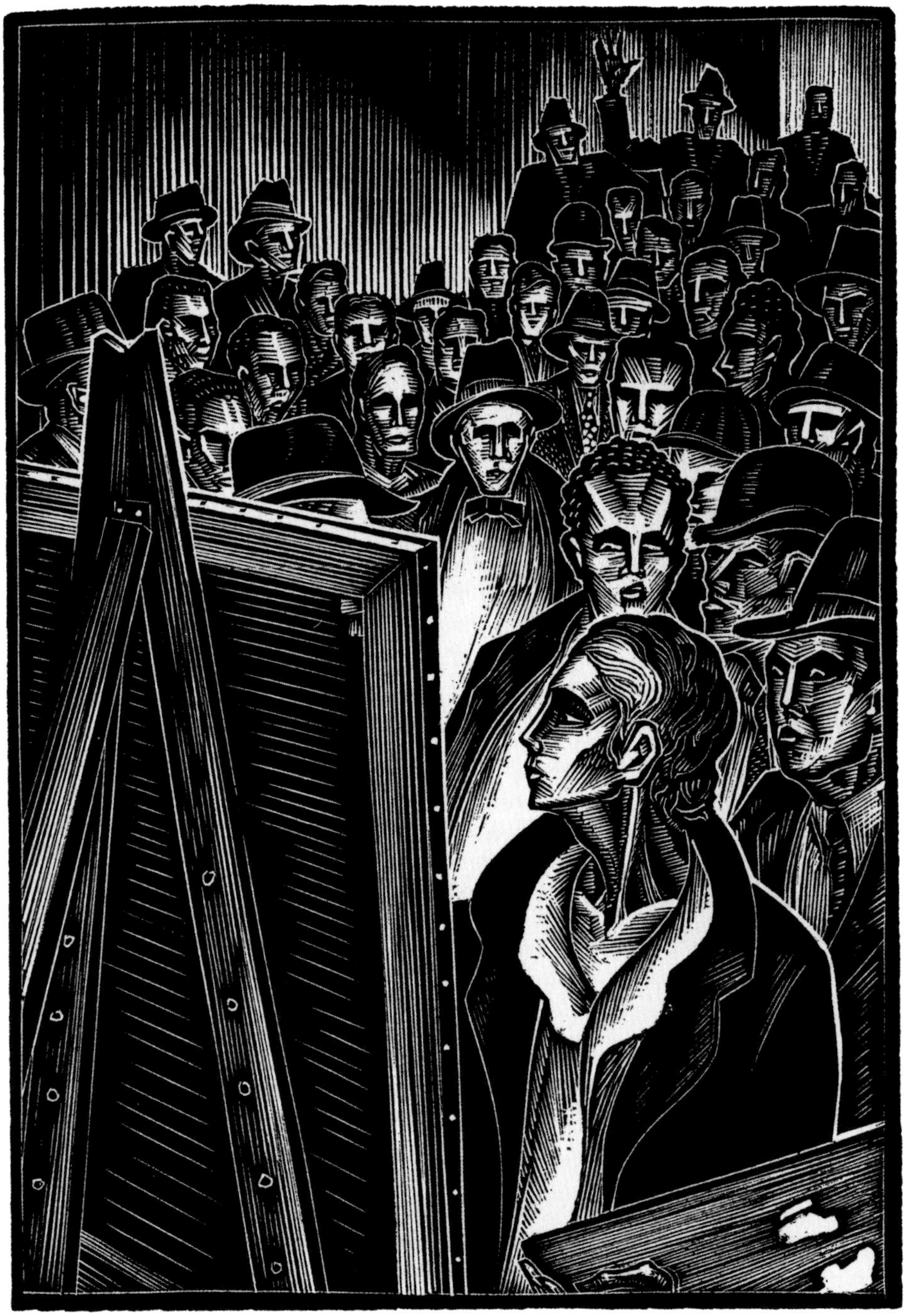

darkness in the city is the natural light Ward depicts in the country scenes (page 49) and the portrayal of bathing, which conveys an almost refreshing liquid feeling of sunlight as it drenches the artist (page 50).

Another striking element of Ward's pictorial composition is his use of space. By placing a different shape in the midst of similar shapes, a greater sense of isolation is apparent. Ward shows the intense isolation of the artist by depicting him standing behind a throng of glasses raised in his honor (page 51, bottom). The isolation of the artist would not have been as effective if Ward had displayed the figures of the men and women holding their glasses. The glasses as a group frame the artist and more dramatically center the focus on the artist.

Ward also varies the dimensions of his pictures. His largest prints (6 x 4 inches), placed as the opening and closing pictures in each of the five chapters, provide the basic framework for the narrative. Within this structure of the ten largest prints, the body of each chapter is filled with other prints of various dimensions, which fall at various lengths from the top of the page. This simple device is effective in providing readers with a visual diversity as each page is turned (in contrast with Masereel, who used a static dimension throughout many of his narratives and uniform margins on each page).

In addition to space, Ward displays his own unique style in the exaggerated expressions of his characters in order to communicate a feeling or reaction without the aid of words. Ward already developed a certain manner of seeing things that he would later advise young artists to follow, like artist and book illustrator Michael McCurdy, who received a letter from Ward that "advised me in drawing to interpret what I saw but then add a little of what I don't see."

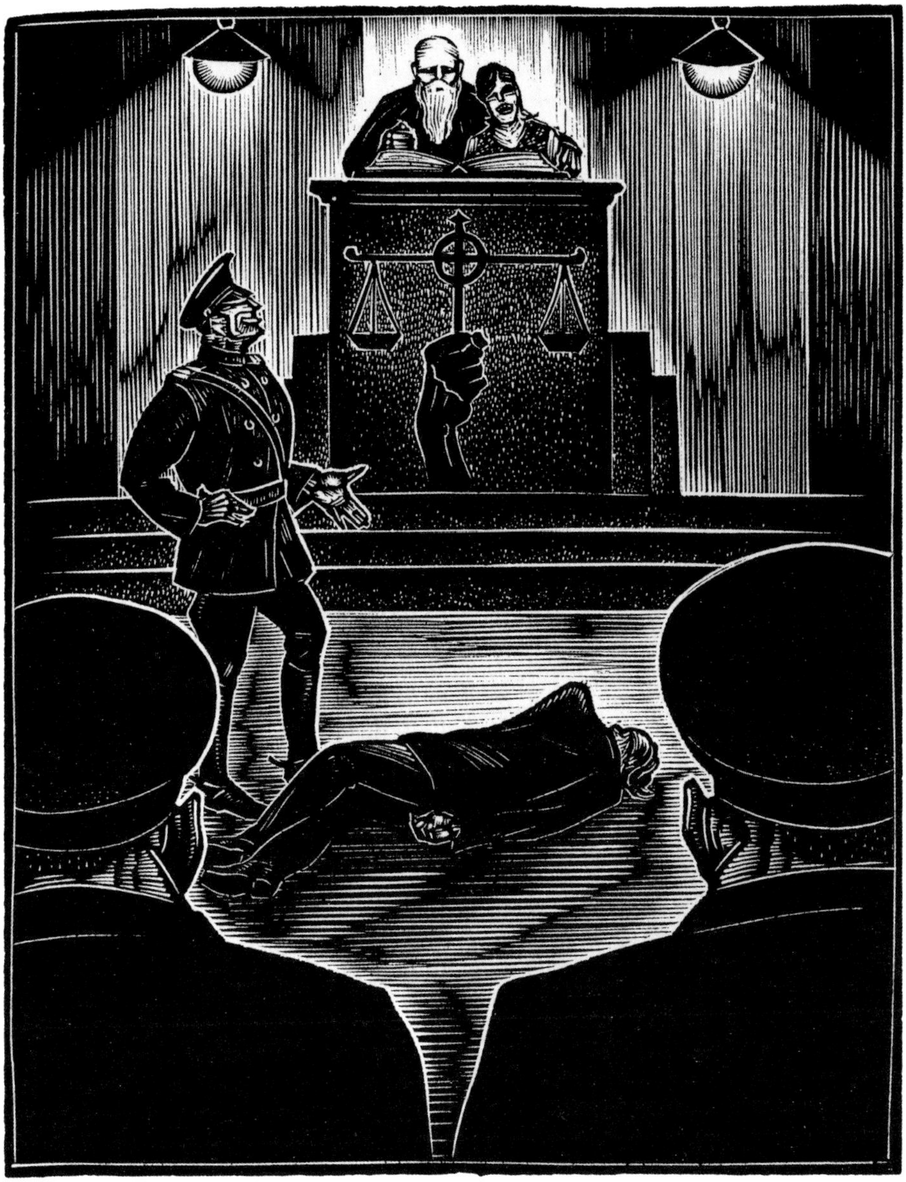

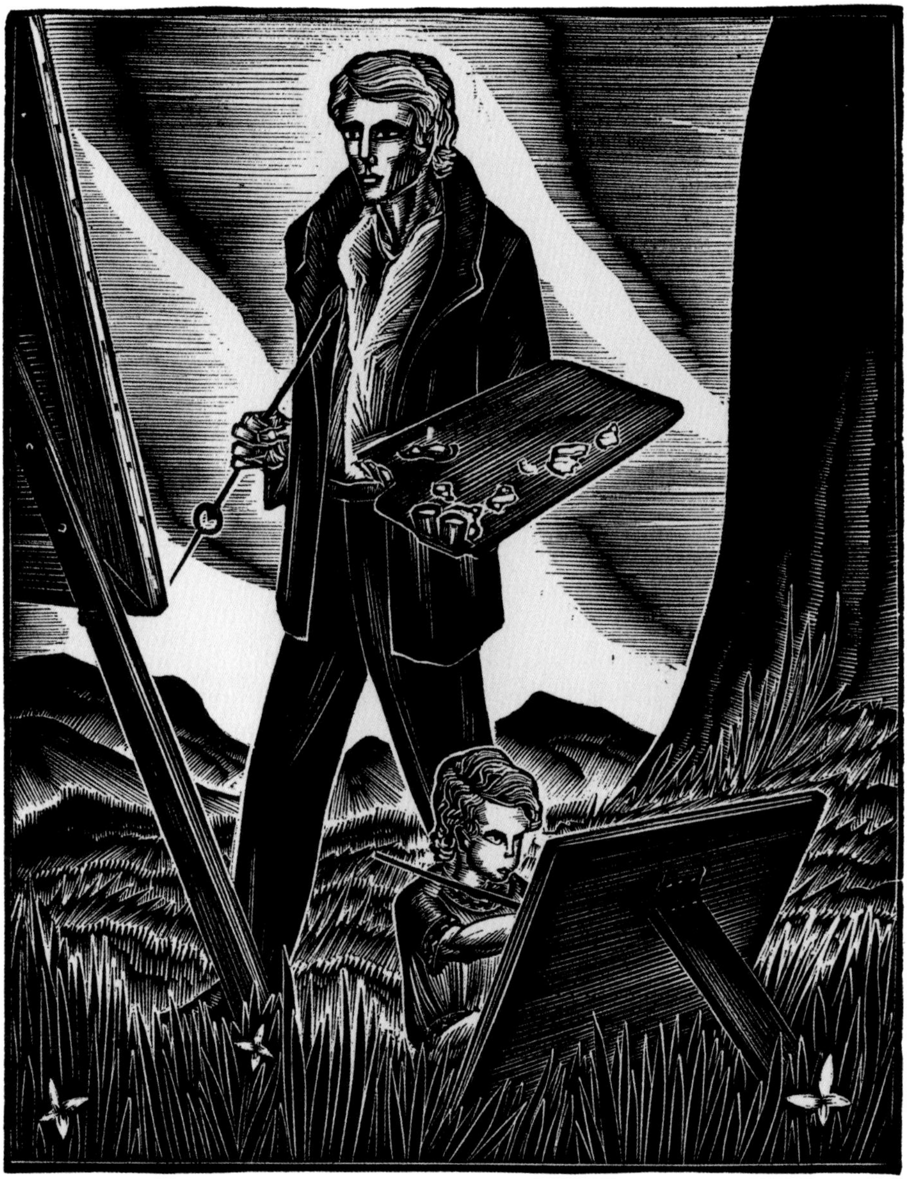

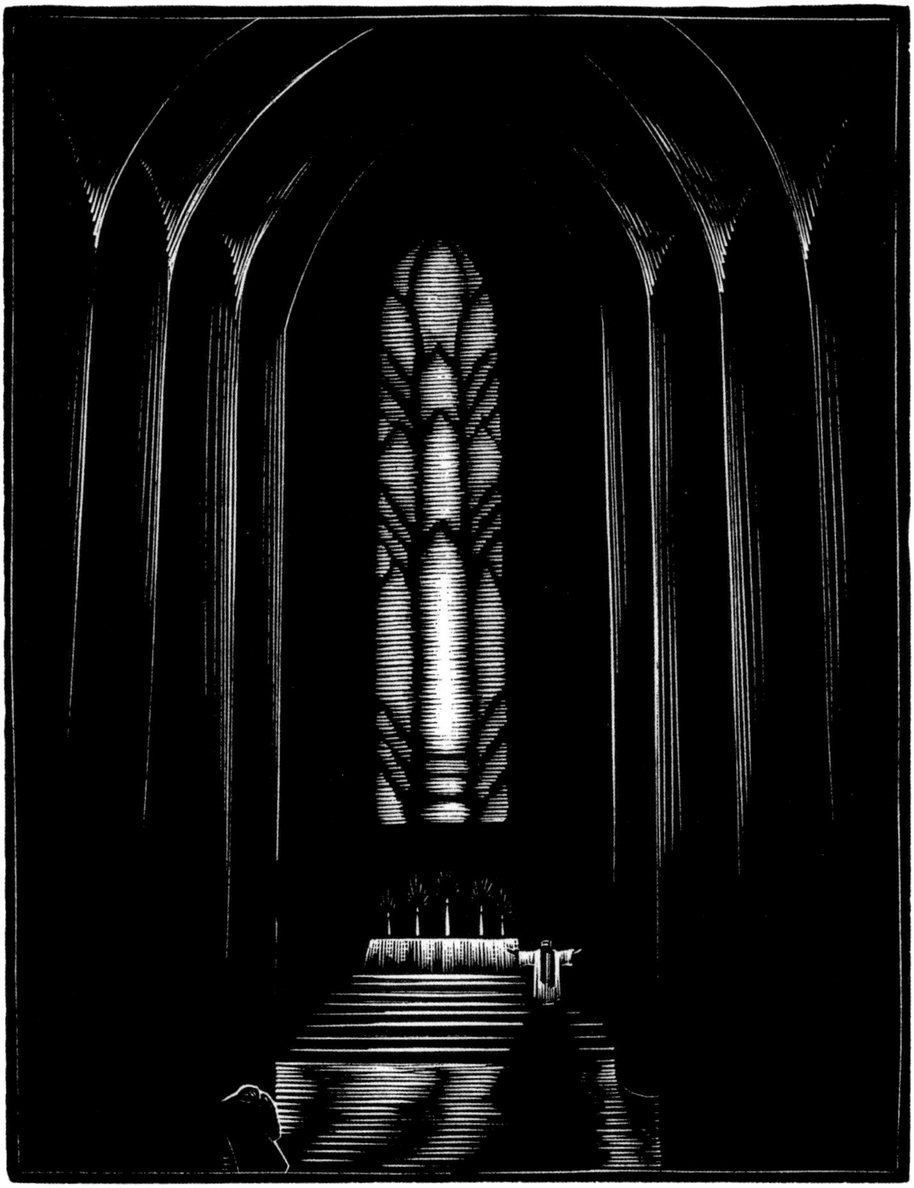

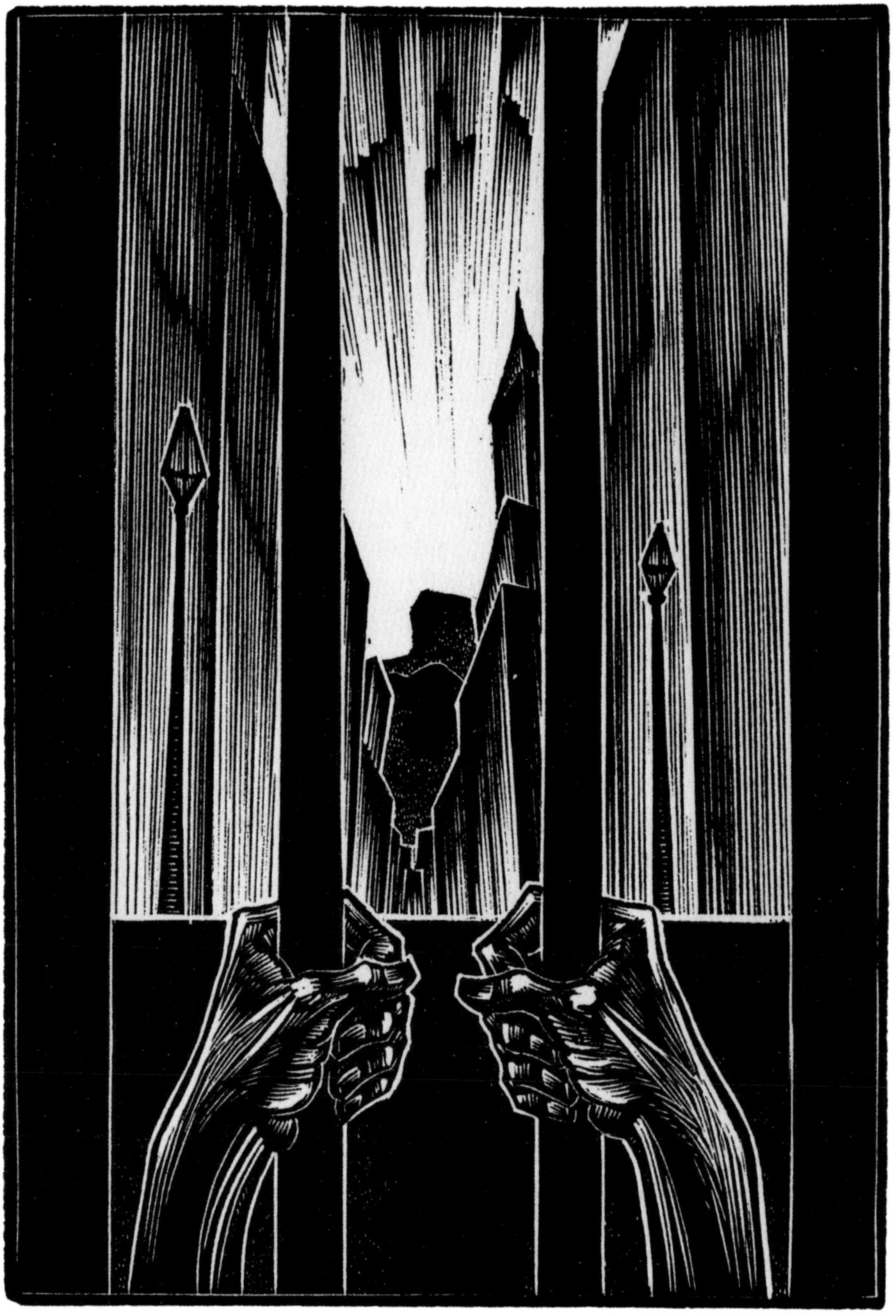

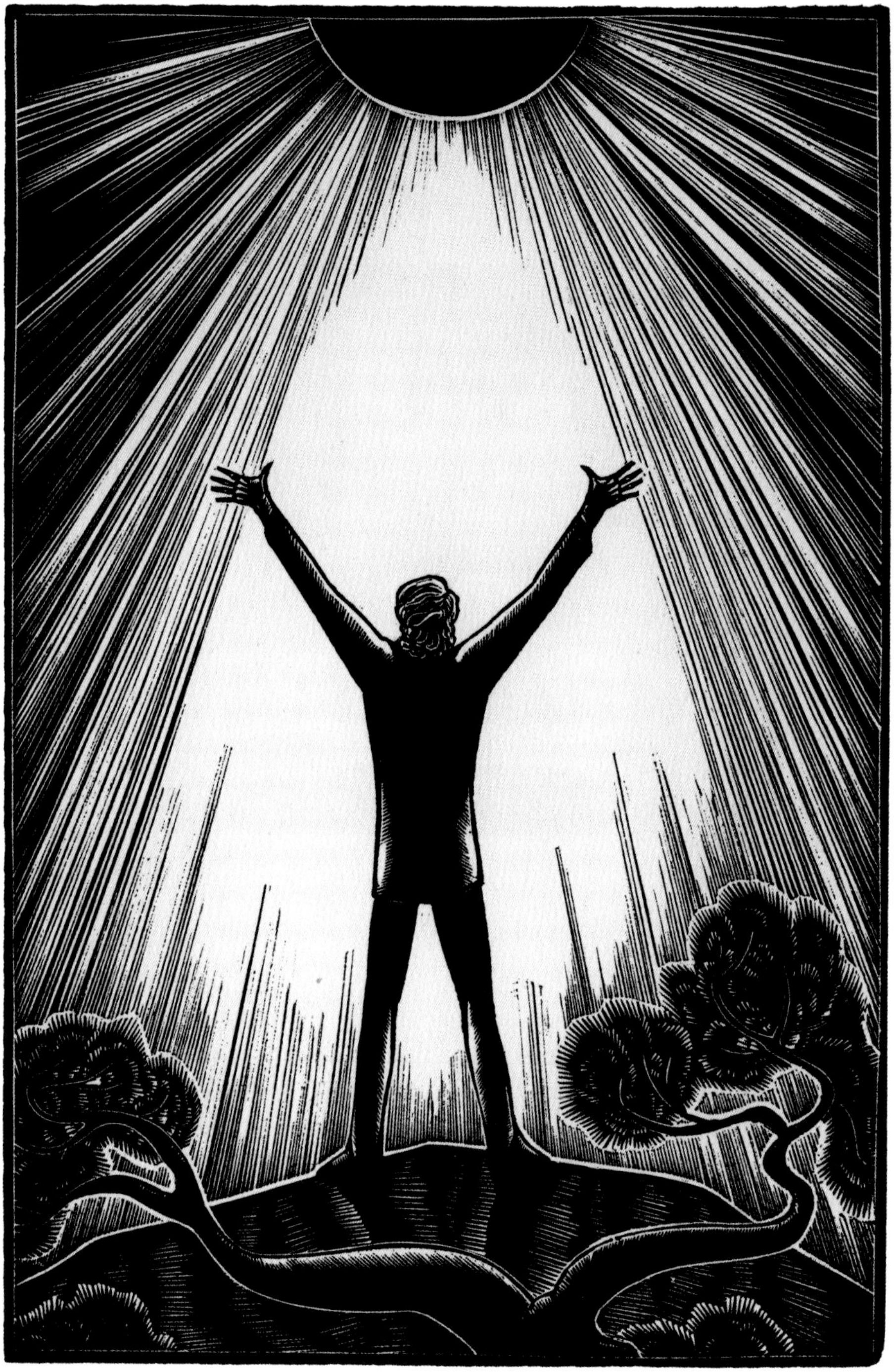

Madman's Drum (1930)

The plot of *Madman's Drum*'s is more complex than *Gods' Man*. This book, consisting of 118 wood engravings ranging in size from 4 x 3 to 5 x 4 inches, involves a family's slave-trading past and the next generation's quest for scientific knowledge.

This novel centers on a slave trader who kills an African man and steals his drum, which is engraved with a distinct face of a demon. With the wealth acquired in the slave trade, the slave trader purchases a mansion for his wife and son. He displays the sword he used to kill the African and the stolen drum over the hearth like a hunter's trophies. When he discovers his son playing with the drum, the father responds violently and beats the boy, insisting that he read books rather than waste his time playing. The son grows into an adult, isolating himself from his friends and his carnal desires (opposite and page 54). He rejects religion and turns his attention to science. He achieves recognition in the academic community, courts a woman, and after their marriage, raises two daughters (page 55). His wife's and daughters' lives end tragically, and with a demented expression on his face (page 56), he ends up walking away hand-in-hand with the jester.

Ward expands his pictorial symbolism in this book and used more engraving tools to achieve detail in his characters and settings (page 57, top). Ward uses the symbol of a flower on the daughter's waistband to indicate her purity. Her innocence is taken by a young man with numerous flowers decorating his vest (page 57, bottom). The drama in this picture is further developed with the placement of curved tree limbs in the foreground in contrast to the linear background. In addition, Ward jabbed out areas in the foliage and the fields, like a watercolorist who skillfully uses white space to bring attention to certain details.

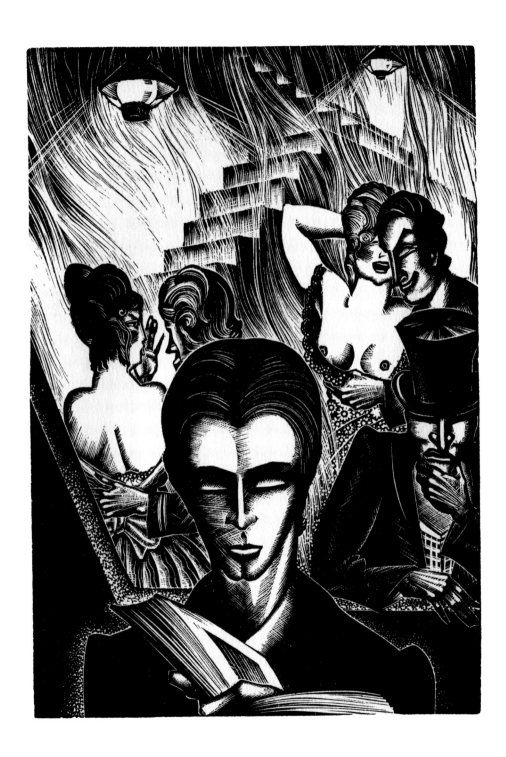

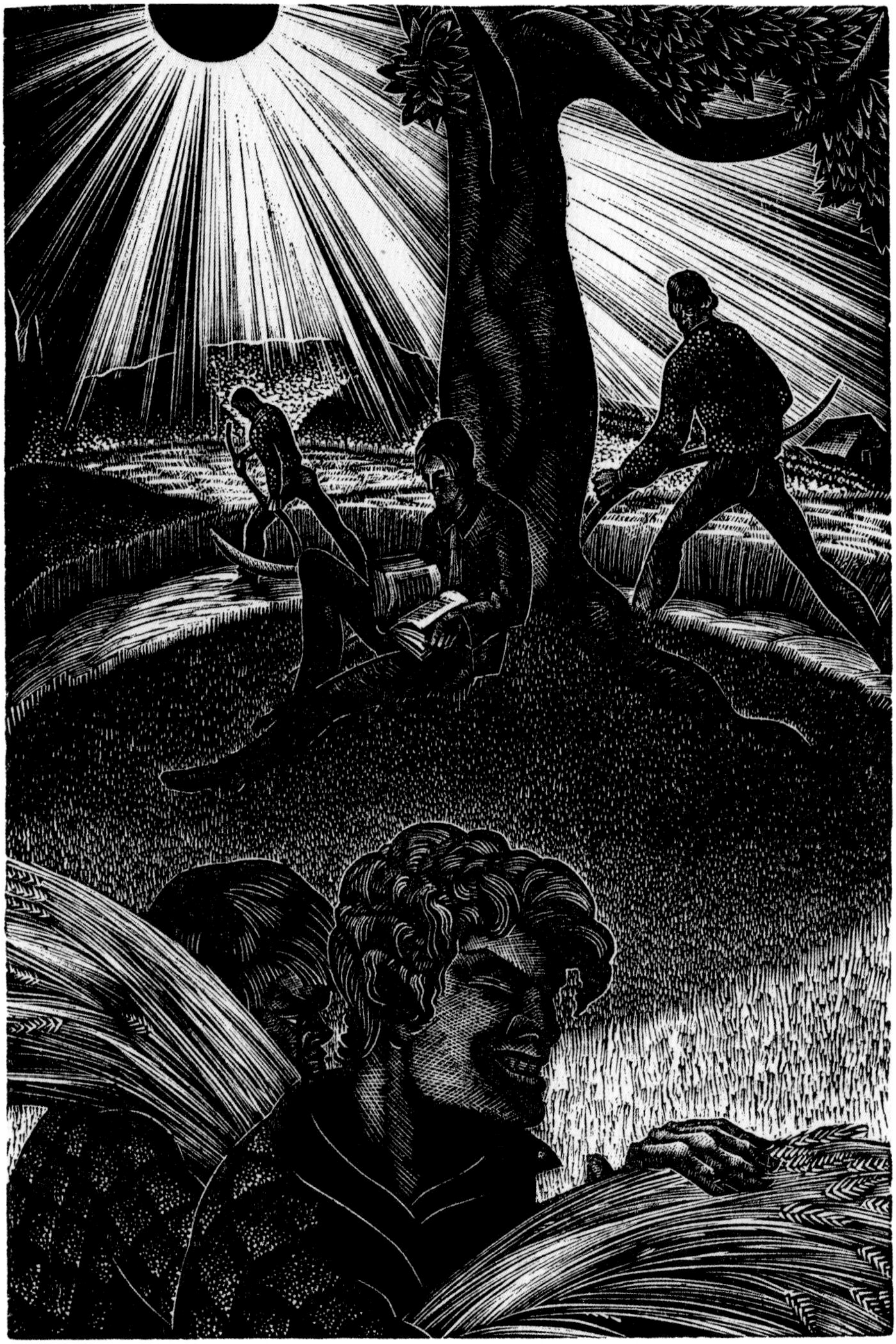

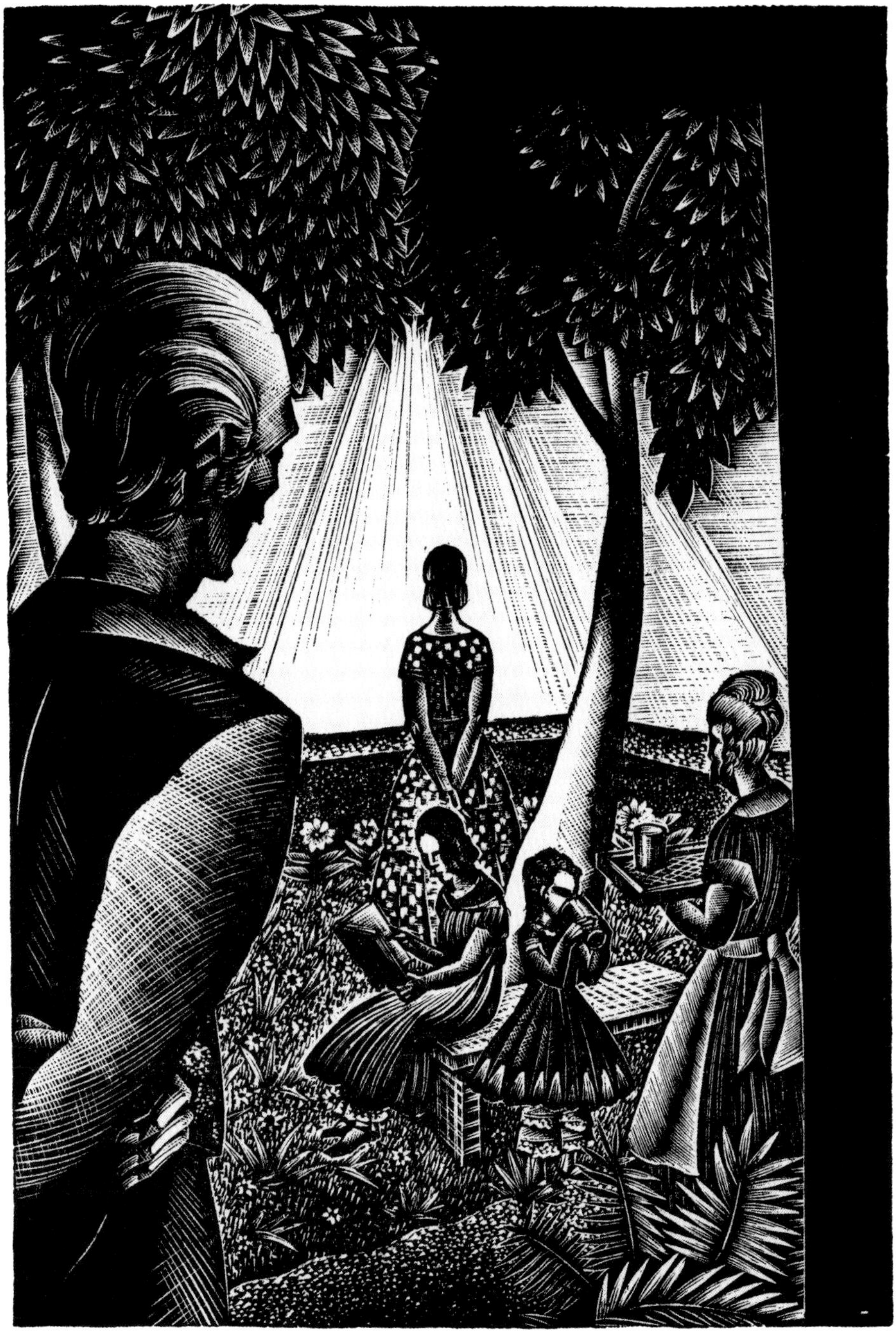

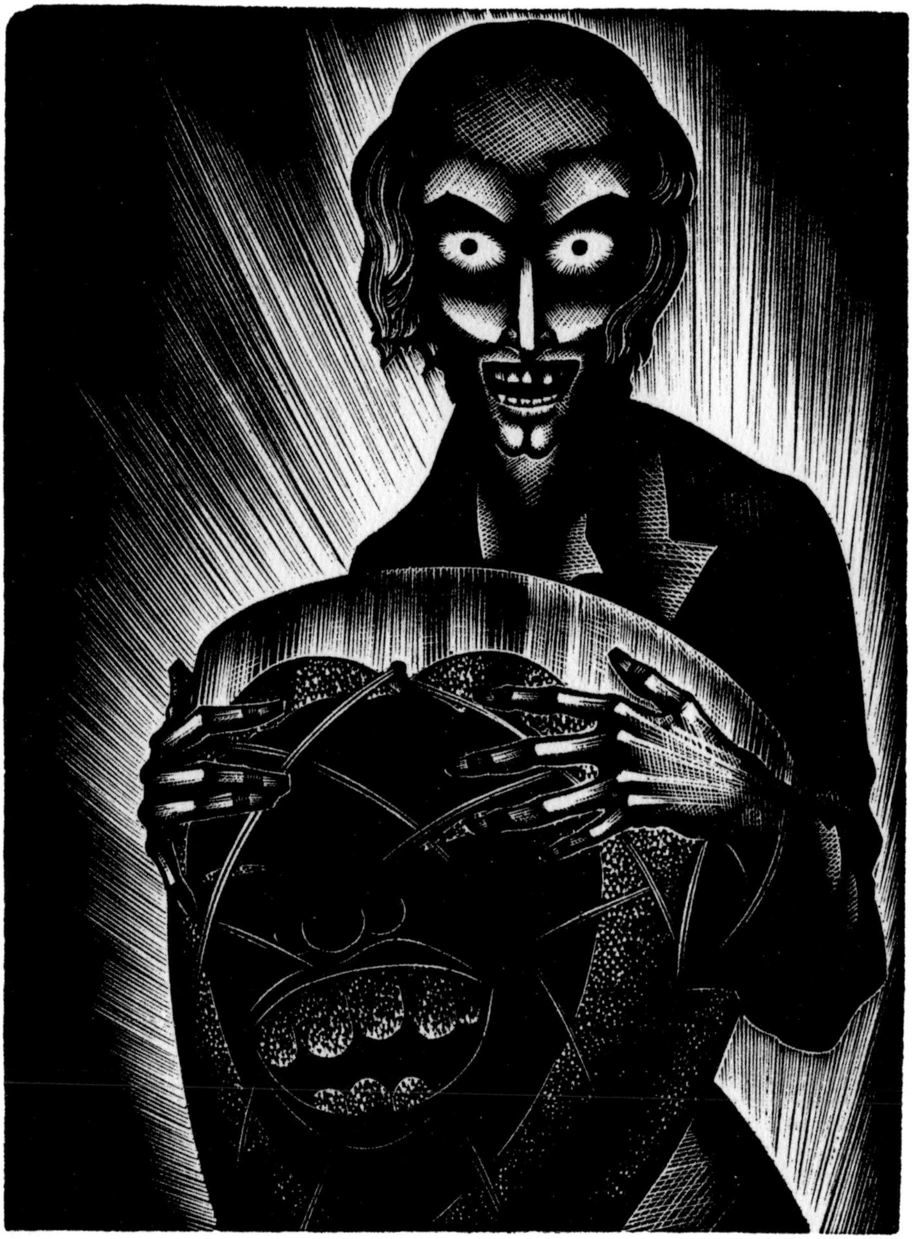

Wild Pilgrimage (1932)

Wild Pilgrimage consists of 105 wood engravings and is Ward's first and only woodcut novel printed in two colors to convey the psychological mood of the protagonist. The dimensions of these prints were enlarged from the previous two novels, increasing the size of the book to 10 x 7 inches. Ward not only enlarged the dimensions of the prints but also the scope of his plot and characters.

In this novel, Ward develops a psychological profile of a lone man during the Depression who attempts to escape the injustices around him. The protagonist is a factory worker who decides to leave the confines of a factory town to discover a liberated life in the country (page 60). He does not go far into the woods before he witnesses the lynching of a black man (page 61). This incident drives him deeper into the country, where he eventually finds work with a farmer. However, when the protagonist begins to act out his sexual fantasies with the farmer's wife, he flees to escape the wrath of the farmer. The protagonist discovers a homestead hidden even deeper in the woods, where an old hermit offers him a place to stay. He learns from the old hermit how to grow fruits and vegetables and listens to the hermit describe the knowledge he has gained from reading books (page 63, top). While lying down in front of the fireplace, the protagonist fades away into a fantasy in which he crawls out of a cauldron, wherein a figure of a fat capitalist reins in his slaves. With the hermit's aid, the protagonist rolls the giant cauldron off the earth and sends it like a comet into space. The protagonist sees himself as a savior battling the injustices in his factory. Supported by his fantasies, he goes back to the factory town, where he joins a labor rally that clashes with armed factory guards. As he battles against the guards (page 62), he has another fantasy where he strangles the factory owner and cuts off his head. When he raises the severed head of the owner, the head he holds in his hand is revealed to be his own. When he returns to reality, he is killed in the fighting.

In order to make the transition from reality to the protagonist's subconscious, Ward uses orange ink instead of the standard black ink (page 237, top). This jump from reality to fantasy allows Ward to effectively portray the protagonist's hidden sexual obsession and his fantasy to escape from the social inequity in reality. Ward termed these two states the "inner" and "outer" worlds.

Many of the images in the protagonist's inner world are copied from and sometimes enhanced by his outer world. In one fantasy, the towers surround the protagonist like giant redwood trees, though the foliage in this case is blasting fire and smoke. The protagonist, the size of an insect in comparison to the smokestacks, raises his arms in defiance. At his feet are dead or slumbering figures. The iron fence in the next picture is another object taken from his outer world. The protagonist is trapped inside the fence with a towering smokestack. The sun shines below the menacing clouds of smoke in the sky, offering the protagonist a glimmer of hope (page 225). The protagonist bends two of the bars on the gate and jumps down from a cliff to a river below, where he floats on his back, allowing the current to take him swiftly downstream.

The final picture in this sequence is a highly charged sexual scene (page 238). In contrast to the erect smoke stacks in previous pictures, the tree trunks sway diagonally over a reclining figure of a nude woman. The protagonist is bare to his waist, his left arm resting on the raised roots of a tree. The arms and legs of the reclining nude are displayed with the same bending lines as the roots near the protagonist's groin. The flow of lines in the picture is worth noting in regard to the tension that Ward presents. The towering trees are in direct contrast to the smokestacks in the first picture, and the lines of the tree trunks point toward the reclining woman. The protagonist raises himself out of the horizontal river, and the multiple lines in the river's current provide contrast to the basic outlines of the tree trunks. The diagonal shape of the protagonist, directed toward the woman, creates tension against the bordering horizontal lines in the river and the vertical lines of the trees. The opening in the trees, with the grassy knoll where the woman reclines, shows the overall direction of movement in the picture. In addition to the suggestive composition, Ward drapes tentaclelike vines from the trees, sweeping the protagonist toward the woman.

As shown in the above fantasy, each inner-world sequence is developed from the previous sequence in the outer world. For example, while the protagonist is staying with a farmer and his wife, he observes the farmer's wife standing outside under a full moon. The color of the page changes to orange, indicating a dream sequence. He approaches her, standing between two long, erect, and smooth trees whose top limbs are symbolically intertwined. The couple walk together over a barren landscape hand in hand. He grasps her. She moves away playfully and stretches herself out naked in front of him. He falls to his knees and she brings her head down and kisses the top of his head. The protagonist reaches behind her and presses his head between her breasts (page 237, bottom). The color of the next page changes back to black, indicating his outer world. The farmer's wife thrashes her arms at the protagonist (page 63, bottom), who has acted out his fantasy and inappropriately approached her. Her eyes open wide in alarm. This is a startling revelation to the protagonist, who recognizes that his inner world has crossed over to his outer world.

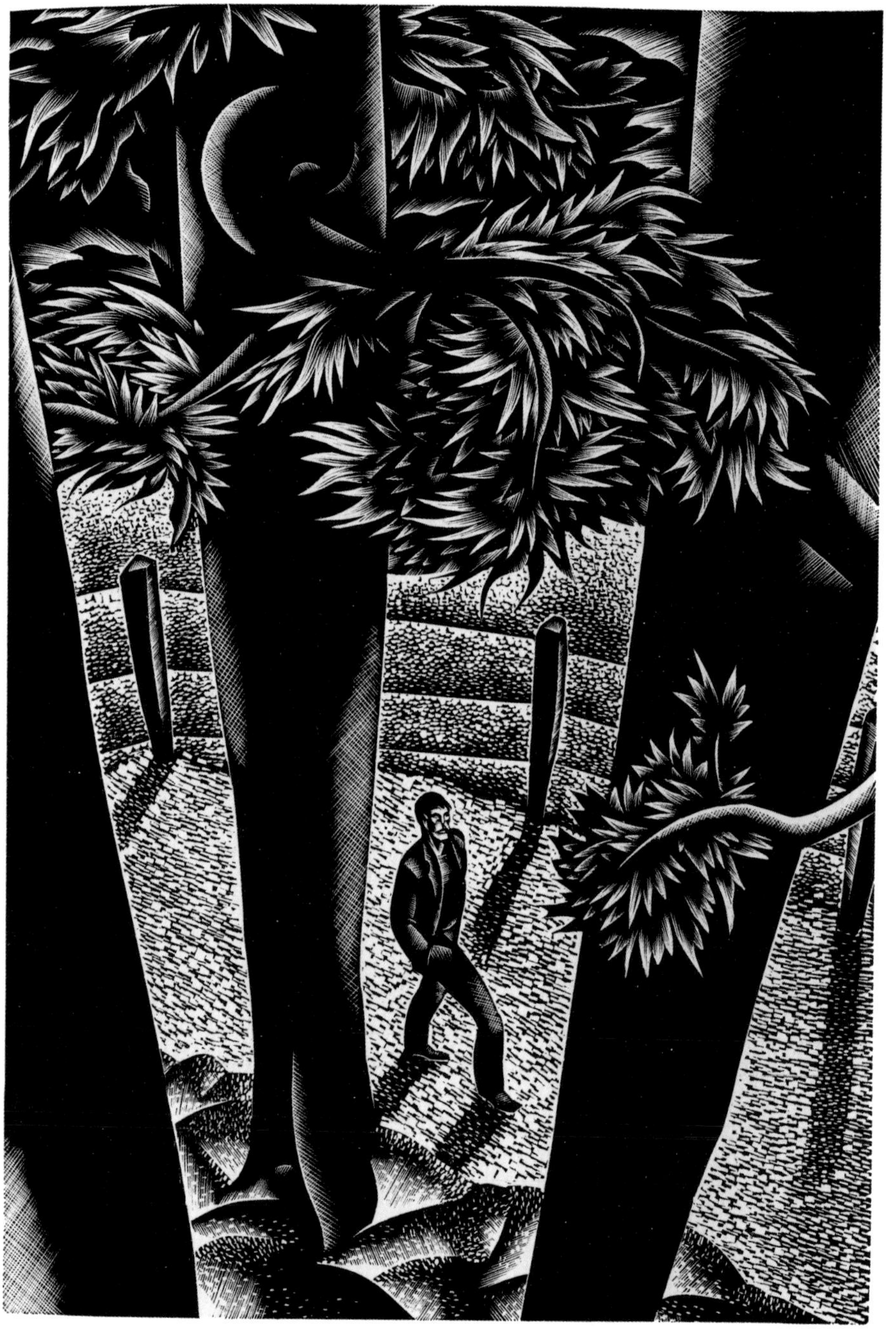

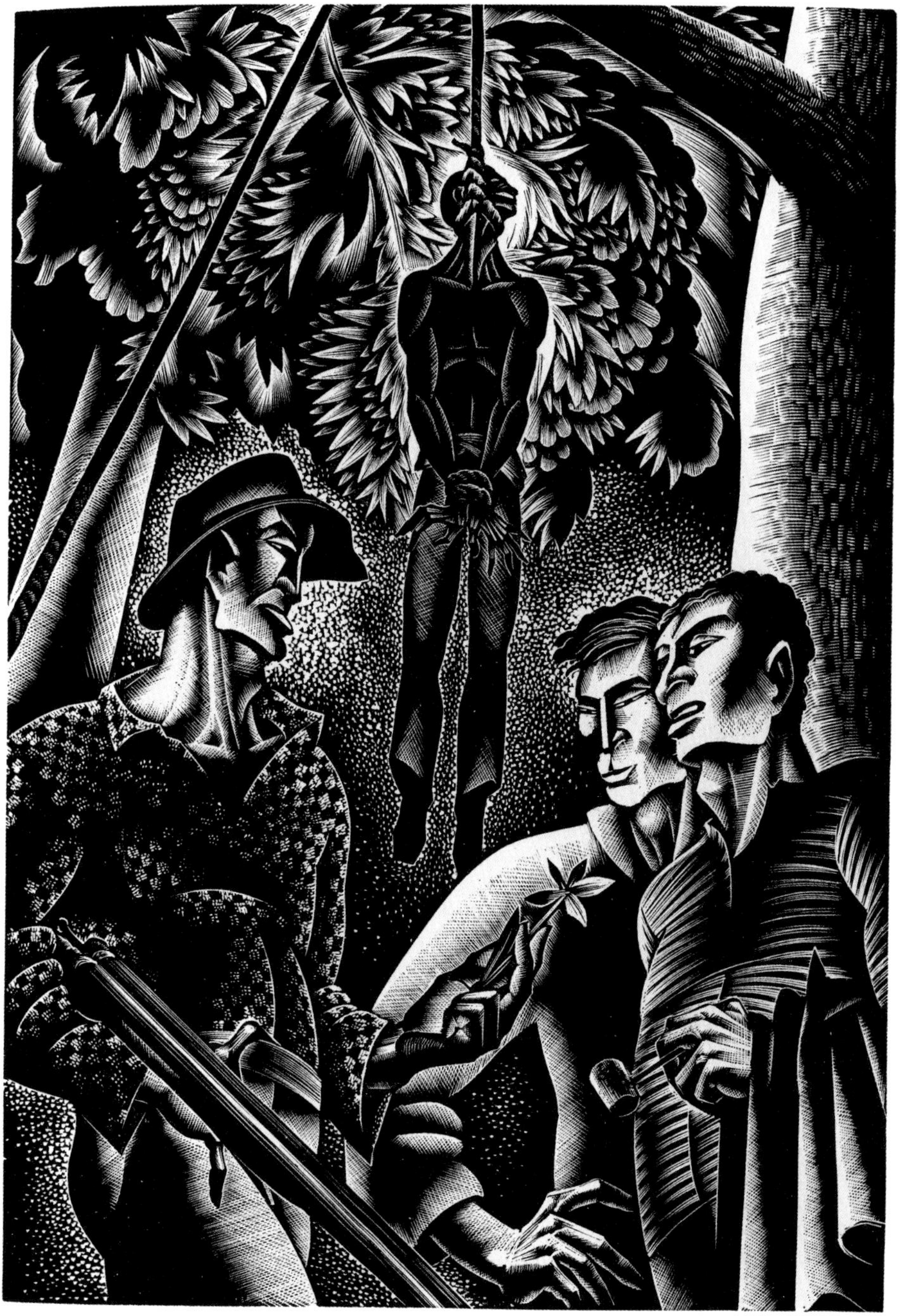

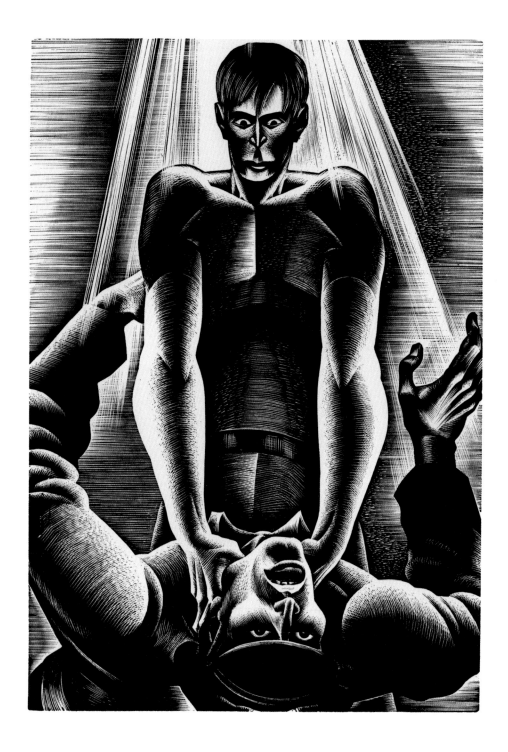

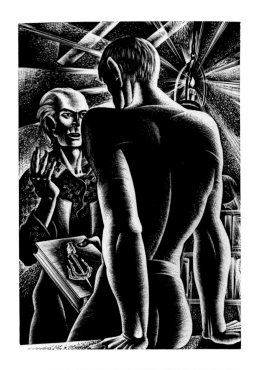

Prelude to a Million Years (1933)

Ward's fourth wordless novel, *Prelude to a Million Years,* includes thirty wood engravings printed from the original blocks in a limited edition of 920 copies. It was published by Equinox Cooperative Press, which was conceived by Ward and included a number of New York's finest artists and printers who were interested in reviving the art of quality bookmaking. The Equinox Cooperative Press's publication of *Prelude to a Million Years* provided the financial success the company needed to continue for a few years before its demise in 1937, after it had published sixteen quality books.

Prelude to a Million Years revisits the theme of *Gods' Man.* In this case, Ward's romantic ideal of the artist is revised. Ward displays the idea of living art for art's sake. Ward places his artist—in this novel a sculptor instead of a painter—in the backdrop of the Depression. In direct contrast to the myth of Pygmalion, in which a statue comes to life in a loving embrace with its sculptor, Ward's alienated sculptor kneels in despair at the foot of his sculpture as his room is engulfed in flames (opposite).

This short novel is filled with symbolism, including city buildings that signify capitalism, the American flag that denotes patriotism, and a fire hydrant that suggests the incendiary mood on the streets in a crowd of patriots and strikers (page 66).

Pulling together his skillful engraving and his expert narrative skills, Ward creates some memorable, distinctive scenes. One example is the sculptor's associations with the representation of the female in this novel. The first is the sculpture, which is an unrealistic symbol of mother/lover chiseled out of stone by the sculptor (page 67, top). The second is the sculptor's former lover whom he visits, discovering her passed out drunk and naked on her bed because of his neglect (page 67, bottom). And the third is the woman across the hall whose husband beats her (page 68) until she falls unconscious on the floor. The husband's raised hand is large like a hammer in obvious association with the sculptor's mallet.

In another example, in a three-page sequence, the sculptor walks past a flag-waving event. His darkened figure shows his singularity and his separation from others even on a crowded street.

All the men in the crowd have their hats off around raised American flags. One man confronts the sculptor. In the next picture, the sculptor has taken off his hat. An officer grips his neck and forces his head down in allegiance to the flag, which is draped over the groin of the military officer (page 69). The soldier to the left of the sculptor looks appeased and the man in the right foreground who originally confronted him has a smug expression on his face in contrast to his agitated expression in the previous picture. In this highly suggestive scene, an erect flagpole in the background stands over the officer and sculptor.

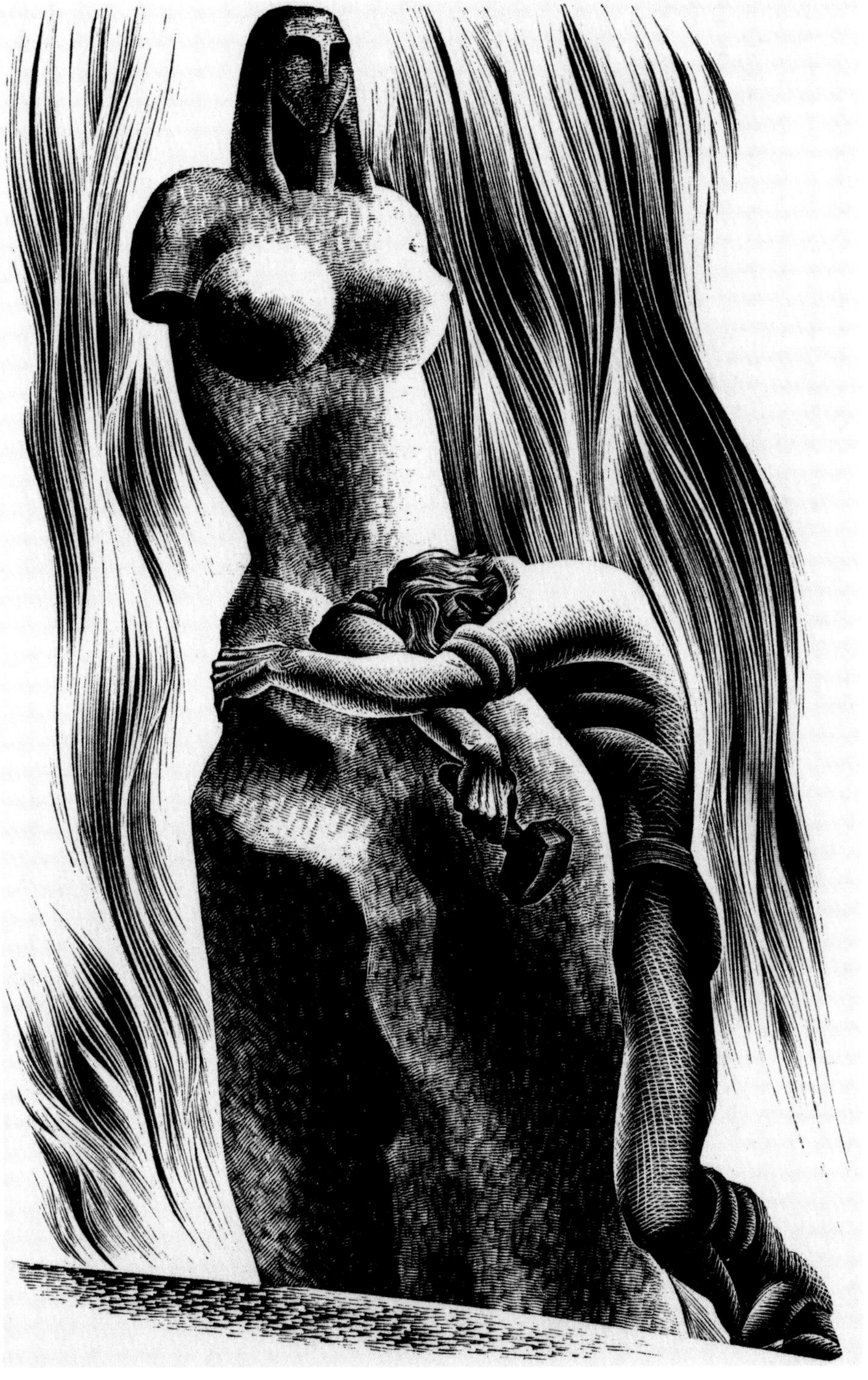

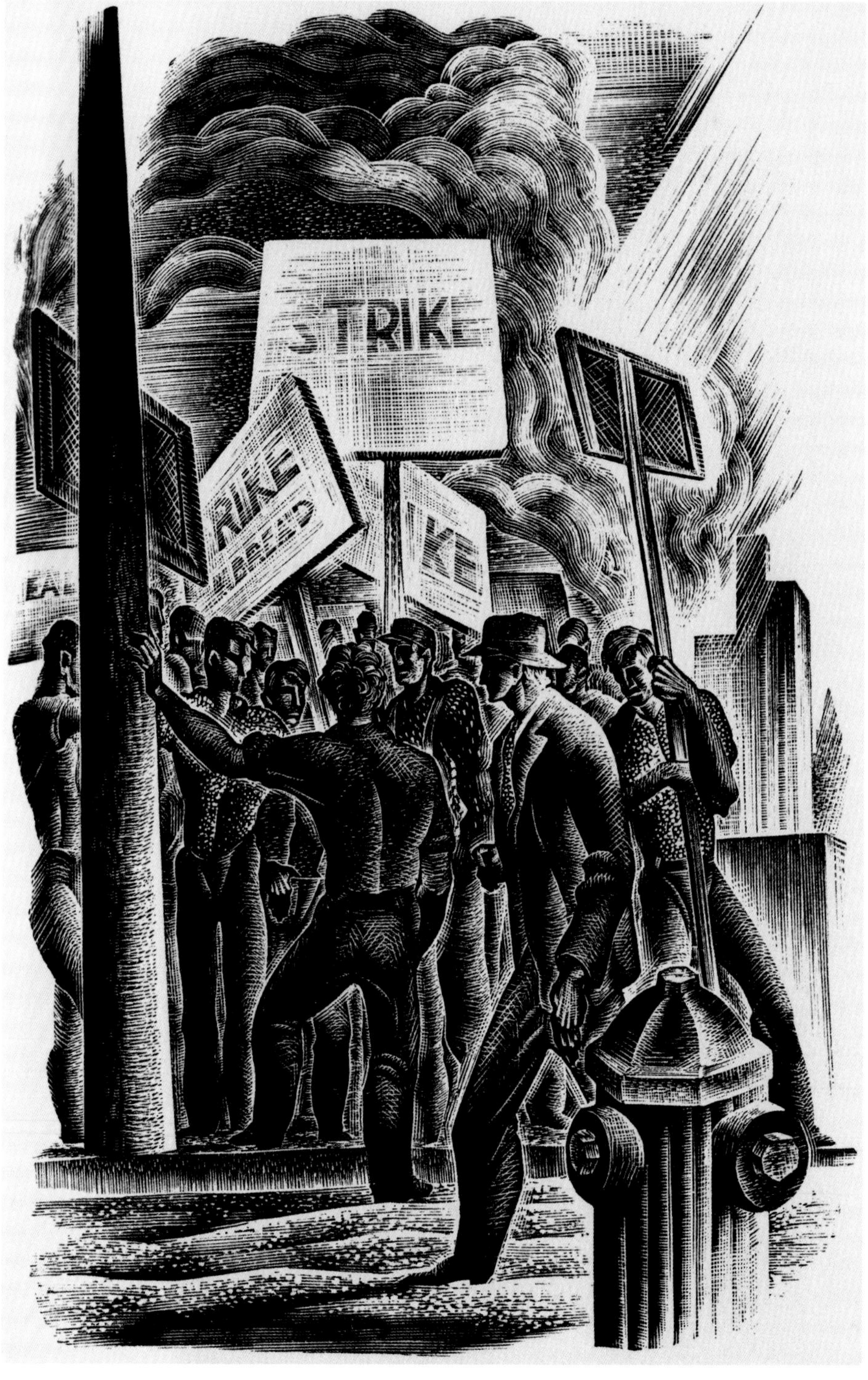
STRIKE

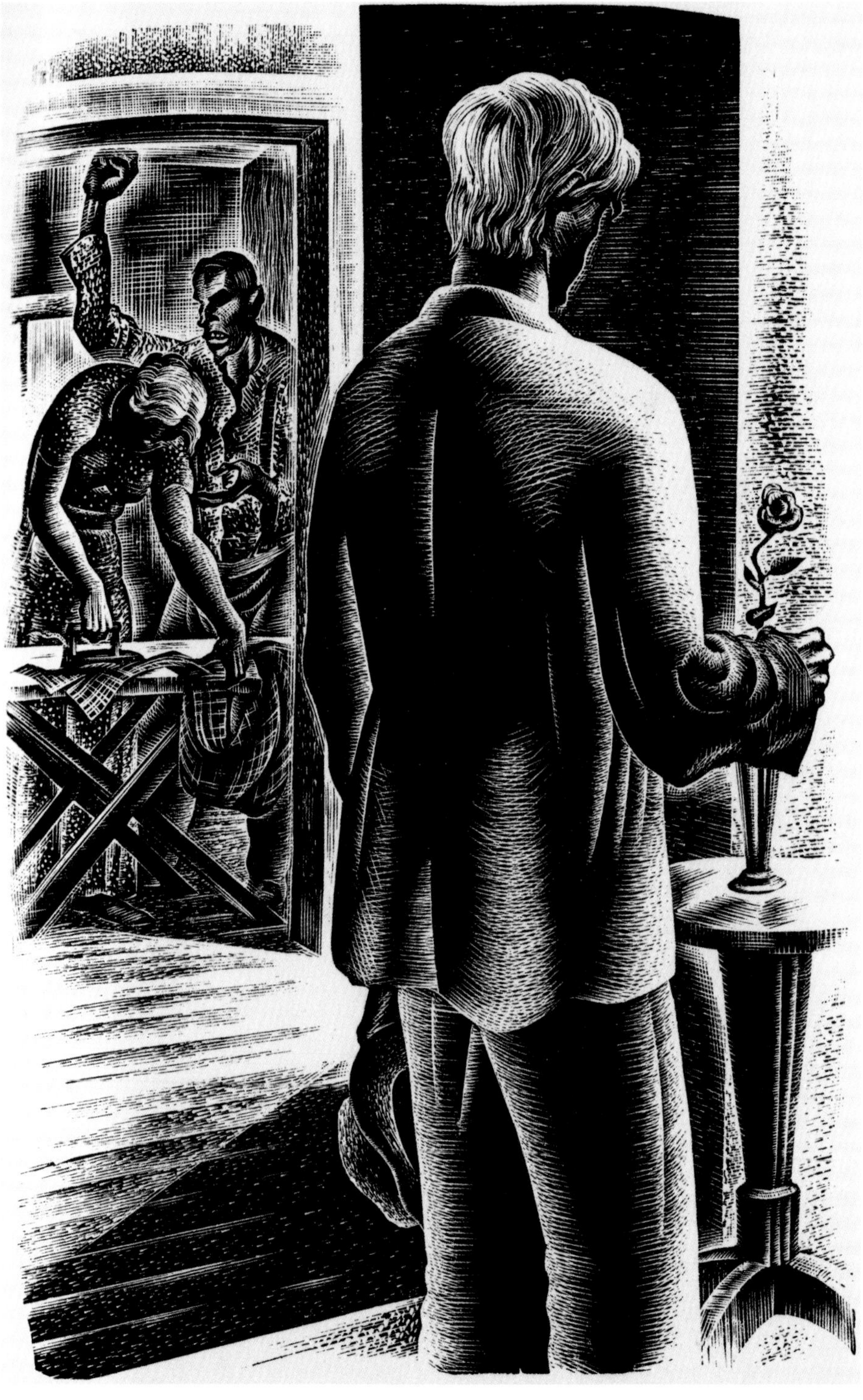

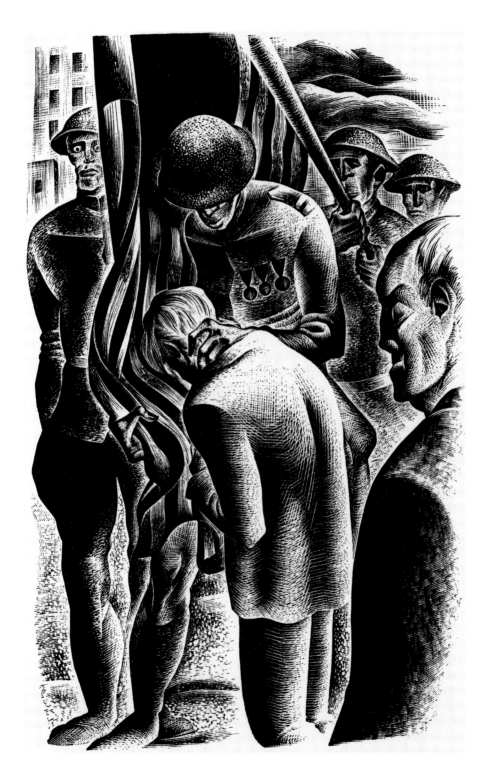

Song Without Words (1936)

Song Without Words, with its controversial metaphors, was printed directly from twenty-one blocks in a limited edition for Random House. Like *Prelude to a Million Years,* this book displayed the crisp quality of Ward's printed blocks. *Song Without Words*, which Ward referred to as a prose poem, focuses on the moral dilemma of bringing a child into a world clouded with the ills of the Depression and the growing threat of Fascism. The story follows a woman who has conceived a child (opposite) and ponders giving birth in a Fascist-ruled world where people are abused, imprisoned, and murdered. The woman spins around and falls into a nightmarish sequence filled with wrenching fears (page 72). Ward's disturbing and impassioned engravings include an image of ants crawling over the skin of a baby impaled on a bayonet (page 73, top) and the woman standing in rebellion against a large skull. In the end, though, she raises her fist in defiance of her fears and gives birth to her child. Her spouse crawls down into her world and remains at her side. Their union on the final page, with his naked, muscular figure enveloping her and their child, offers the reader a glimmer of hope for the future (page 73, bottom).

As in his previous woodcut novels, Ward uses standard symbols such as the looming city buildings and fat capitalists to eclipse the individual. In this novel, Ward adds vermin and scavengers like rats, vultures, and ants to heighten the unpleasantness of the mother's fears. A swastika is displayed in a banner above the barbed-wire fence, which wraps around a concentration camp of starving children (page 74).

Perhaps no other single picture combines the elements of Ward's themes and symbolism better than the eighteenth wood engraving (page 75) in this novel. The mother comes face to face with the skull that looms above her. On closer examination, this skull, more than just a symbol of death, displays tombstonelike teeth that are the jutting tops of city buildings. The city represents oppression and death, and capitalists slink comfortably inside the eye sockets. The mother stands posed in the foreground, her right arm raised high in defiance.

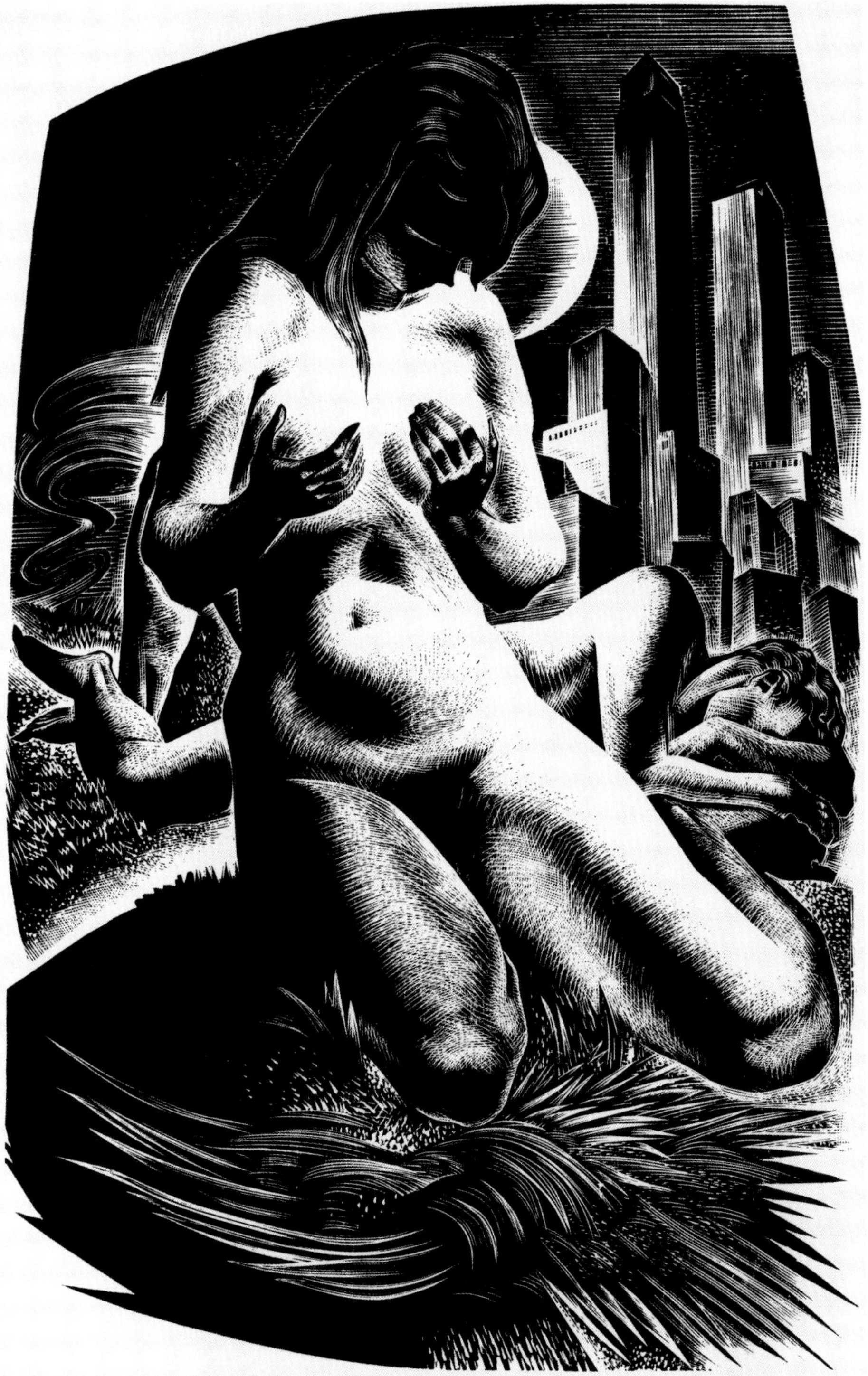

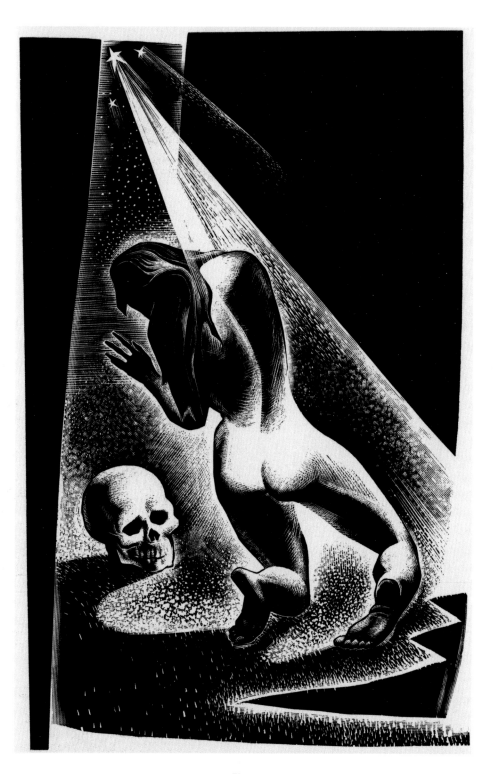

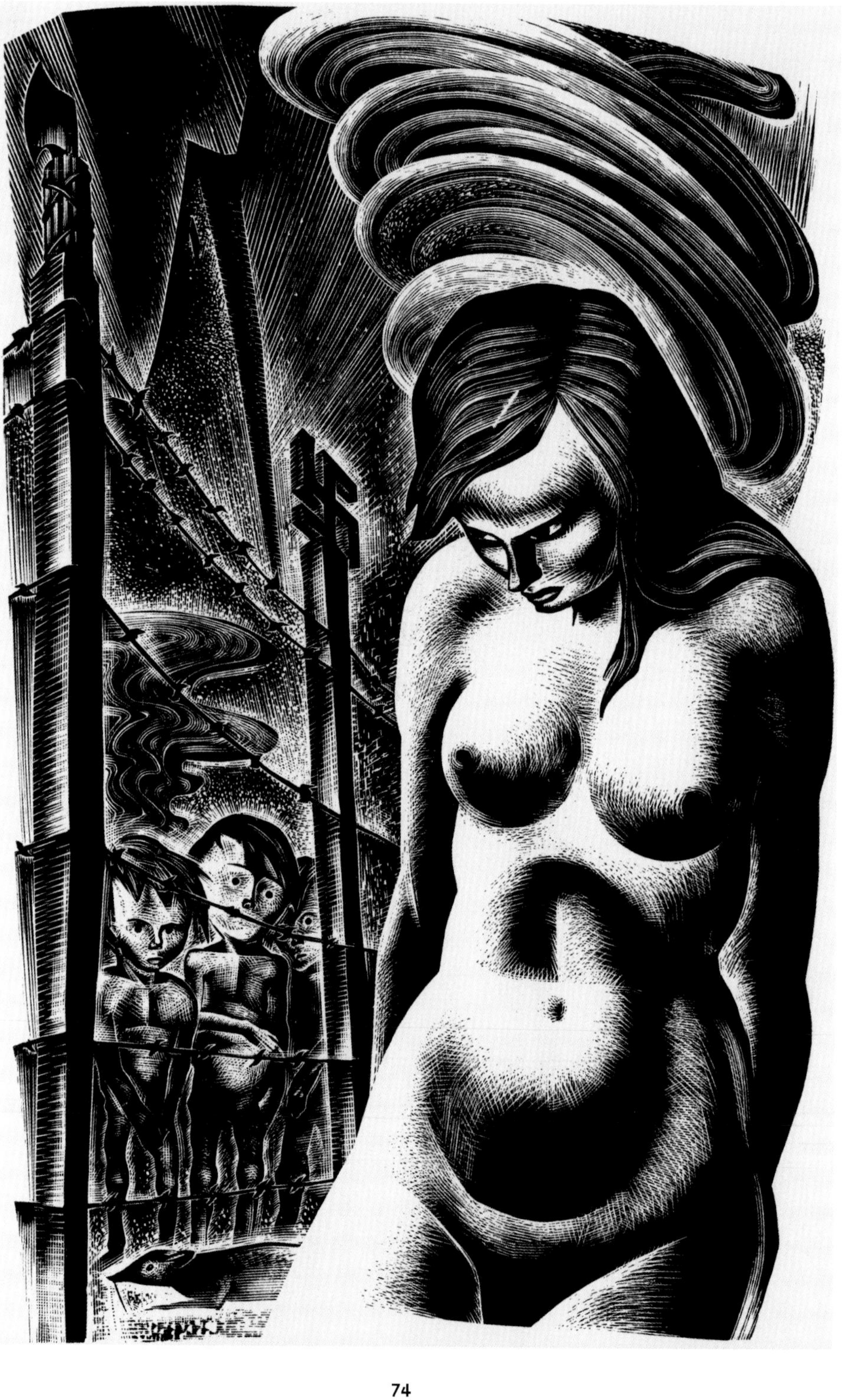

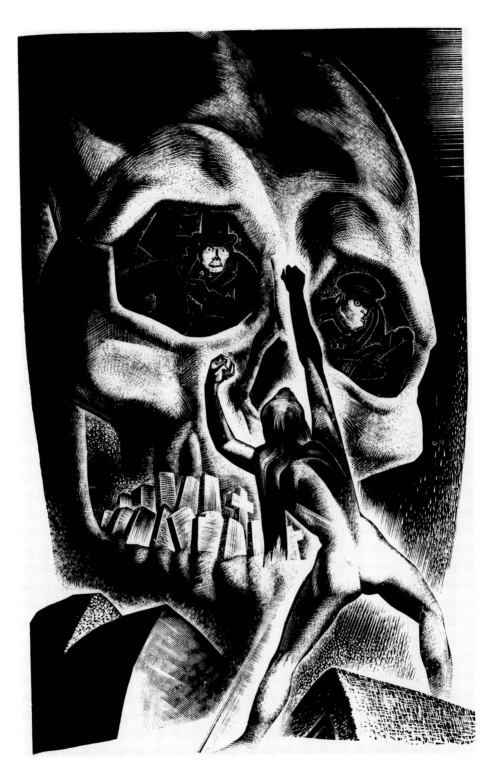

Vertigo (1937)

Ward's sixth wordless novel, *Vertigo*, is a colossal book, and considered his masterpiece, with 230 wood engravings that took two years to complete. In this novel, Ward examines the effects of the Depression, specifically through the lives of three characters—a girl, a boy, and a rich, elderly gentleman. Since the plot of *Vertigo* is so involved, Ward breaks the narrative into three parts, each following the three main characters and the way their lives cross during the years from 1929 to 1934. Ward examines the life of each character against the backdrop of the Depression. Like the evolving proletarian fiction that emerged at this time, *Vertigo* was Ward's political declaration of a dying capitalistic system.

Ward's focus and detail with the single figure and the crowd scenes is remarkable. For example, the nude figure of the girl that opens the novel is portrayed in realistic detail (opposite). The lines that capture her body are thin and crisp—almost fragile—in comparison to the traditional bold lines in many of his other wood engravings. She is shown stretching her arms high above her head, which is tilted to one side. Her eyes are closed and her young breasts are raised high on her chest. In the background, the dresser mirror reflects her figure from the back. A curtain of etched lines lights up the curves of her stretching figure. Her eyes are closed as though she has just risen from bed. Ward allows us to gaze cautiously on her naked figure knowing she may open her eyes at any moment.

Ward's restriction to three main characters allows for fuller depiction of them in readily displayed comparisons and contrasts. For example, Ward displays a full nude picture of the elderly gentleman that is in direct contrast to the youthful figure of the girl. He wears his wrinkled and sagging skin like an overcoat hanging from his bones (right). The girl, in striking contrast, is displayed with hands raised up in the air with an energy that makes her ready to spring off the page onto the reader's lap. Symbolically, she represents the enthusiasm of youth and a hopeful future following World War I. Both she and the boy initially share these dreams of the future and carelessly dance, confident that nothing

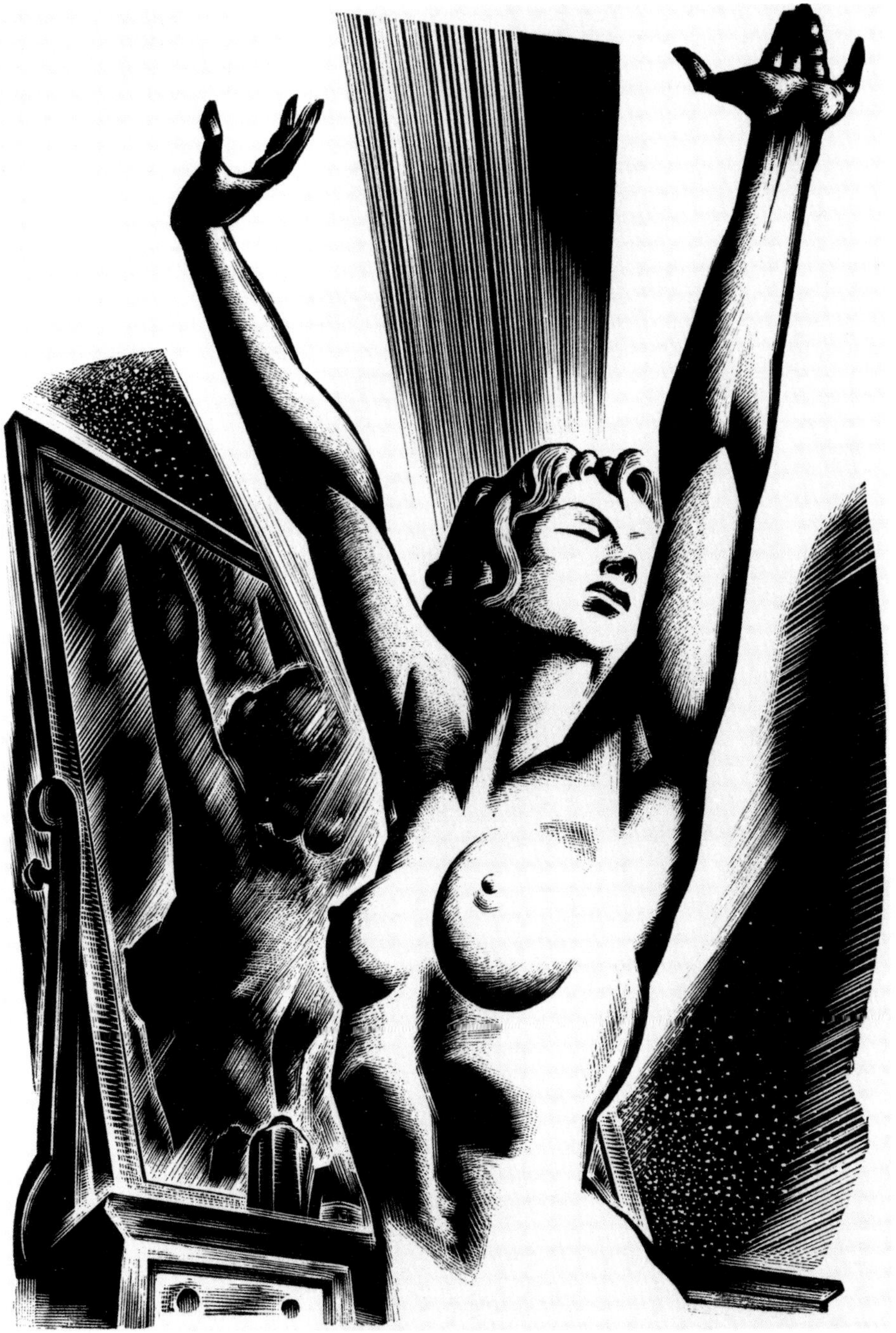

can interfere with their hopes (below). Their world is represented as an amusement park with a roller coaster that rises into the clouds. Their enjoyment is interrupted by a storm that represents the beginning of the Depression era (page 80), which ultimately brings tragedy into their lives. When they reunite at the end of the book, they are shown embracing each other in fear on this roller coaster, which now appears foreboding as it speeds down into darkness (page 81).

In addition to the contrast between the younger and the older generations, Ward shows how the Depression strips the girl and boy of their individuality and forces them into a large, anonymous mass of desperate men and women standing in relief lines for the simplest of needs such as food, clothing, and shelter. Ward displays this gradual erosion by showing the girl standing in a bread line under the watchful eyes of a policeman (page 82).

In *Vertigo*, the small number of characters encourages us to perceive them as cultural caricatures of that era. For example, the elderly gentleman is dressed in the classic clothes of a wealthy man of the era who values a work of art based on the price tag and whose public charity consists of giving Thanksgiving food baskets to the needy. This character is the product of the traditional industrial system of master and slave, a representation of traditional America further emphasized by his company, "Eagle

Corporation of America." The father of the girl is a white-collar worker who is laid off from this corporation. His layoff eventually leads to his unsuccessful suicide attempt and eviction from their home (page 83).

In the winter, when the snow covers the city, the elderly gentleman takes a train south, where he lies on a solitary beach with palm trees. The title of "elderly gentleman" seems appropriate, and his solitary figure almost brings a moment of compassion, which is quickly forgotten in the ensuing chapters as he proves to be anything but gentle (page 84, top). With the threat of a strike in his company, he enlists the support of politicians (page 84, bottom). Action against the striking workers increases until the leaders of the strike are gathered up (page 85) and murdered by a group of hired thugs (page 86). When the elderly gentleman is informed of this outcome, he places the phone back down on its cradle and the cord, like a lifeline, goes horizontal, indicating the death of the workers.

Another feature that Ward skillfully develops is the use of expressions and gestures to convey mood. Perhaps the most memorable facial gestures are those of the five board members of the Eagle Corporation of America as they gloat over the upward trend in profits at the expense of the workers (page 87).

One of the more interesting developments in the plot is the subtle overlap in the three characters' stories, and how the presence of each in one chapter foreshadows future involvements and events in another chapter. For example, while he is delivering groceries, the boy catches a distant glimpse of the girl with whom he later falls in love (page 88, top). We know it is the girl from the first chapter, "The Girl," because she is carrying a violin case—an instrument that she dreams will take her to celebrated heights. Later in the third chapter, "The Elderly Gentleman," when the gentleman is dying, we discover that the boy is the figure depicted on the street in front of the elderly gentleman's mansion, which is based on the exact setting from the previous chapter (page 88, bottom). The doctors see the boy from the gentleman's window. The boy is questioned by one of the doctors and provides a transfusion of life-sustaining blood (page 89) for the gentleman in exchange for money (page 90, top).

Ward makes use of signs and our own capacity to fill in the broken or missing letters in certain pictures, which contributes to the unfolding narrative and provides further insight into each character. He masks the letters in many signs with objects or figures, and our understanding of the text within the context of the picture makes it easy for readers to fill in the missing letters.

Some of the textual signs in this novel that support the narrative are the "insti[tute of] mu[sic]" that the girl attends; a "Free S[oup]" sign that stands over a crowd; and a sign that reads "The Army has Vacan[cies] for young [men] of chara[cter]," which is considered by the boy who travels from one placement bureau to the next looking for

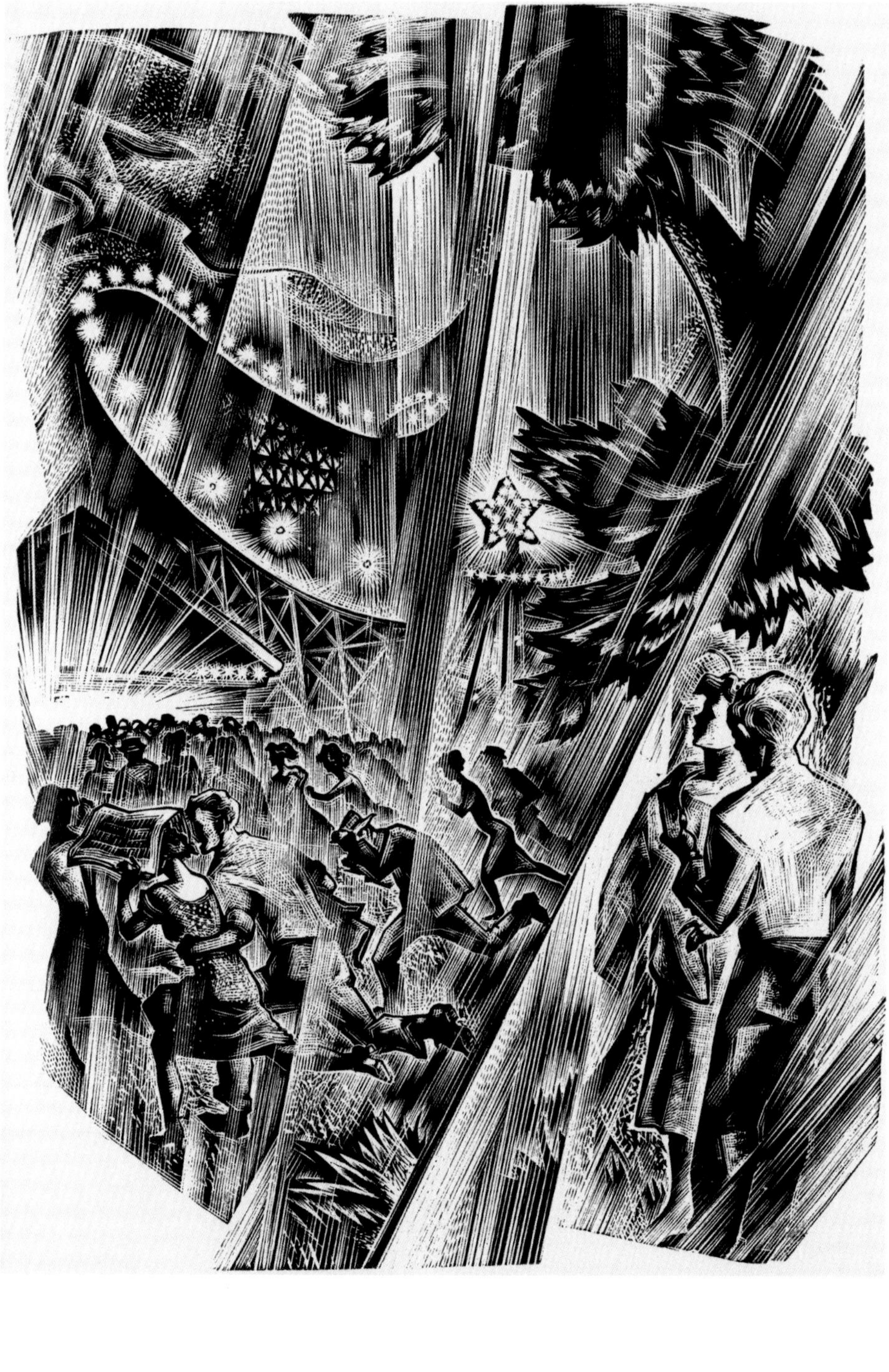

food and work and stands in line with other men to fill an opening. An ironic sign is displayed (page 90, bottom) over the line of men that reads "Your job is our job."

In addition, Ward displays clearly understandable text, such as the posting at the Eagle Corporation factory during layoffs. In a series of pictures the postings get progressively worse. They begin with "All wages are hereby reduced 10 per cent," followed by "All men on night shift laid off until further notice. Day shift will have 15 minutes for lunch and will work all day Saturday." This prompts action by the workers who raise signs reading "Fight for the Union/the Union fights for You. No [W]age Cut." This ignites a bloody strike ending in the death of many workers (page 91).

These textual blocks are numerous in this novel and show a migration from pictures alone to a mix of word and image. Ward's pictorial narratives are far from incorporating the traditional interdependence of word and image recognized in comics, but the use of text in *Vertigo* brings this novel closer to the medium of comics and suggests the affiliation of Ward's wood-engraving novels with the graphic novel.

Ward's distinctive contribution to the graphic arts was his development of the "pictorial narrative," which is what he preferred to call his wordless novels. His use of

visually dynamic objects, consistent symbols, and thematic threads in his pictorial narratives results in first-rate storytelling. In addition to developing a pictorial vocabulary for lengthy storytelling, Ward's experimentation with two-color printing opened the investigation of the psychological world of his characters. In this form, Ward established the basis for storytelling that is used today by artists of picture books and graphic novels.

Finally, in his pictorial narratives, Ward documented the injustices in the American economic and social system during the Depression era. Ironically, the social ills Ward displayed in his novels seventy years ago are evident in today's culture. Though not as readily visible as the soup lines, today's economic uncertainties, the breakup of the family, a shortage of traditional blue-collar jobs, and a general sense of spiritual isolation are realities just as crucial as they were for Americans during the 1930s.

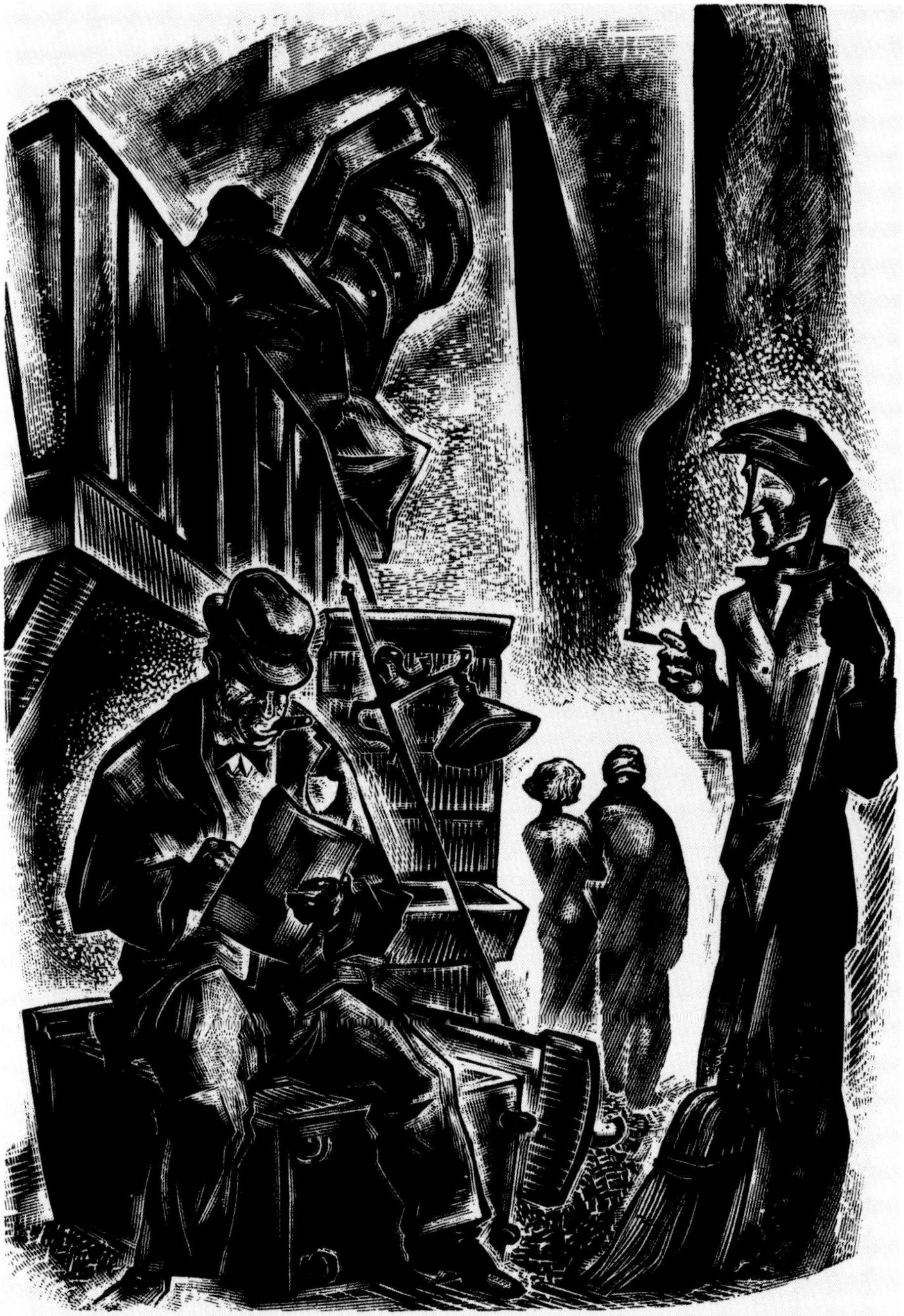

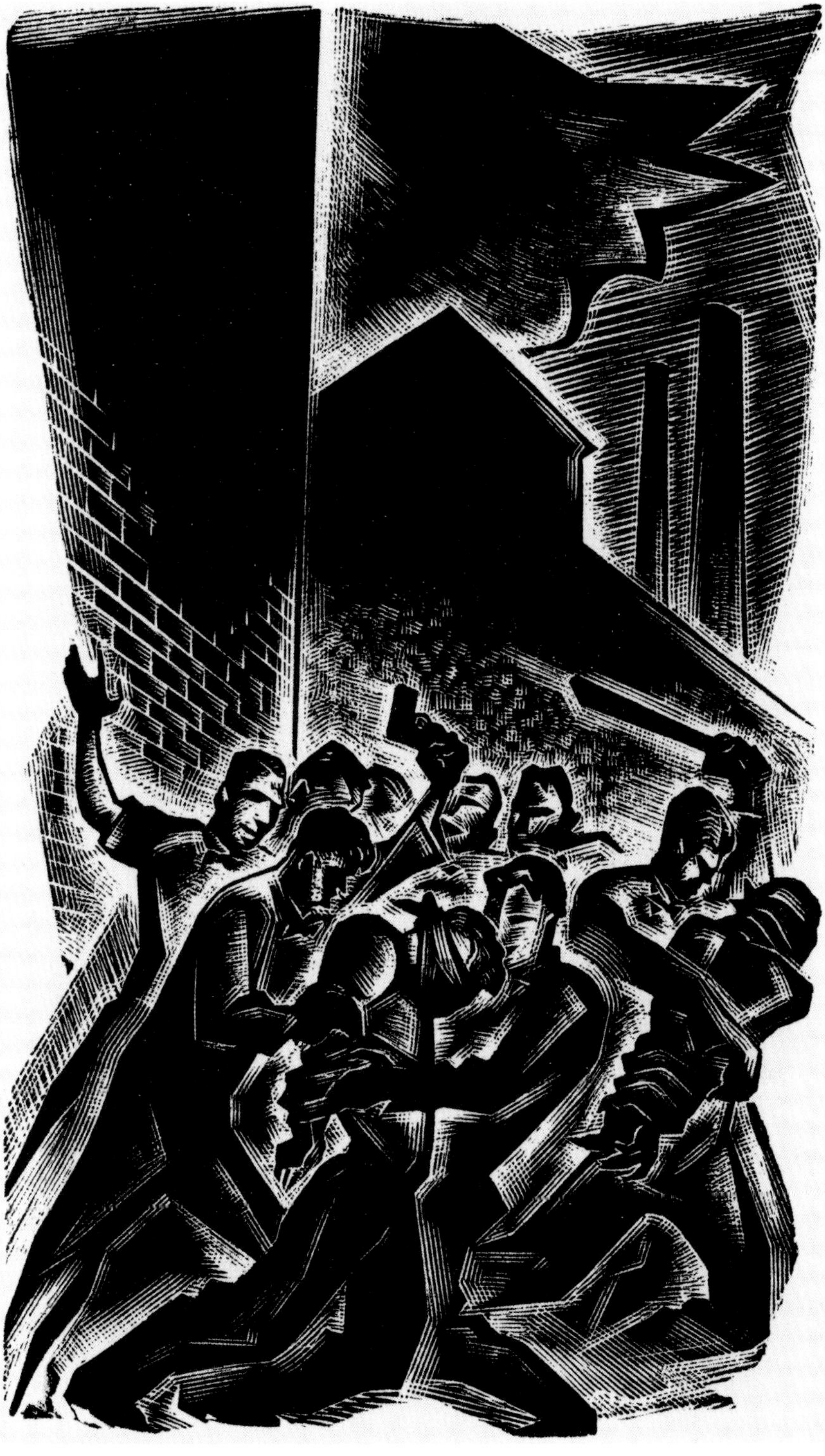

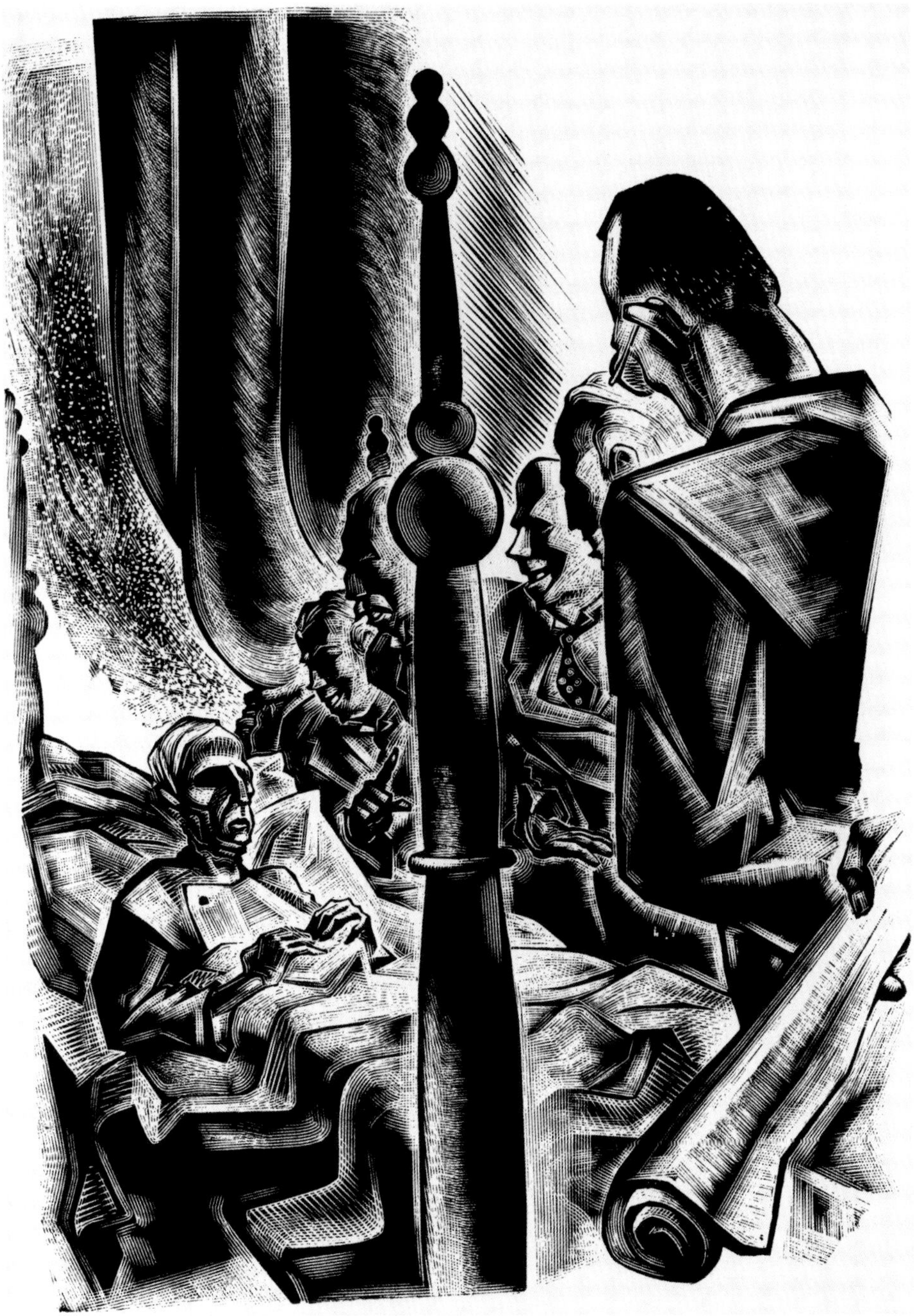

CORNER
GROCERY

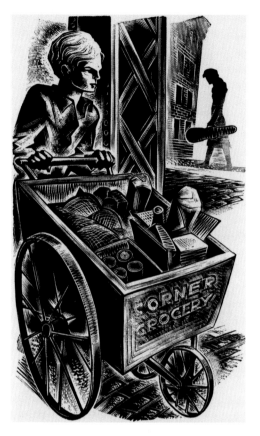

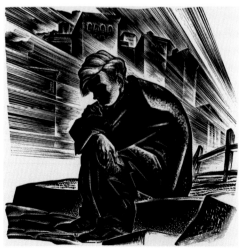

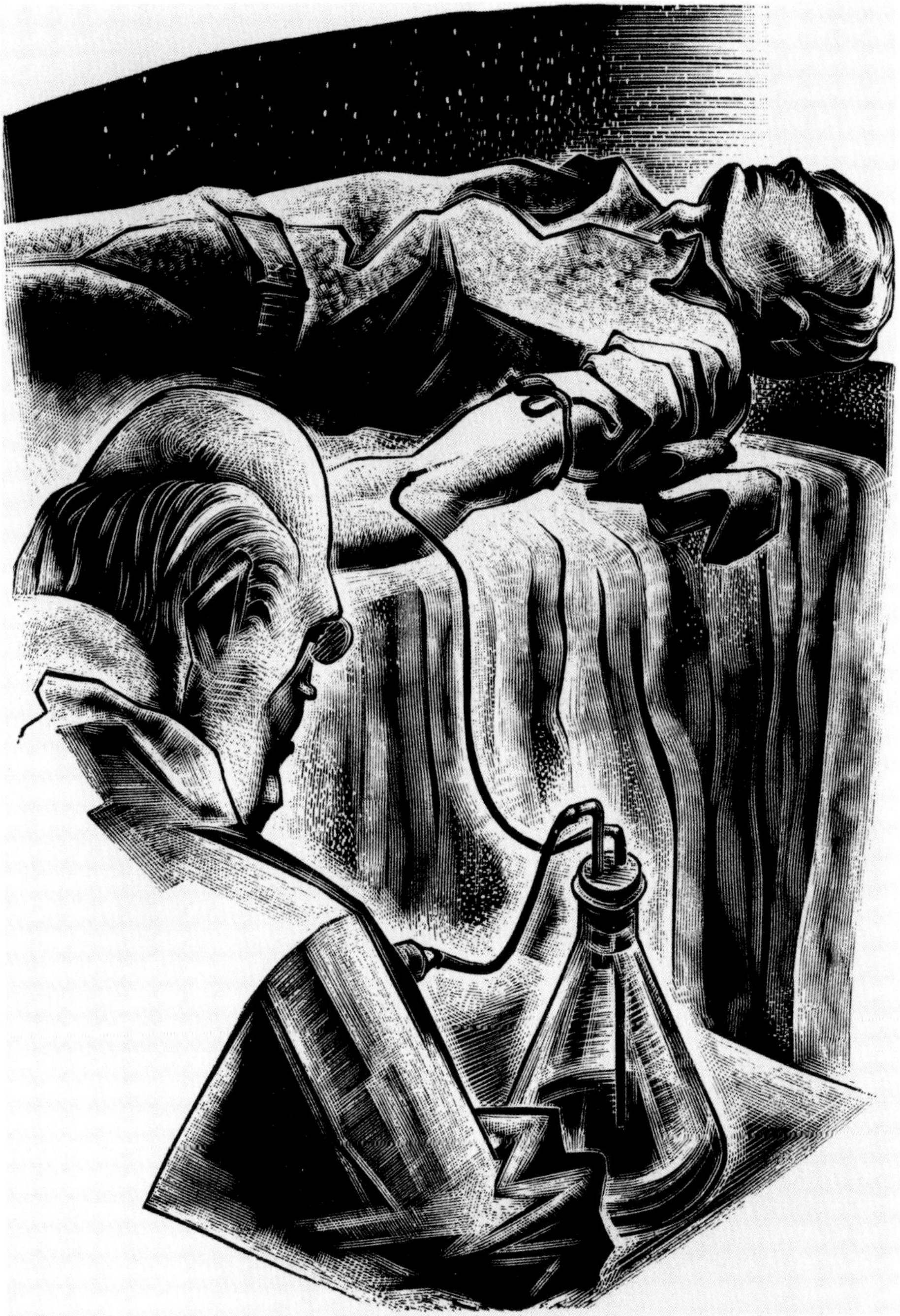

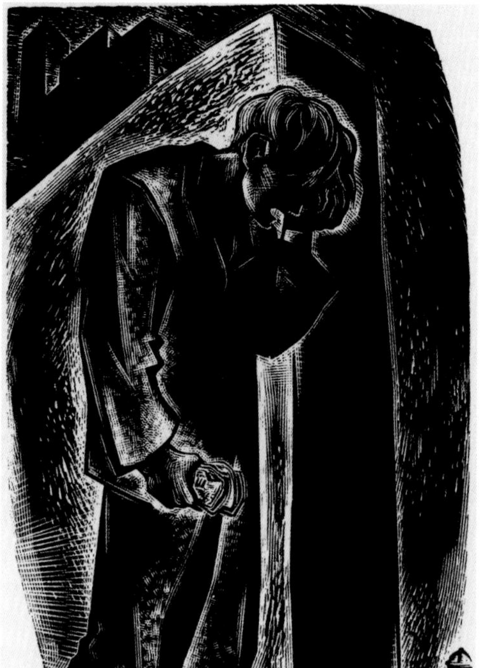

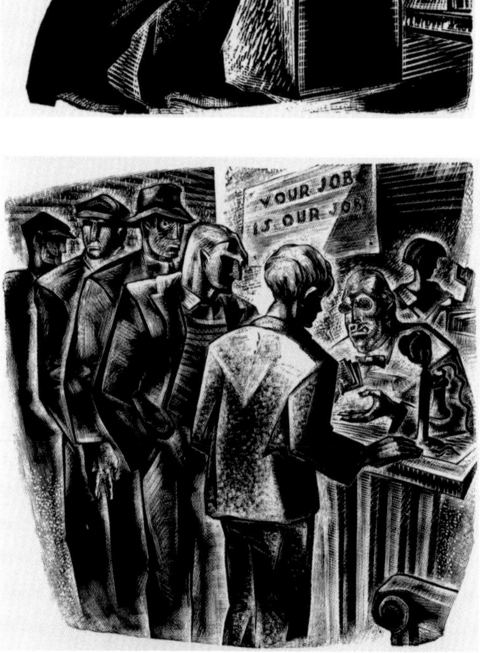
YOUR JOB
IS OUR JOB

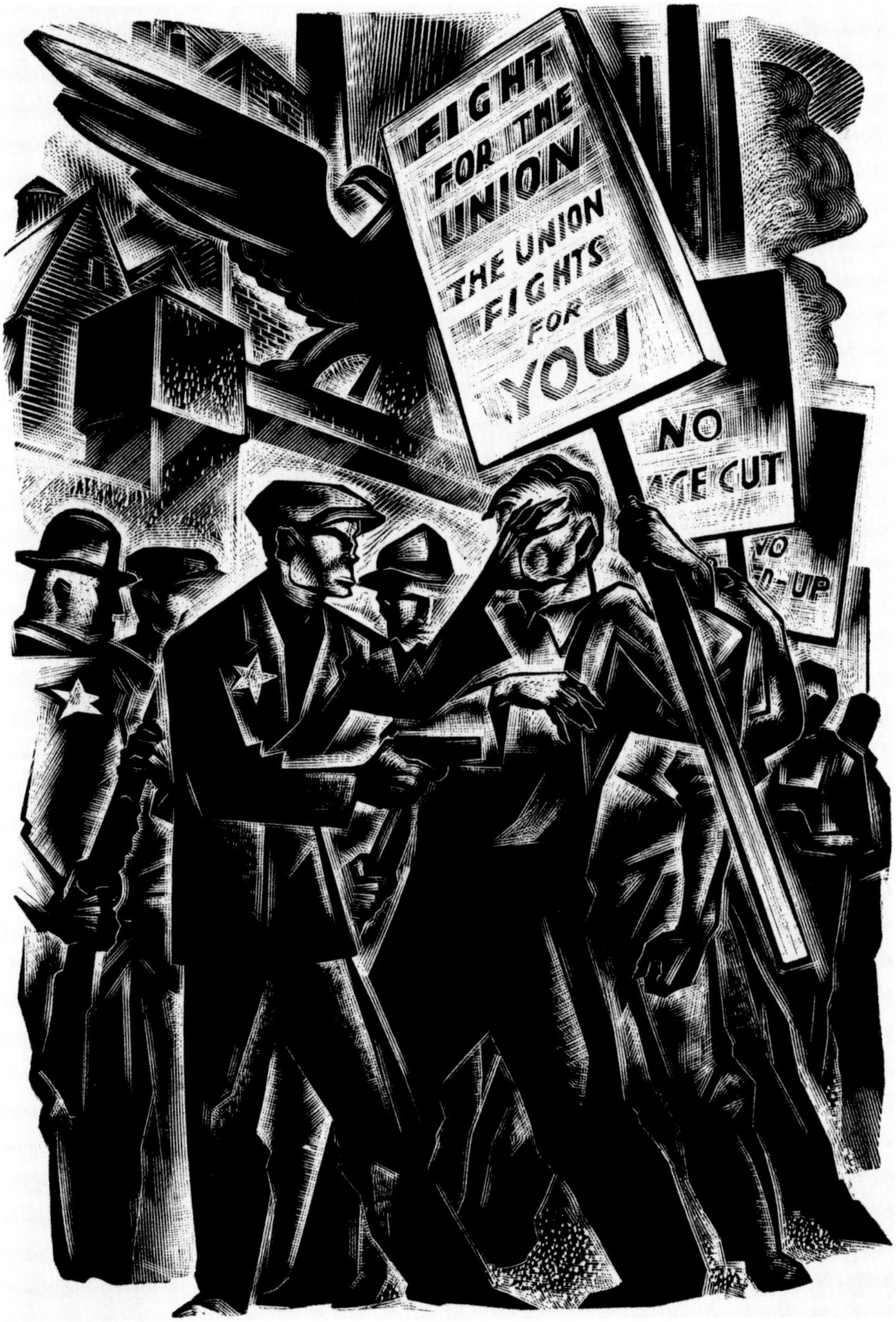
FIGHT FOR THE UNION
THE UNION FIGHTS FOR YOU
NO

Chapter Four

Otto Nückel

(1888–1955)

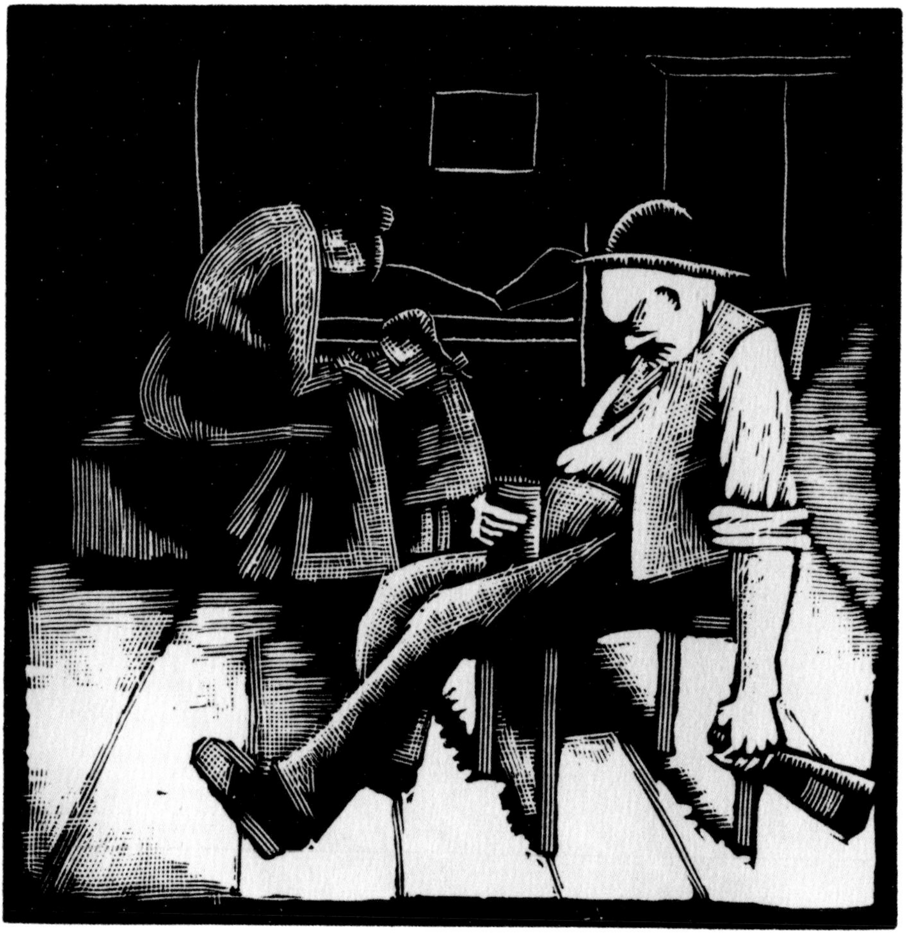

Otto Nückel was born in Cologne, then moved to Munich, where he worked as a painter and illustrator after dropping out of medical school. His early illustrations include books by Thomas Mann, Alexander Moritz Frey, and E. T. A. Hoffman, using leadcuts. Nückel created numerous illustrations and cover artwork of political satire and caricatures of artists for the journal *Der Simpl*.

Nückel is recognized as the first artist to use lead instead of wood to create picture books. The critic H. Lehmann-Haupt observed that Nückel "took to it in the days of war, when there was no proper wood available in Germany, and he has become so familiar with it that he has never gone back to wood."

Destiny (1930)

Destiny, in over 200 black-and-white leadcut prints, is a masterpiece of drama that reveals the social milieu of women in Western civilization during the nineteenth century. This melodramatic novel traces the tragic life of an impoverished woman who is consistently victimized not only by men but by a culture that offers little opportunity for women to survive. The heroine's drunken father and overworked mother die early in her life, leaving her alone to survive (opposite, pages 95, 97, 98). She works for a farmer in a village where she is seduced by a traveling salesman (page 99, top), resulting in an unwanted pregnancy (page 99, bottom). After imprisonment for the murder of her unwanted child, she works as a prostitute, forsakes a chance for a traditional relationship, murders a man with an ax during a drunken revelry (pages 100–102), and is shot by the police (page 103) as she jumps to her death from a window of an upper-story room (page 104).

Nückel's use of light and shadow is effective in setting the mood throughout this startling narrative. Unlike Masereel, who used flat images in his woodcuts, Nückel's use of lead in these prints provides a finer line. The use of the engraver's multiple tool, which normally gives a mechanical effect on the page, gives depth and creates a focus for the action in Nückel's skillful hand. It is no surprise that woodcut artists have been profoundly influenced by Nückel's work. Lynd Ward felt that Nückel "surpassed Masereel both in complexity of plot development and in subtle psychological interplay between characters." Will Eisner affirms the assessment that Nückel's novel "was more sophisticated and the graphic narrative more complex," in comparison to Masereel's work.

Nückel achieved a unique level of storytelling with a mixture of melodrama and symbolism. The heroine in this novel is trapped in a life of deceit and misery that ends tragically. The remarkable mix of black-and-white space unfolds a complex drama through both simple and detailed arrangement of characters and objects on the page. Nückel's composition and the resulting interplay of black-and-white space are displayed in numerous prints, such as when the heroine's mother climbs the steep stairs (page 105, top). The mother's stooped figure is held in the grip of the surrounding darkness in the stairway. Her head is downcast, and her grip on the banister is highlighted in the strip of white space. There is no one meeting her at the door or walking alongside her. She is alone with a heavy weight, climbing steep stairs in the darkness. Nückel presents a realistic depiction of the destiny of women in this stark picture of solitude. Other examples of the successful contrast of black and white that stir up an emotional response are presented in the print with the mother on her deathbed (page 105, bottom). The barrenness of her life is shown in the emptiness of the room. She is alone on a single bed in an attic with only a chair, where objects like a bottle and bowl are at her side rather than a person, such as her daughter or a friend. Her hand drops down to her side, lifeless. The surface of the beams is highlighted, which accents her projection into the background of darkness and death. The view outside the small window is not inviting. There is not a tree limb or a cloud in the sky, only a white emptiness. This square of white space is in stark contrast to the blackness of the walls and ceiling, depicting a thin line between life and death for this woman. It is ironic that the novel concludes when this mother's daughter jumps to her death from an upper-story window.

One of the more striking uses of black and white, beyond its indication of squalor and limited options in life for women, is found in Nückel's depiction of motion. In one print (page 106), a wagon filled with firemen is highlighted by street lamps and lanterns in the firemen's raised hands. Motion is achieved by depicting streaming flames from lanterns being pulled in the wind, which in turn is indicated by ellipses highlighting the accelerating wagon wheels. If one were to cover the print and hide the flames from the lanterns and the ellipses behind the wagon, the galloping horses would suggest a static display of motion, especially when compared to the dynamic uncovered print.

Another feature of Nückel's work is the presentation of light and the use of lamps and lanterns. Characters can only navigate the oppressive dark environment with lamps as a means of illuminating their paths or predicaments, such as when the heroine is shown looking in a mirror confirming her misbegotten pregnancy (page 107). Her hand is shown drawn over her stomach in front of a candle she has placed facing a mirror, and her dire situation is expressed in the dark background—her secret exposed only in the privacy of the candlelight. Like her mother, the heroine is left alone to deal with the consequences of her actions with irresponsible men—in this case, her seduction by a traveling salesman.

This effective use of light and shadow in plot and mood is evident in another picture: the one where the heroine drowns her infant for whom she can no longer care. In this image, the infant is discovered in the canal (page 108). The background in the

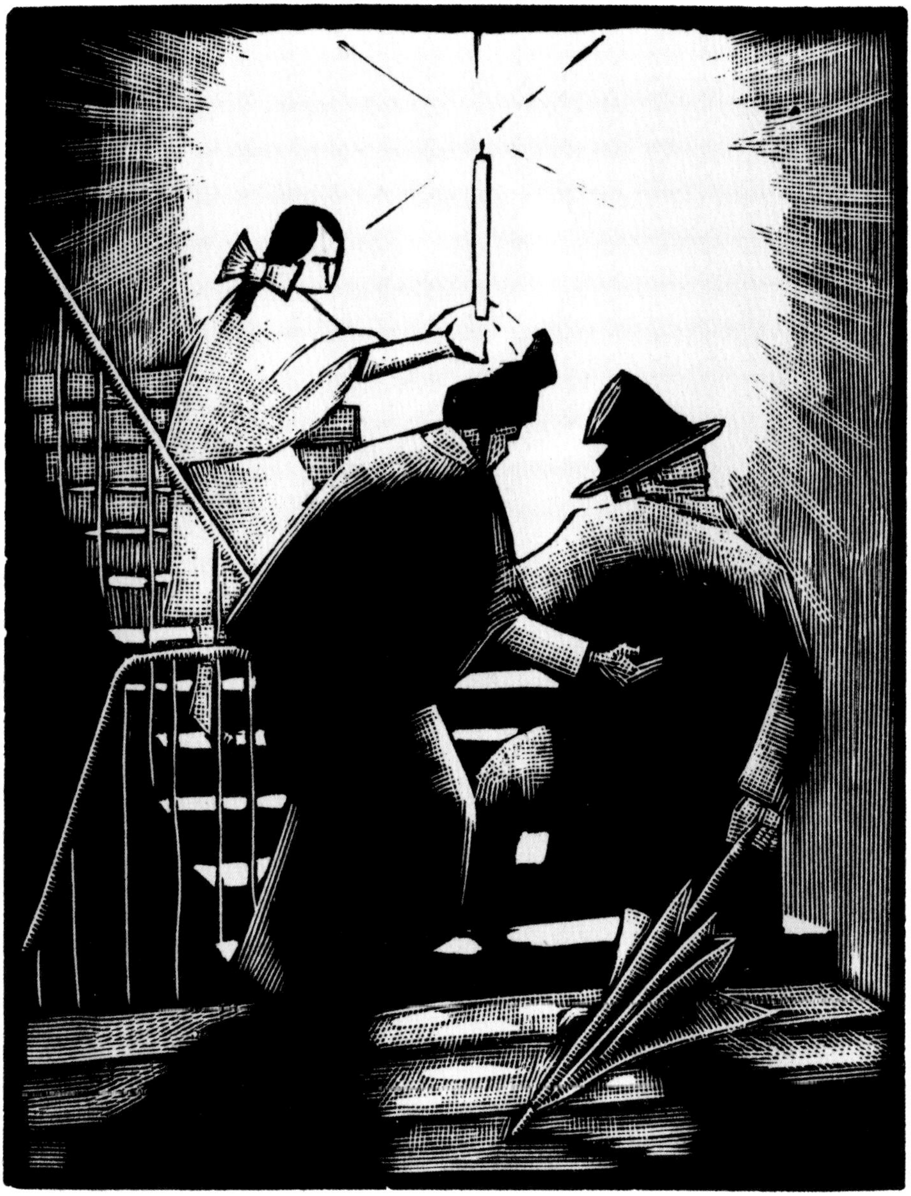

upper-right corner displays flat, primitive trees with enough light in the sky to balance the tiles in the lower left-hand corner of the print. Nückel's use of the multiple tool etches out the shadow falling on the face of a building. The sparse light left on the building from the horizon points down to a man holding a drowned infant he has pulled from the canal. The infant's body is white against the blackness in the canal. This contrast of light and dark and the idle manner in which the man in the boat is holding the body denotes the infant's lifelessness.

There are also moments between harrowing scenes of murder and violence that Nückel inserts symbolically to intensify the plot. No other picture displays the feeling of entrapment better than the picture of the heroine sitting at a table facing a sparrow that has entered her room (page 109). With her head resting in her hand, she looks calmly at the bird. Her other hand sits on the table with her index finger perhaps gently tapping the table, cautiously, so as not to startle the bird. There is only a hint of a smile on her face. In the background is her sparsely filled room that she shares with her elderly husband—reflecting the frugality and rigid order of her middle-class life. Nückel gives readers a moment to feel empathy with the heroine, allowing them to join her wish to fly away like the sparrow from this room. This is one of the few pictures that shows a discernible expression on the heroine's face. In this one picture Nückel displays her discontent. When an old lover arrives in the next scene, it is no surprise that she has sex with him and abandons her husband. When her husband discovers her misdeed, he grieves over his loss and hangs himself (page 110). The joists that he used to hang from are shown in the shape of a stick figure with raised arms, beseeching help in a pitch-black background. A window without any ray of light accentuates the husband's despair. In the center of the picture is his gnarled left hand, and vertical lines on the joists are directed down into darkness.

In another dramatic image, the heroine's isolation is expressed by the inclusion of empty chairs arranged in a restaurant she is cleaning (page 111). Throughout *Destiny,* empty chairs accentuate the isolation of other characters. For example, a solitary chair is set beside her dying mother and is used earlier in the suicide of the heroine's husband.

The only vital relationship in the story occurs when a worker comes to the house of prostitution where he meets the heroine. The worker arrives to hang, ironically, a lamp—an object that gives light and represents hope, therefore the prints that follow their courtship are filled with light as she finally becomes part of the world of light. In this sequence, a festival is shown in detail. The darkness is not oppressive. The heroine is displayed sitting on a park bench in the arms of her lover, the sunset skimming over the surface of a lake and a bird singing on an illuminated tree branch (page 112). Compare this scene in nature with her seduction by the salesman when she covers her face from the sunlight in shame (page 113).

Nückel incorporates the tone of German silent cinema of the era, especially in the tension and atmosphere he creates using shadow and light. Nückel's work pulls together a naturalistic narrative with a strong Expressionistic style. Although the similarities with silent film and wordless novels are identifiable, there is a difference that reflects the essence of the book, which was recognized by critics like H. Lehmann-Haupt when *Destiny* was first published.

> . . . the pleasure is more subtle, for we are alone in this theater and audience and operator are one person. We can make the story run quickly, we can even skip, but we can also stop altogether. Then suddenly it is not so much a piece out of a story that counts, but an individual picture with its own particular qualities. This is where the superiority of the picture novel comes in.

Nückel's complex story line is a good example of the power of pictorial narrative to evoke strong compassion for a character, and represents a pioneering work in the development of the contemporary graphic novel with its focus on social injustice in the tragic life of one significant character.

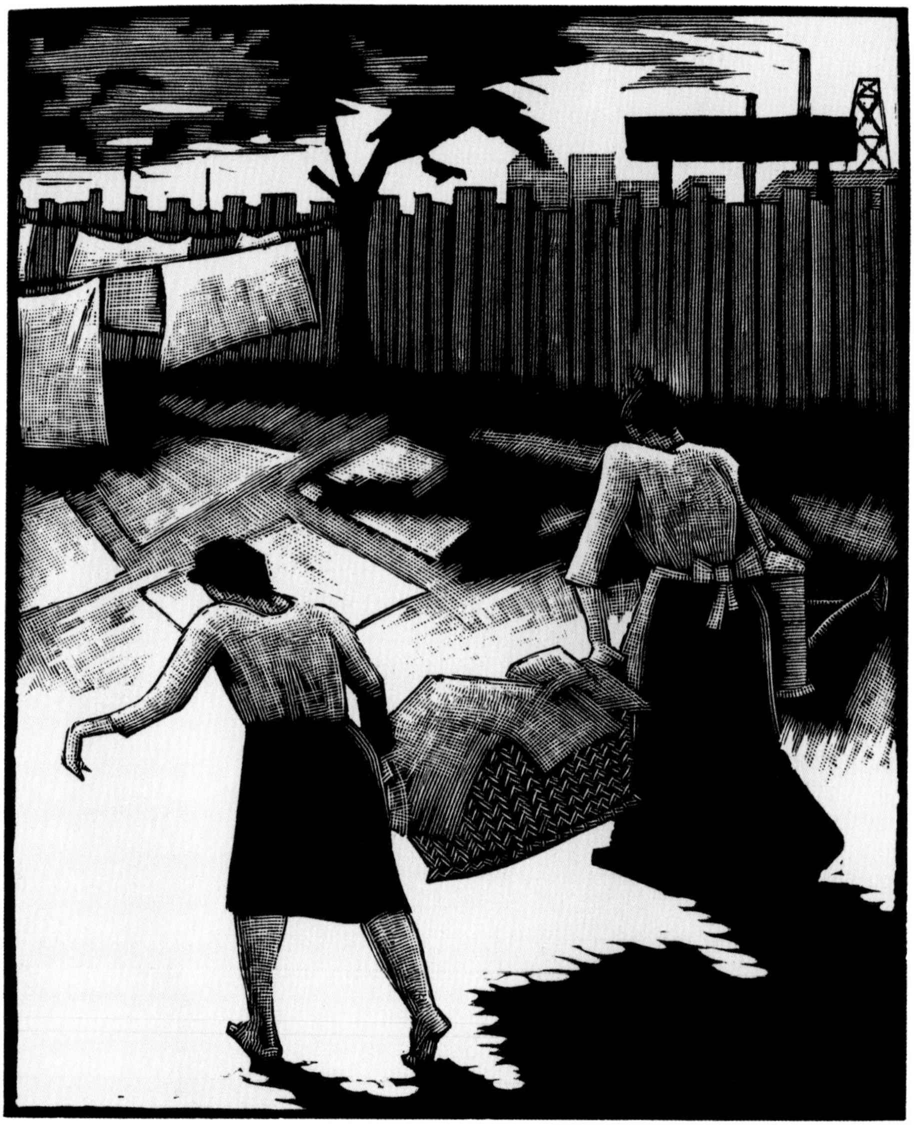

101

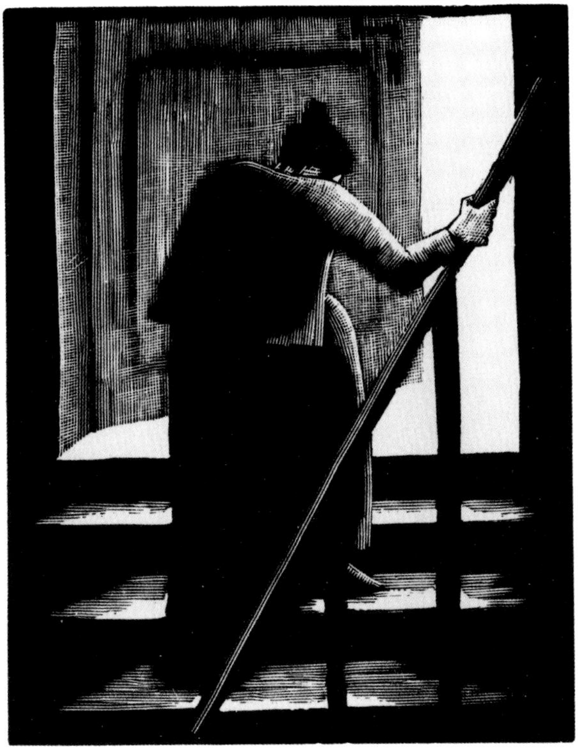

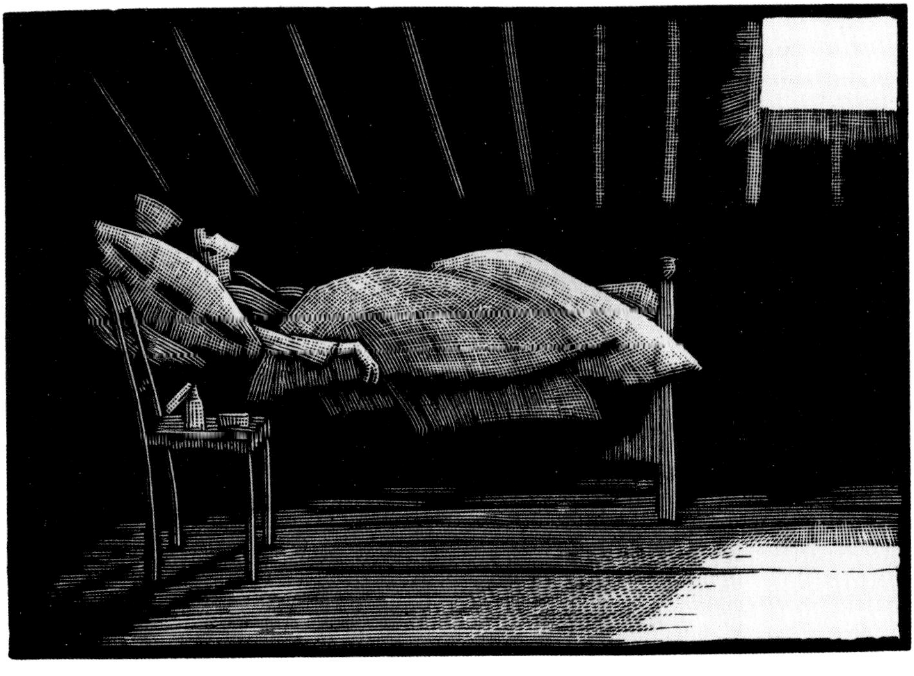

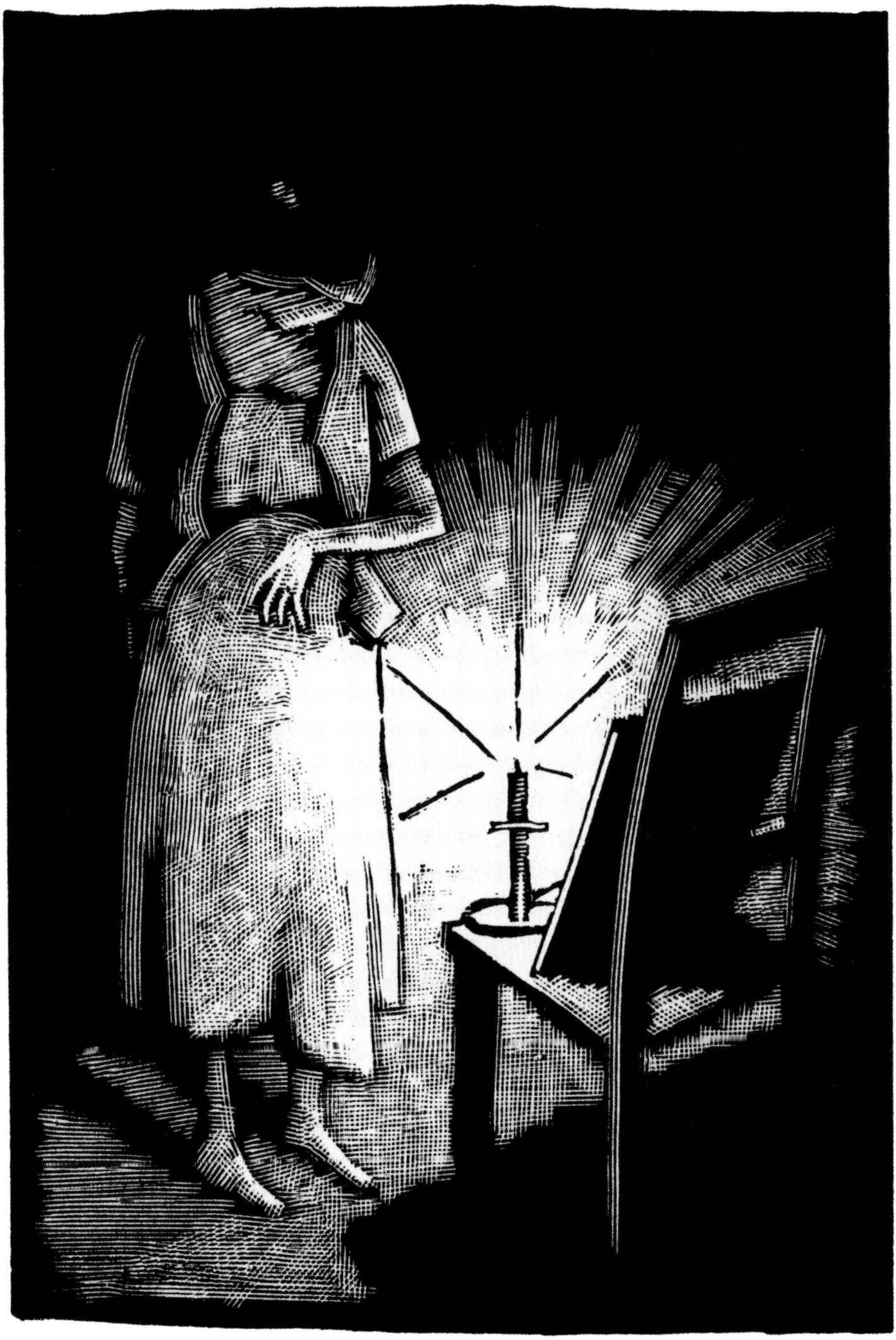

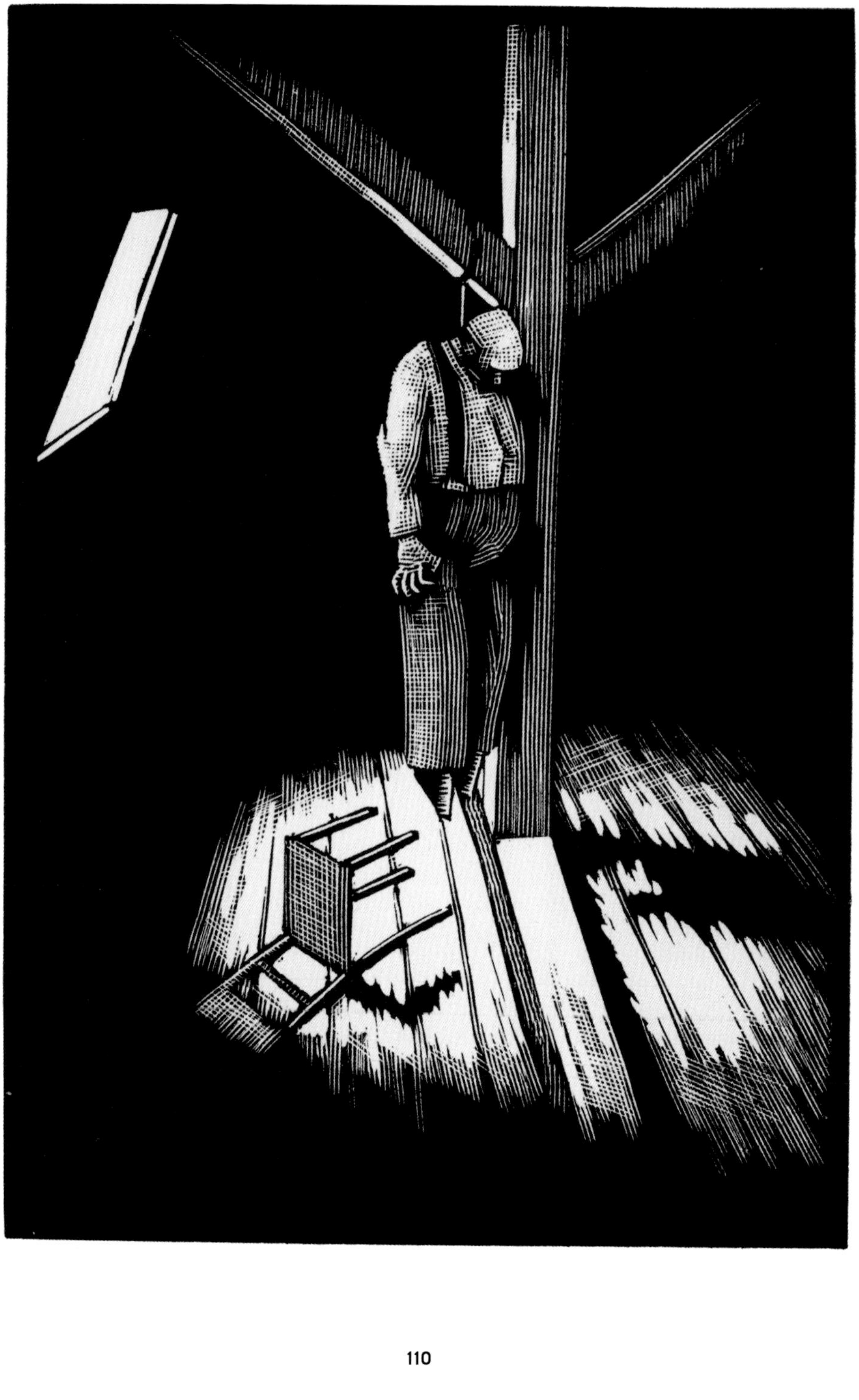

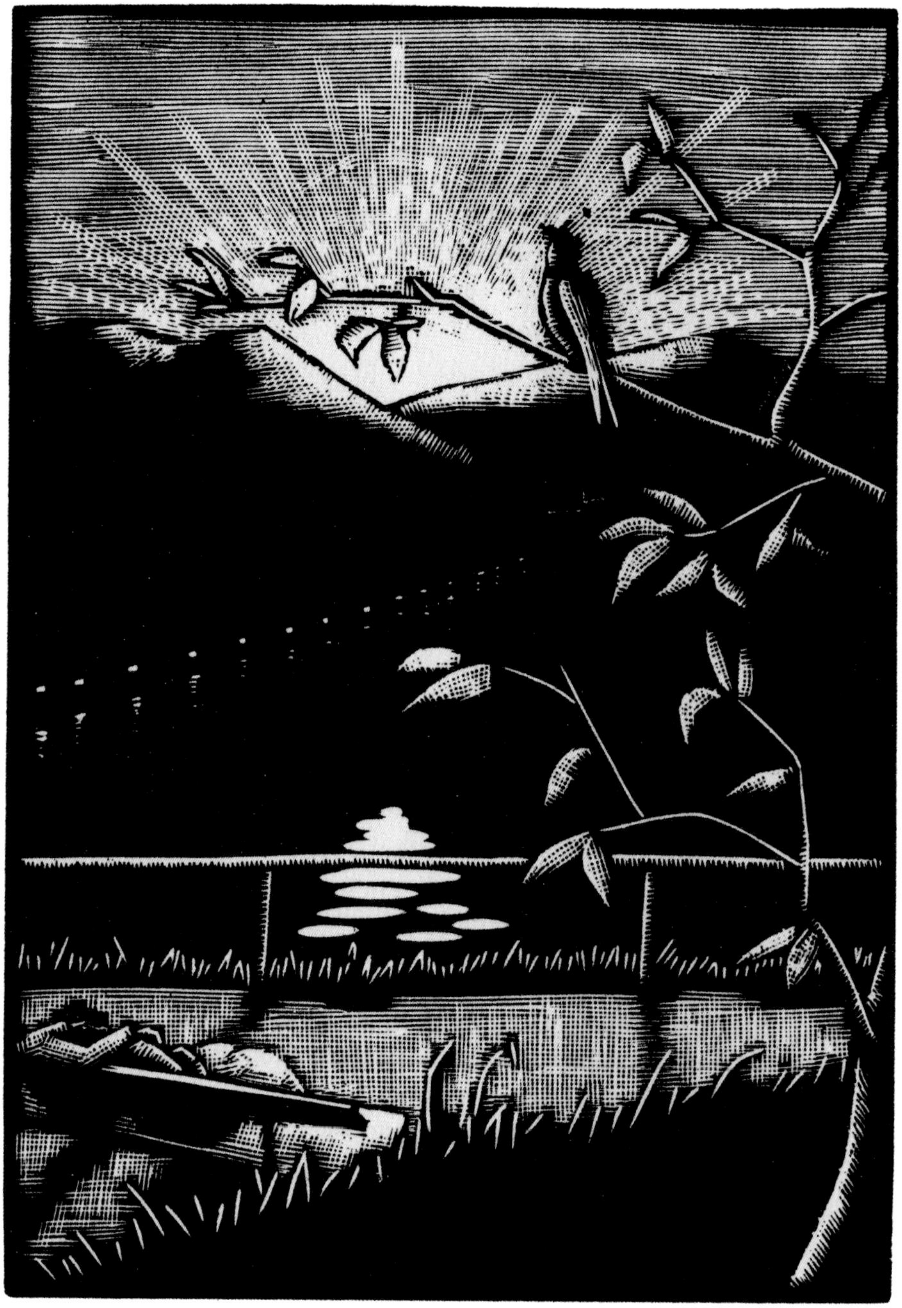

Chapter Five

Helena Bochořáková-Dittrichová

(1894–1980)

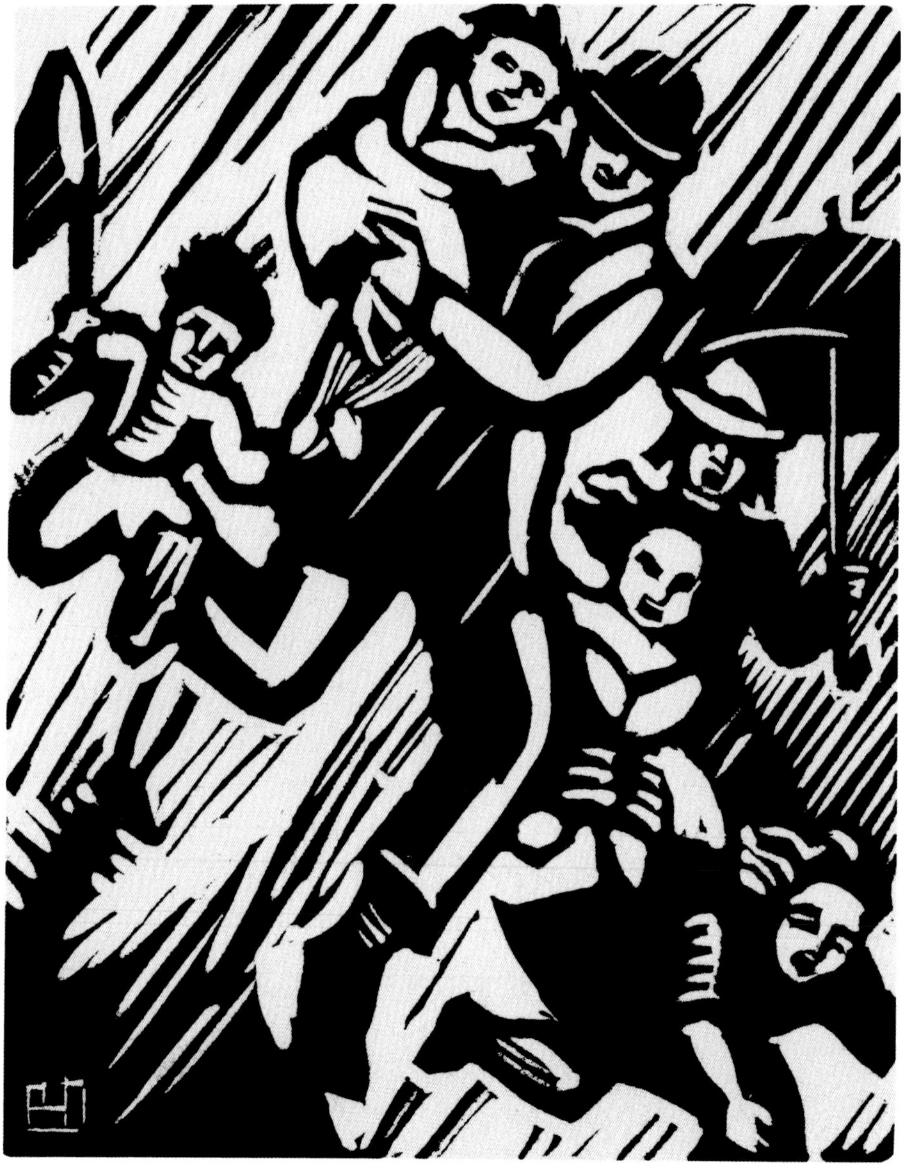

<mark>H</mark>elena Bochořáková-Dittrichová was born in Vyskov, Czechoslovakia, studied at the Academy of Fine Arts in Prague, and received a stipend to study in Paris, where she discovered the woodcut novels of Frans Masereel. Bochořáková's artwork focused on woodcuts and linocuts inspired by social issues and stories from the Bible such as the life of Christ (*Kristus*). She was severely short-sighted and in the 1940s turned to painting, due in large part to her visual disability. In addition to being the first woman to publish a woodcut novel, Bochořáková was a painter, illustrator, and the author of several travel books.

Childhood (1931)

Although Frans Masereel was an obvious influence on Bochořáková, she presents a style and narrative in *Childhood* that is distinct. Bochořáková depicts a realistic picture of middle-class life in the country that has its own set of trials and tribulations—one that is a refreshing divergence from the squalor presented by Otto Nückel and Masereel. Bochořáková's focus is not on the sullen side of life but rather on a childhood protected from the harsh realities of urban squalor. The location reflects the small town of Hana in what is now the Czech Republic where she spent her childhood.

Bochořáková presents the simple day-to-day activities of the middle class. Arne Novák observes in her introduction to the book that the Bochořákov family "is devoted to its daily tasks, modest in its amusements, conservative in its opinions and habits, and in general, disposed to fix its gaze confidently on the sunny side of life."

These sequential images are a youthful work, but instead of judging this as a disordered narrative, it would be best to consider this a novel of impressions.

Childhood reflects Bochořáková's traditional, patriarchal family structure (opposite and page 116). The father is present for religious celebrations such as baptisms, and involved in outdoor activities such as hunting (page 117) and building a snowman with his children (page 118). The mother works solely in the house, scrubbing floors and caring for their kids (pages 119–121). This is a picture of an orderly world with a close bond between the family and church. The children are shown in many liturgical settings such as processions or attendance at sacred ceremonies in the church. Many of the prints reflect common childhood memories that are familiar to many readers, such as begging for the scrapings from a bowl of frosting, or telling ghost stories that stimulate children to imagine monsters hiding behind bedroom doors (pages 122–127).

These prints are good examples of Bochořáková's style. The bare designs in her woodcuts reflect a childlike vision of growing up. She attains a clear definition of facial expressions with simple detail. The expressions of the girls, for example, display a variety of feelings including shock, surprise, and anticipation. She does not need to go into any Goyaesque depiction of imaginative monsters behind a door when the children are playing. The plain stick figures indicate the innocence of the girls' fear, the power of their imaginations, and how the girls would draw these monsters with their own hands. In other pictures, Bochořáková displays her skill as a woodcut artist, effectively rendering detail in the children's dress, room interiors, and the town's architecture. In addition, her use of light is consistent with the sense of innocence she conveys. Many of these woodcuts have steadfast backgrounds, like the sky with even horizontal lines (pages 128, 129). This undisturbed white background reflects the sheltered life in Bochořáková's childhood—secure and predictable. What is immediately apparent in this book is the overwhelming use of white space in her woodcuts that directly relates to the openness in Bochořáková's childhood—sunlight is everywhere!

However, there are moments when this life is shaken as the girls grow older. A woman drowns, though it is not certain what connection she has to the family. And later, when the central character discovers she is going blind, the diminished use of light is significant. The first time she becomes aware of losing her sight occurs during a classroom scene (page 130). All the other children follow the teacher pointing to something on the blackboard—the blackboard, however, is blank. The central character, her back to us, raises her hands to her head in panic. Bochořáková's

arrangement of action in this picture succeeds in showing readers what the central character experiences in the initial stages of her blindness.

The irony of this is that the central character now enters the darkness of her imagination. The fear she shared with her girlfriends about the unseen monsters behind the bedroom door is now replaced with the reality that she cannot see her girlfriends (pages 131, 132). She is, in a sense, behind a door with her own monsters. This feeling is strikingly presented in dramatic detail. The central character, with her head held in her hands in despair, is displayed in simple lines surrounded in darkness. She now lives separate, in literal darkness, her blindness drawing her away from her friends who live in a world of light. These friends are shown playing hand in hand with beams of blazing white light shining down upon them. This light is in direct contrast to the flat, dark world that the central character now inhabits. Eventually, a cure is discovered for her blindness, and in the last picture she kneels in front of the sun with her arms held high. She is a woman—no longer a child—who rejoices in the sunlight that she can now see clearly again (page 133).

In one sense, Bochořáková has shown us that even the middle-class culture—far removed from the urban realities of Masereel and Nückel—experiences death, disease, and despair. Bochořáková presents, in this cycle of woodcuts, the tragedy and joy of life inherent in all cultures.

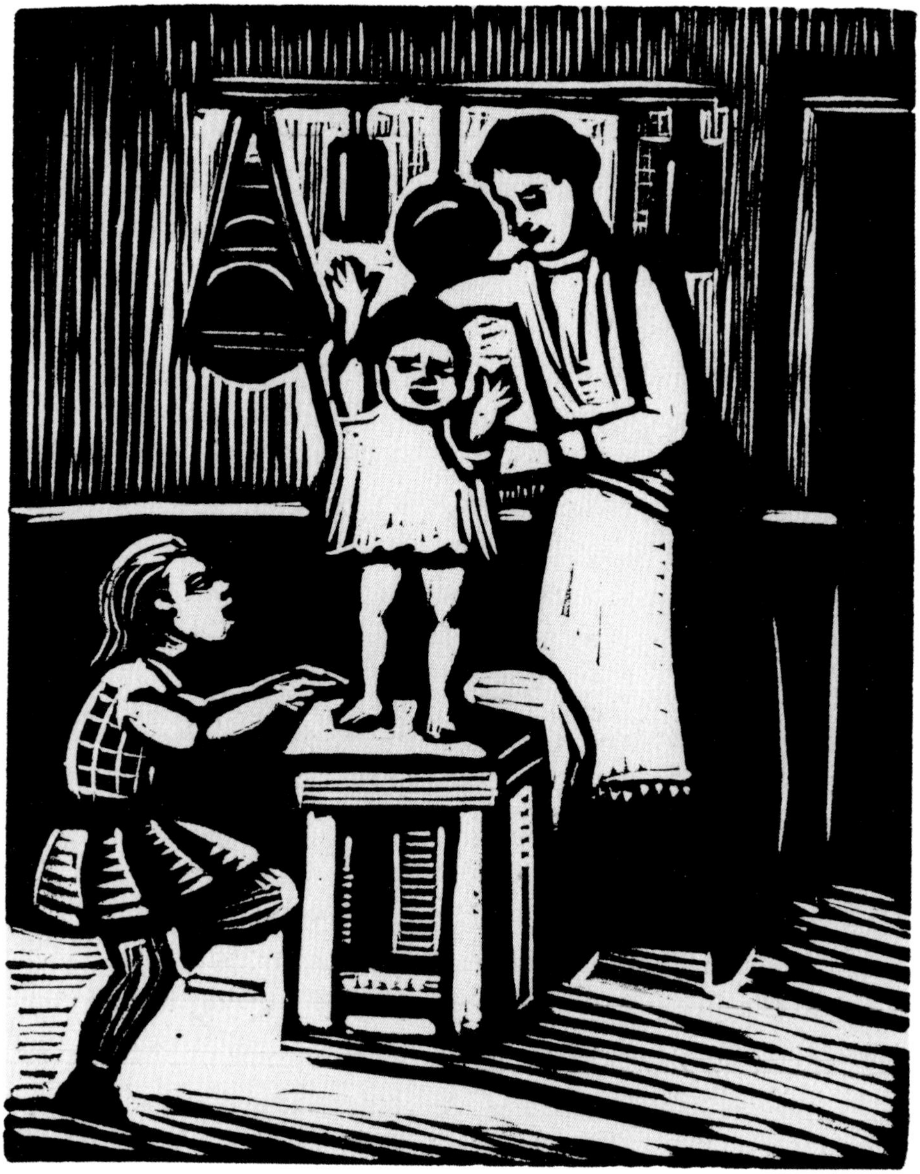

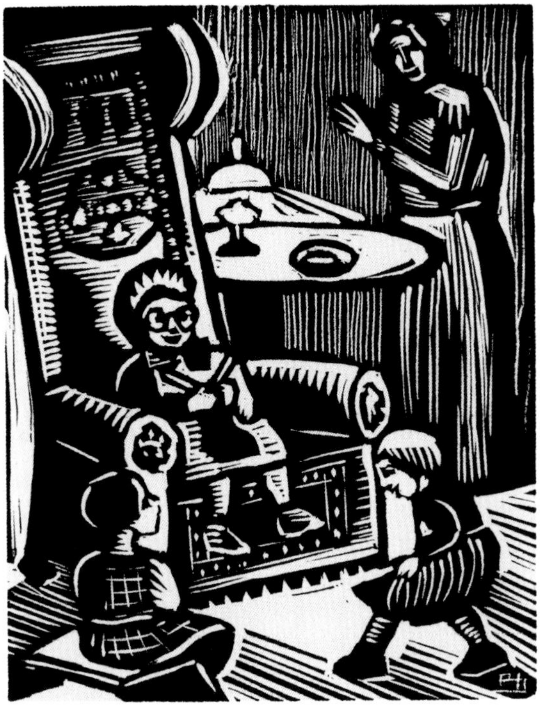

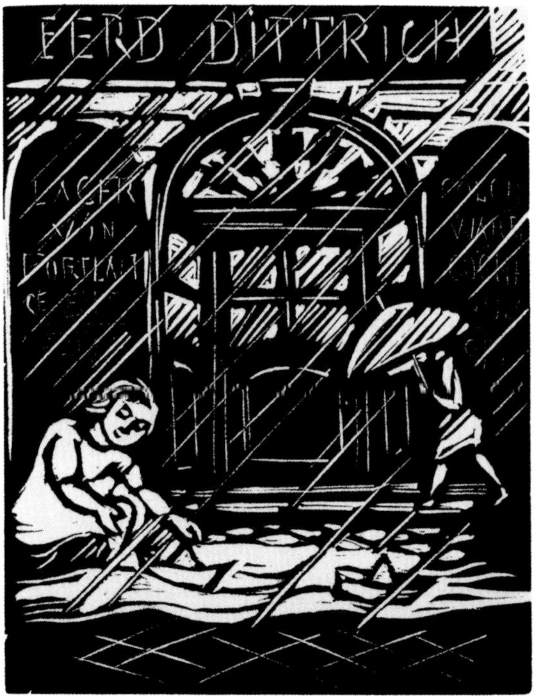
FERD DITTRICH
LAGER
VON

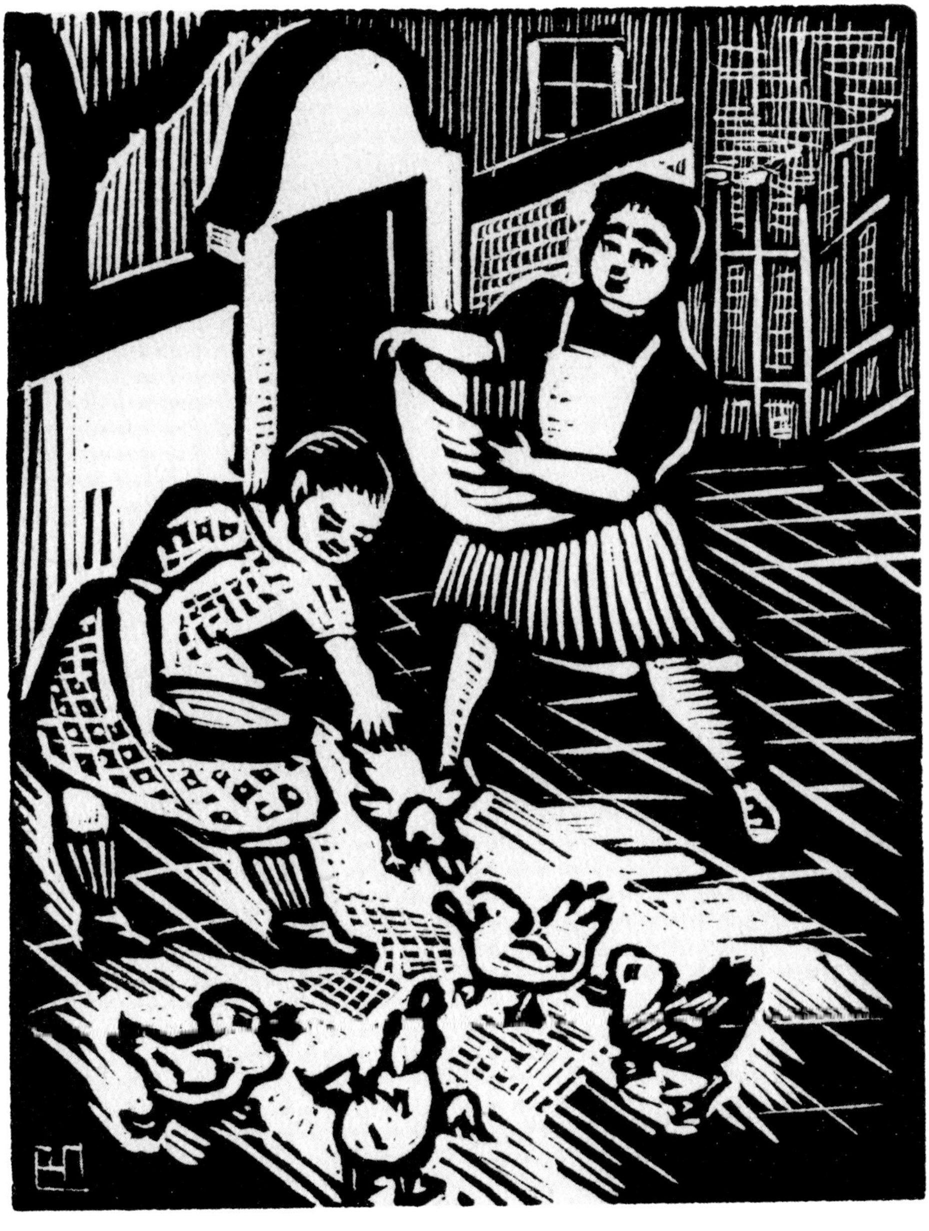

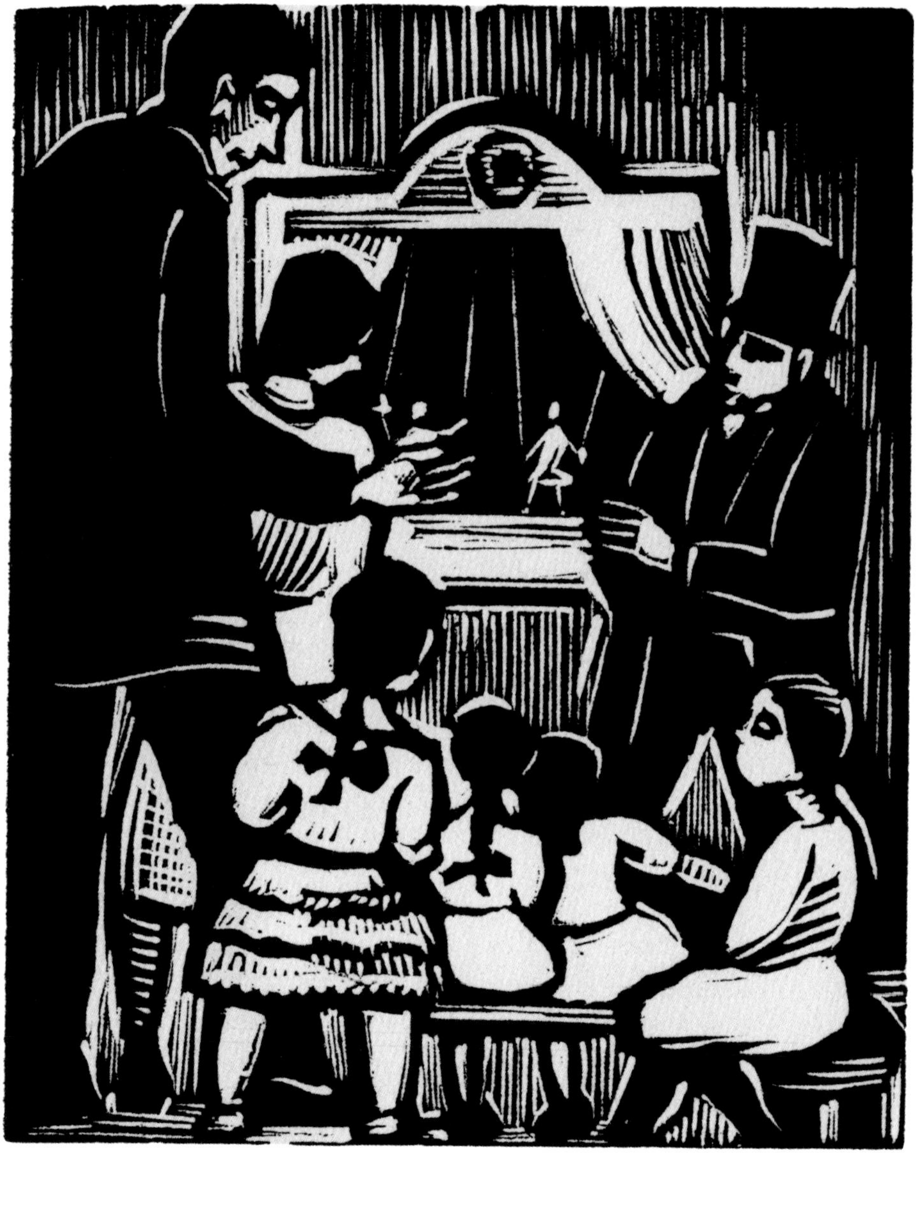

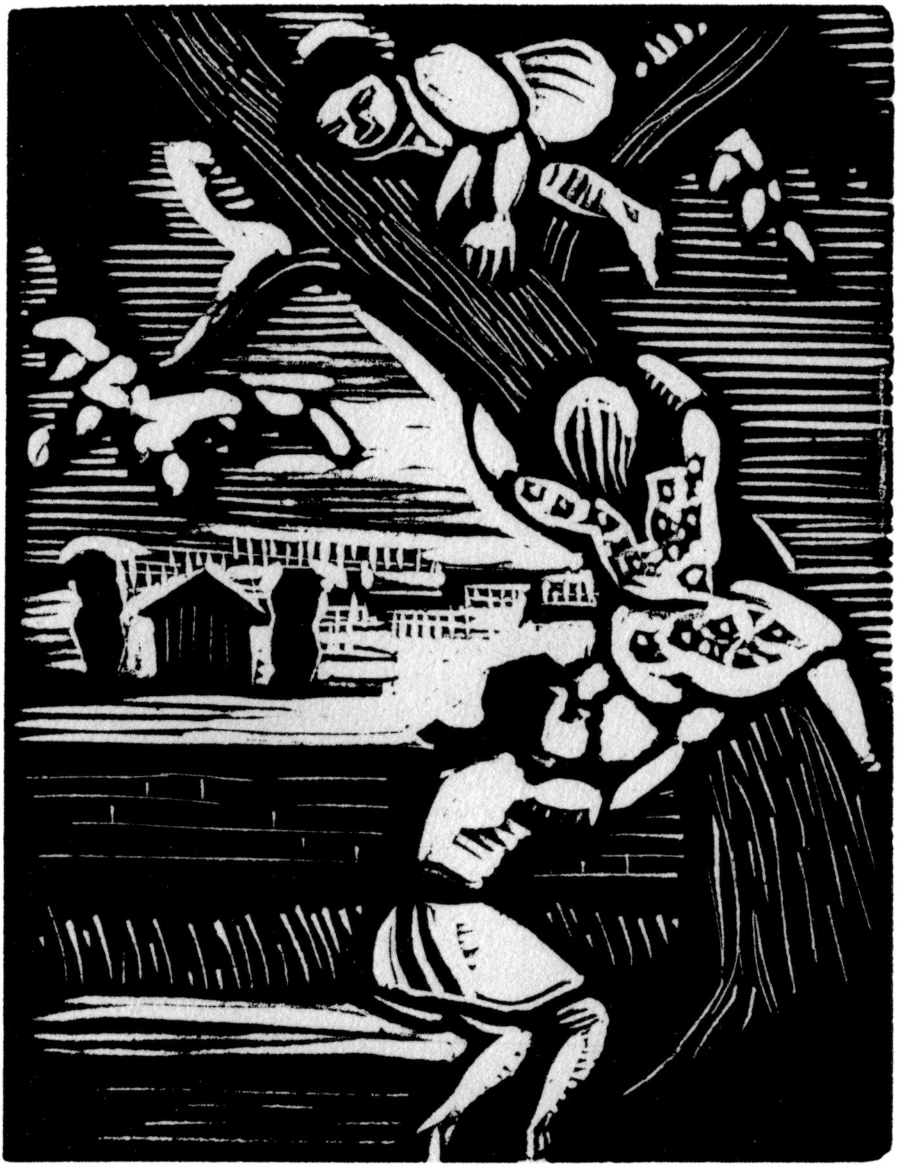

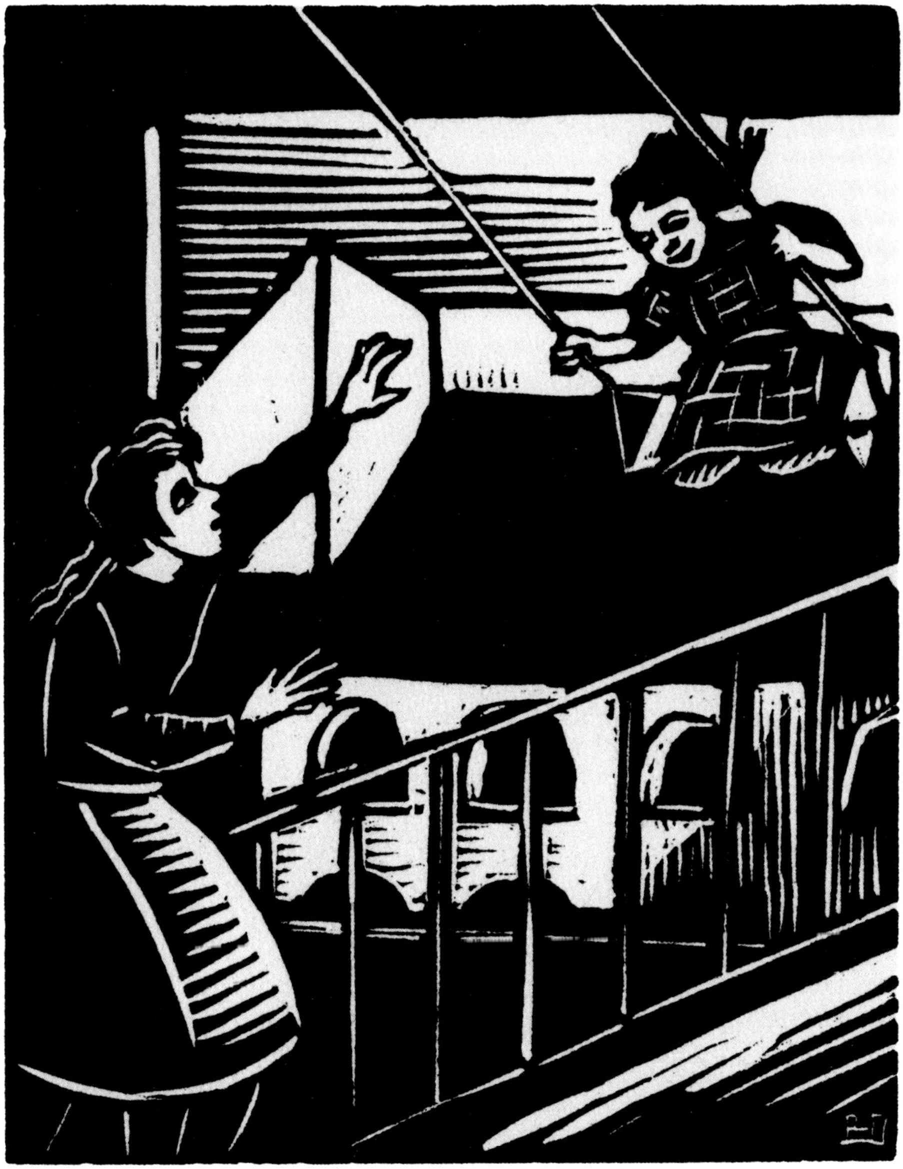

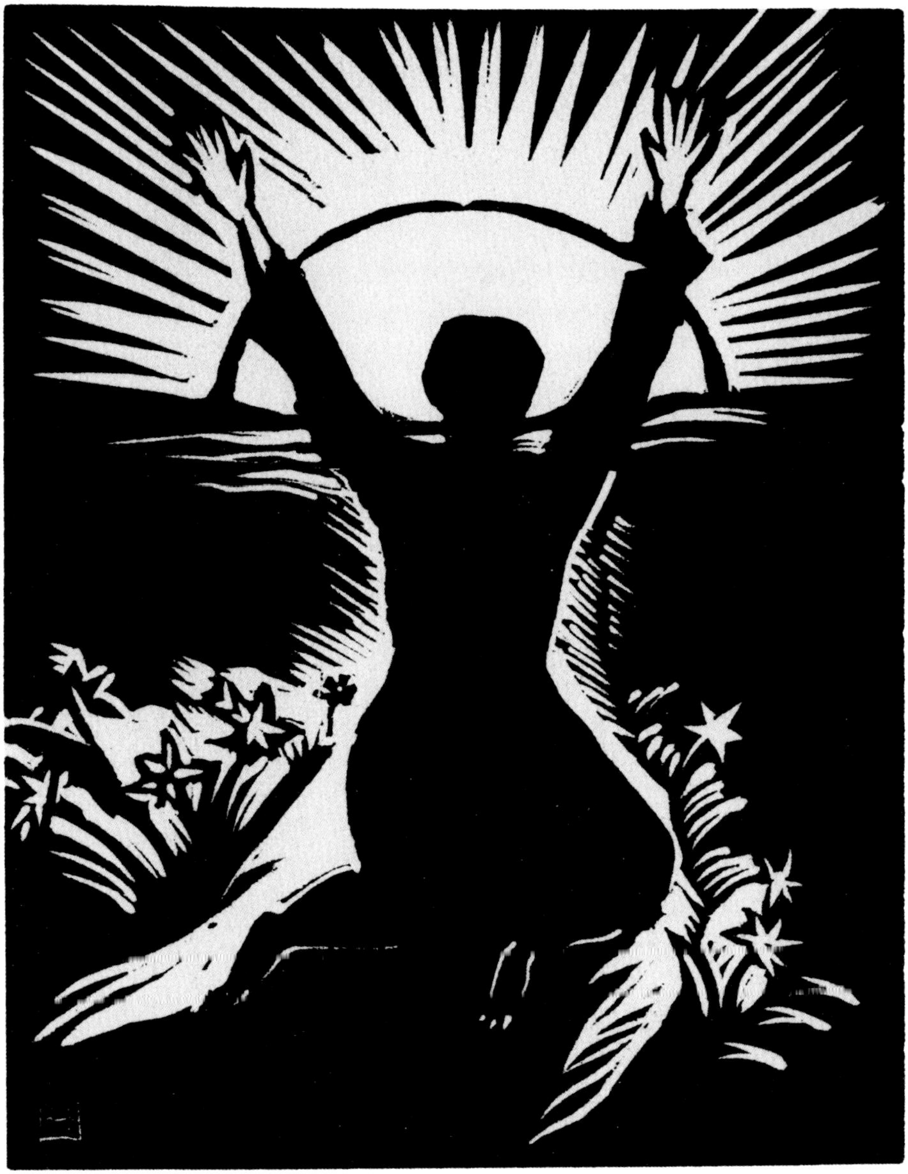

Chapter Six

William Gropper

(1897–1977)

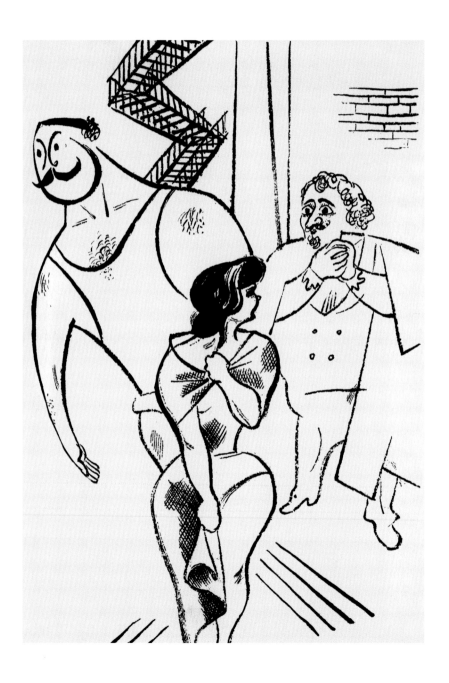

William Gropper was a cartoonist, book illustrator, and painter who had strong ties with the urban working class from birth. As a young man, he worked as a cartoonist for the *New York Herald Tribune* and contributed to journals like the *New Masses*. His cartoons were biting and never shrank from exposing the inequities and realities in the lives around him.

The artist and writer Louis Lozowick praised Gropper's drawings as "a chronicle, a commentary, and an indictment of an era of social conflicts, dislocations, and maladjustments, of repression and protest—and a tiny bit of hope, too."

Gropper's famous caricature of the Japanese emperor Hirohito in the August 1935 issue of *Vanity Fair* provoked the Japanese government to sue the magazine. Gropper refused to apologize for his work in this or any other instance. In 1953 he was called to testify before the Senate House Un-American Activities Committee and refused to appear. Gropper used his storytelling skills and caricatures to uncover social injustices in a series of paintings and prints, most notably in his portfolio of fifty lithographs, *Capriccios* (1953–56), which he created in response to the Cold War and the rise of McCarthyism. Gropper is celebrated as a social artist with unrelenting attention to the plight of the common worker.

Alay-oop (1930)

Alay-oop presents the lives of two acrobats and a portly singer from the vaudeville stage (pages 134, 135, and below) who falls in love with the female acrobat. In a series of picture balloons, the singer begins courting the female acrobat and shares with her his dreams of riches and success (opposite). After a night of troubling dreams, she comes to a resolution and accepts the singer's proposal of marriage (page 138). The male acrobat, rather than feeling resentful, is pleased with his partner's happiness, even though she dissolves their acrobatic act. Her marriage with the singer is anything but glamorous (page 139). After a few years, the couple has two children and lives in a modest, working-class tenement building rather than enjoying the prosperous lifestyle the singer promised his bride. The male acrobat reunites with the couple and they relive their memories (page 140). The singer, bitter with his failed dreams of success, is jealous of the acrobat's charm and his relationship with his wife (page 141). The male acrobat suggests that they bring back their old acrobatic act and include her children (page 142). When the singer returns and sees his wife and the male acrobat demonstrating their routine (page 143), he demands that the acrobat leave his house. After an angry tirade, the singer accuses his wife of infidelity and sends her out on the street with their children (page 144). The three characters go their separate ways, and in the conclusion, the singer ends up selling items from a fruit wagon; the acrobat finds a job as a steelworker on the girders of a skyscraper; and the wife returns to the circus, where she performs with her two children in an acrobatic act.

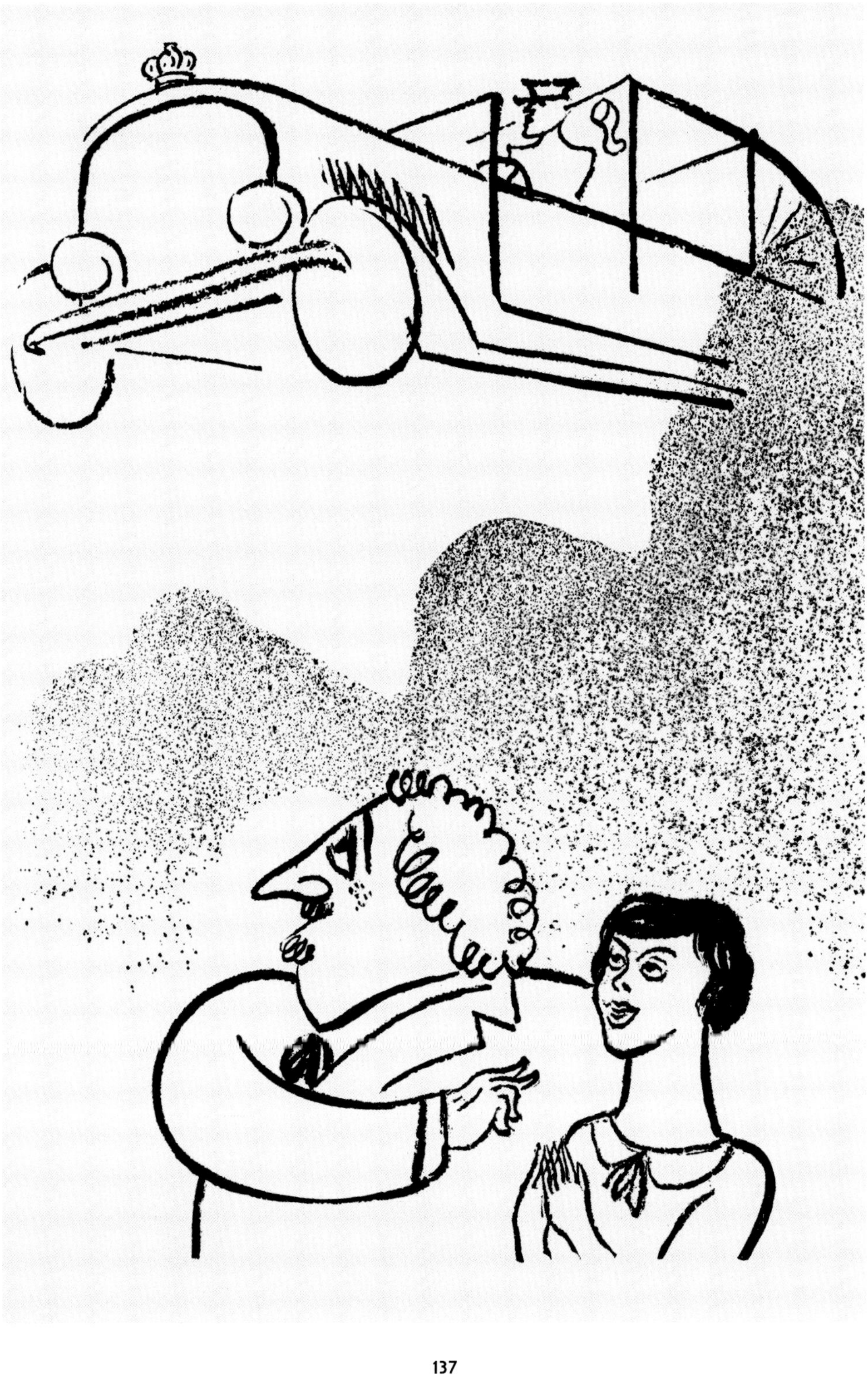

Gropper's drama is told with straightforward symbolism and innuendoes, such as the display of wash hanging from a clothesline, which brings back the singer's memory of the female acrobat flying in the sky (page 145).

Alay-oop is a running narrative, with the action bleeding off the full page rather than enclosed in a panel or a border. Gropper's use of crayon, pen and ink, and brush—with a splattering effect on the page—is effective in isolating characters and events and narrowing the visual focus on particular objects. This is especially effective in the representation of picture balloons. For example, when the singer suspects his wife of infidelity, he imagines his two children with moustaches, implicating the male acrobat as the children's father (page 146, top).

One of the more interesting additions to the unfolding of this drama is a dream sequence (pages 146, bottom, through page 151), reflecting a curiosity with the nature of psychology and the impact of dreams—a subject that dominated popular books and movies during the era.

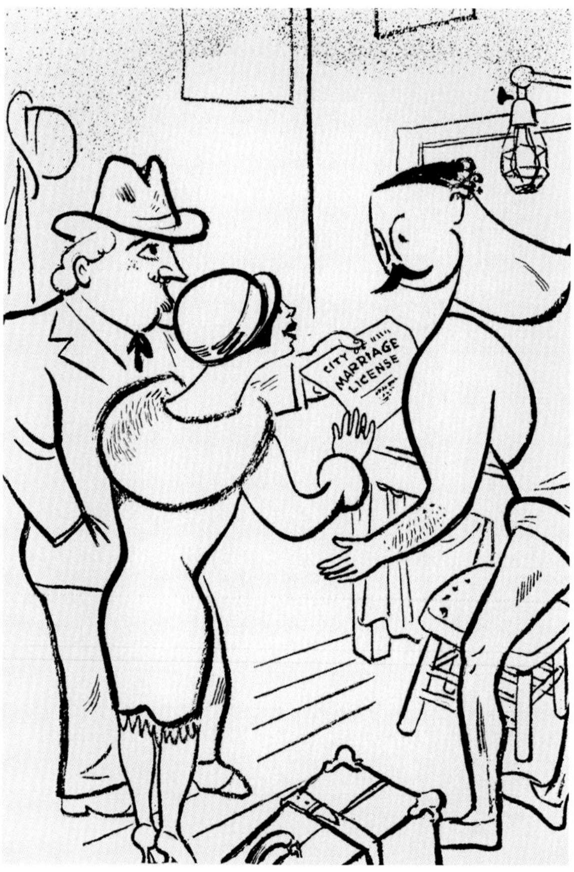
CITY
MARRIAGE
LICENSE

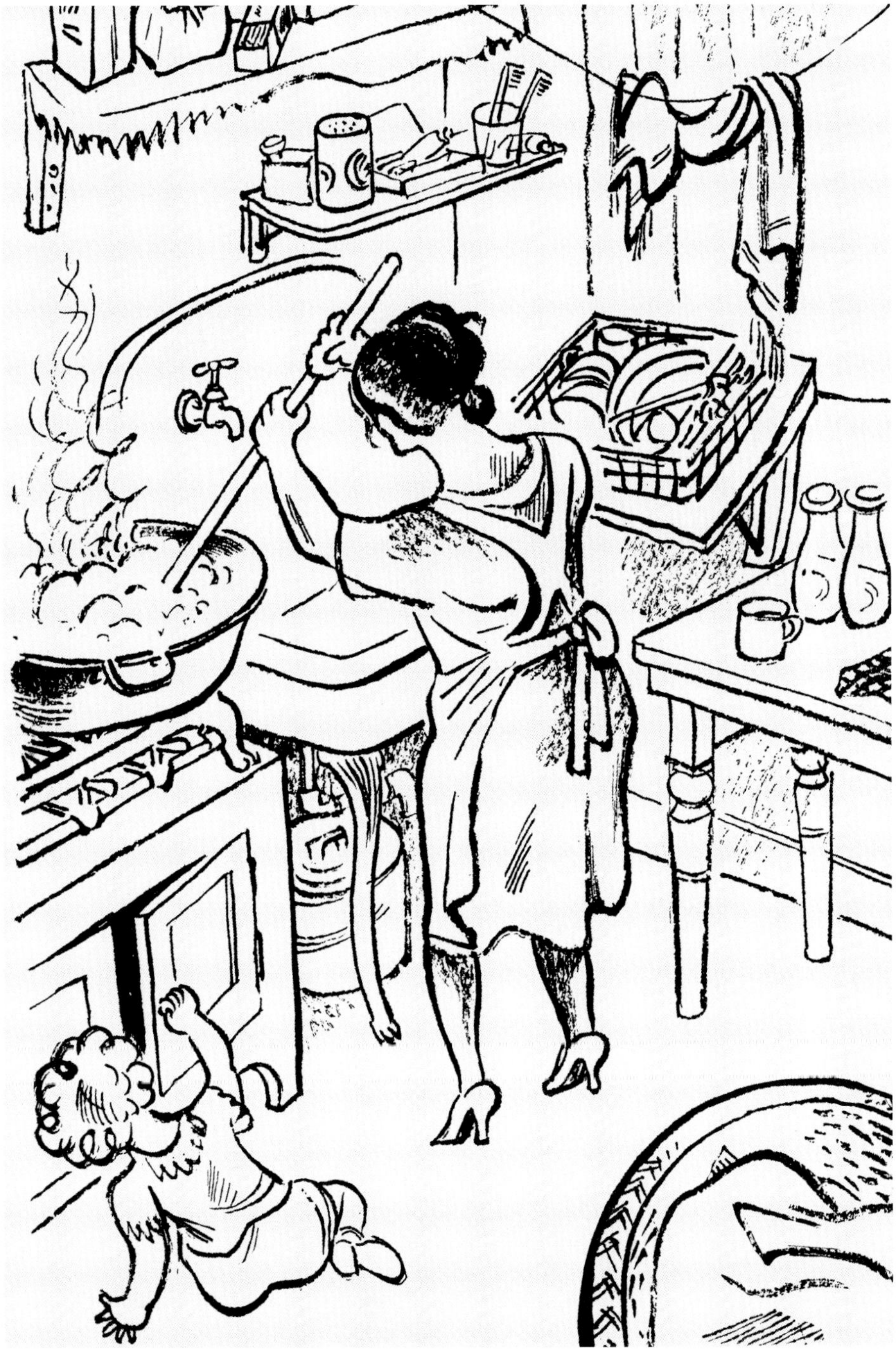

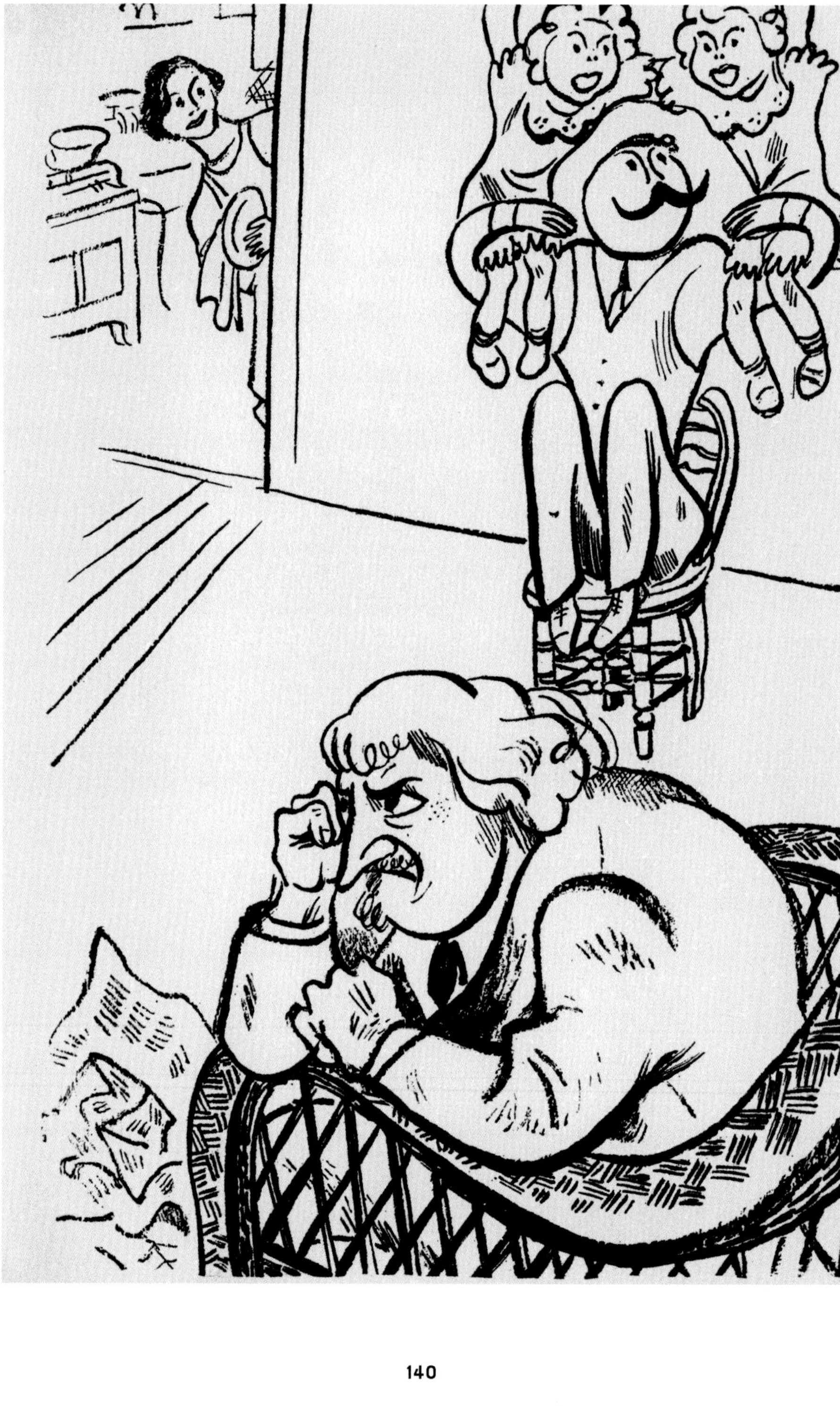

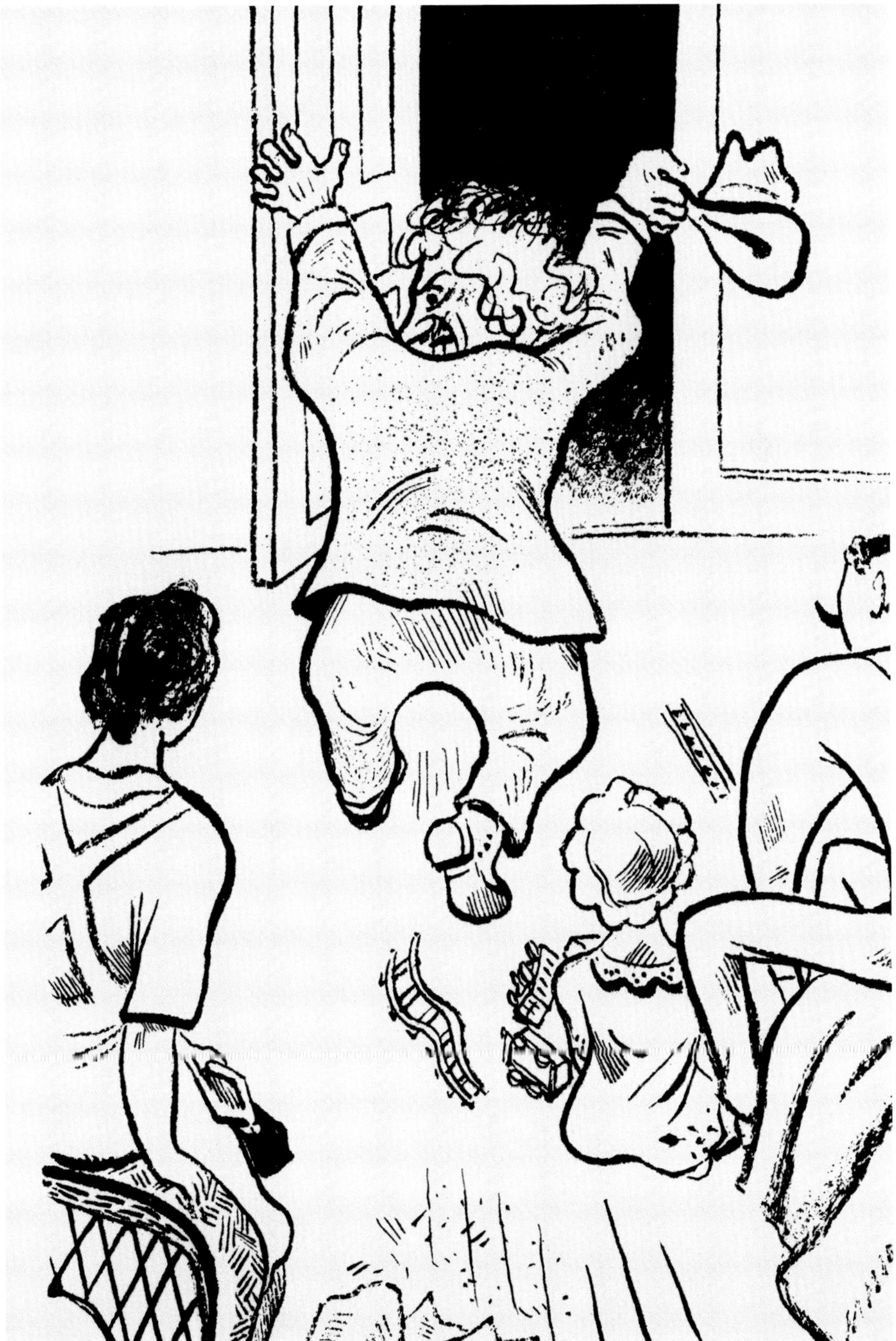

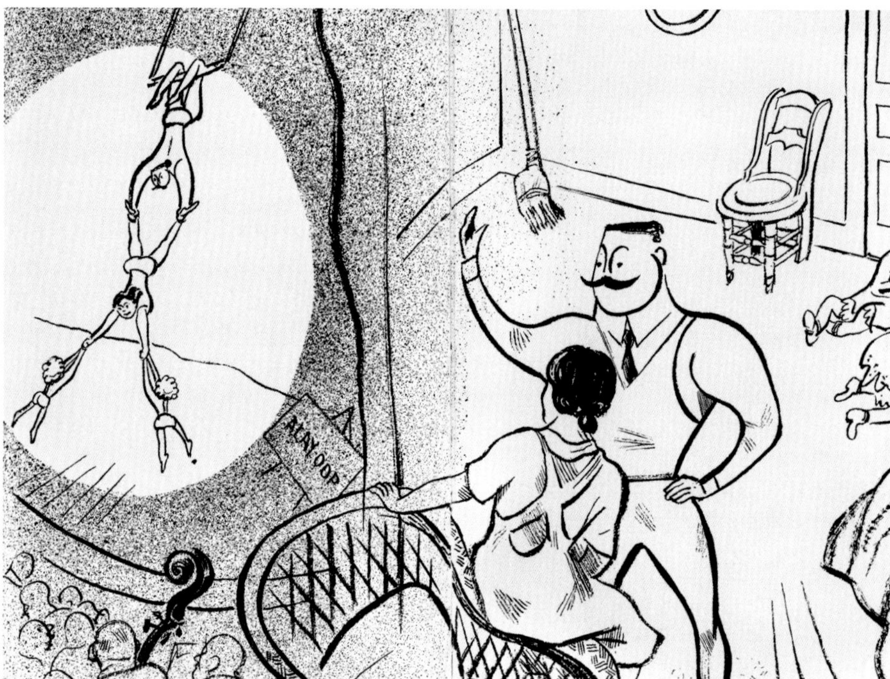
ALLAY-OOP

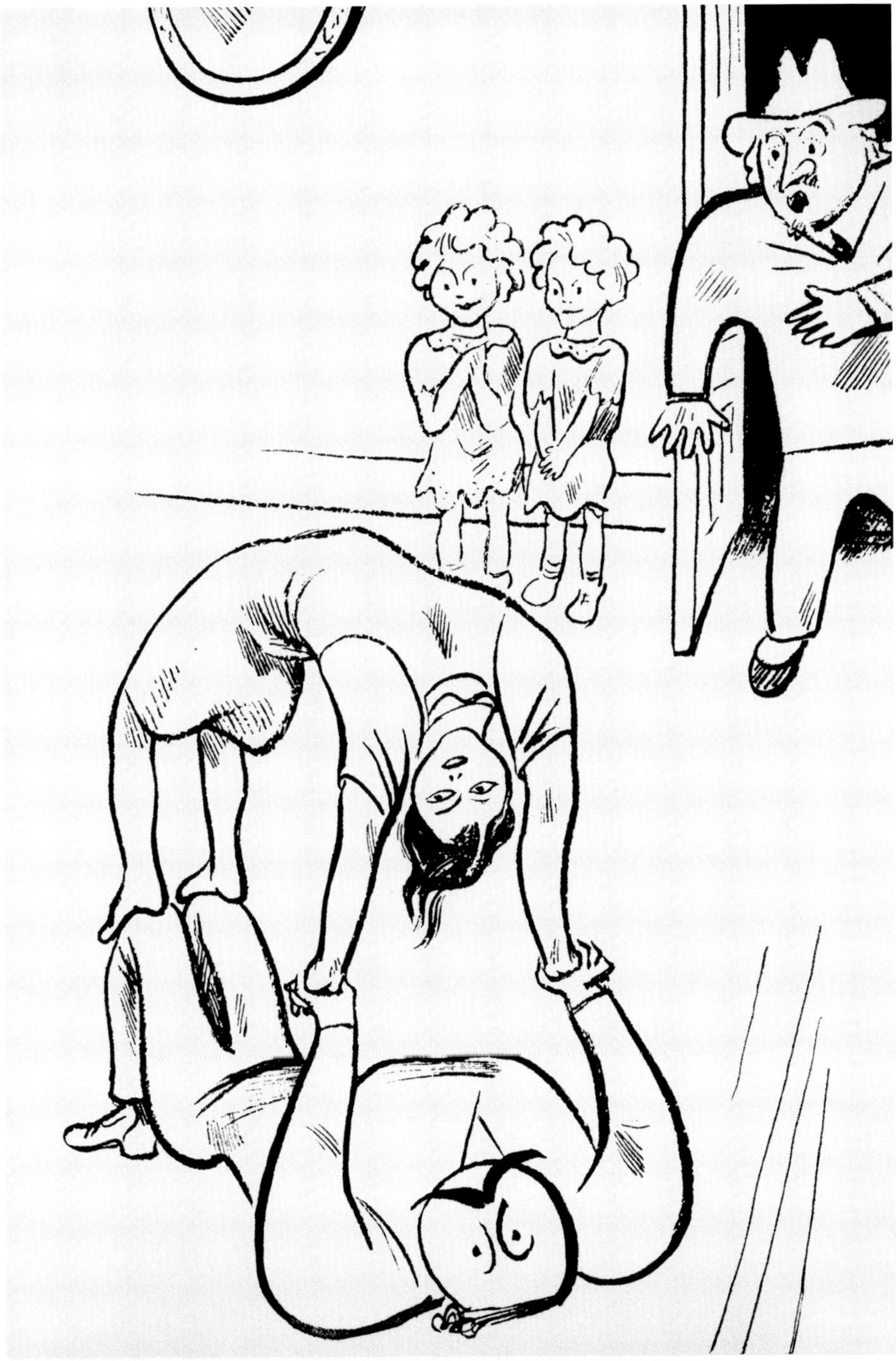

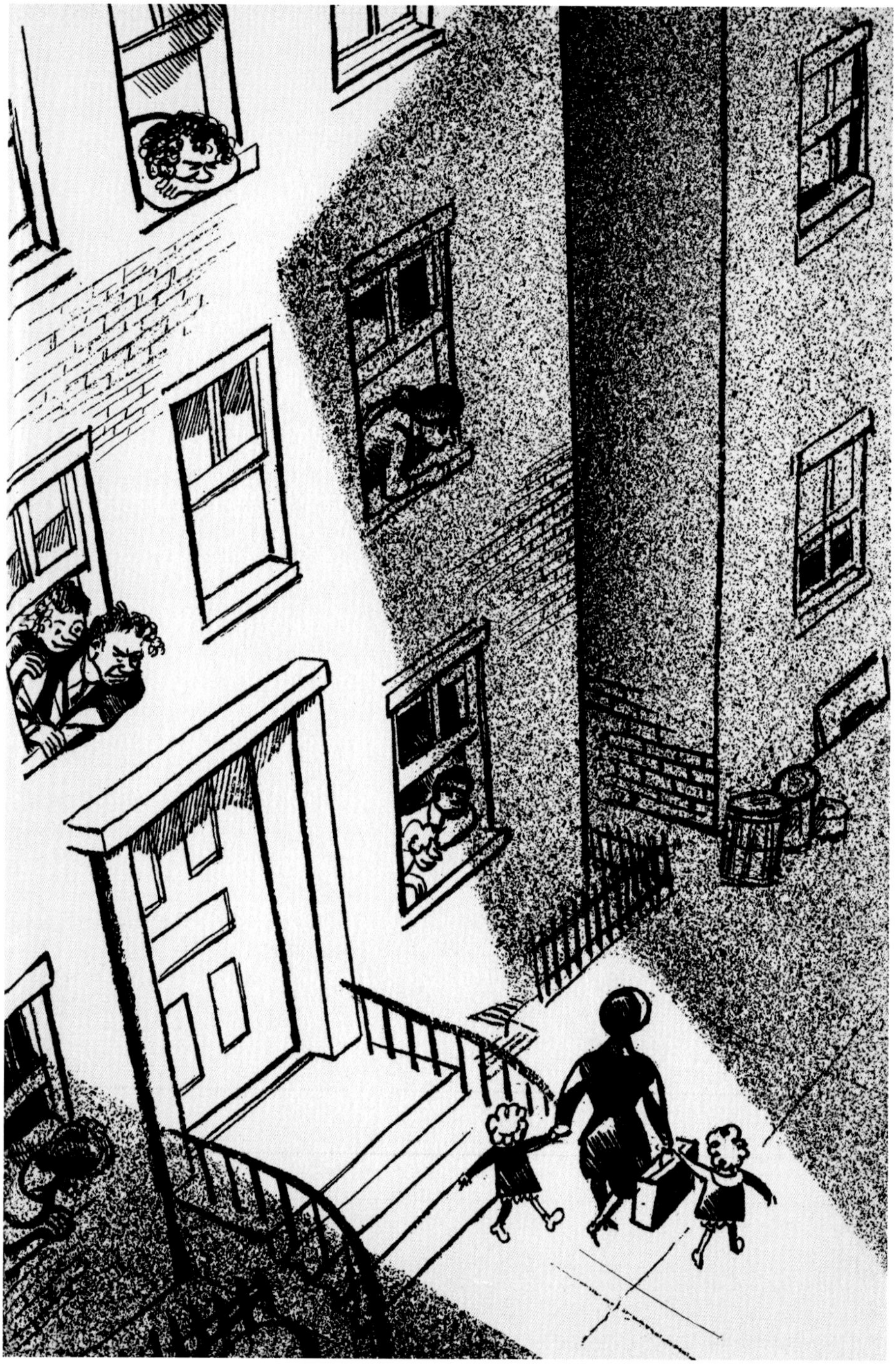

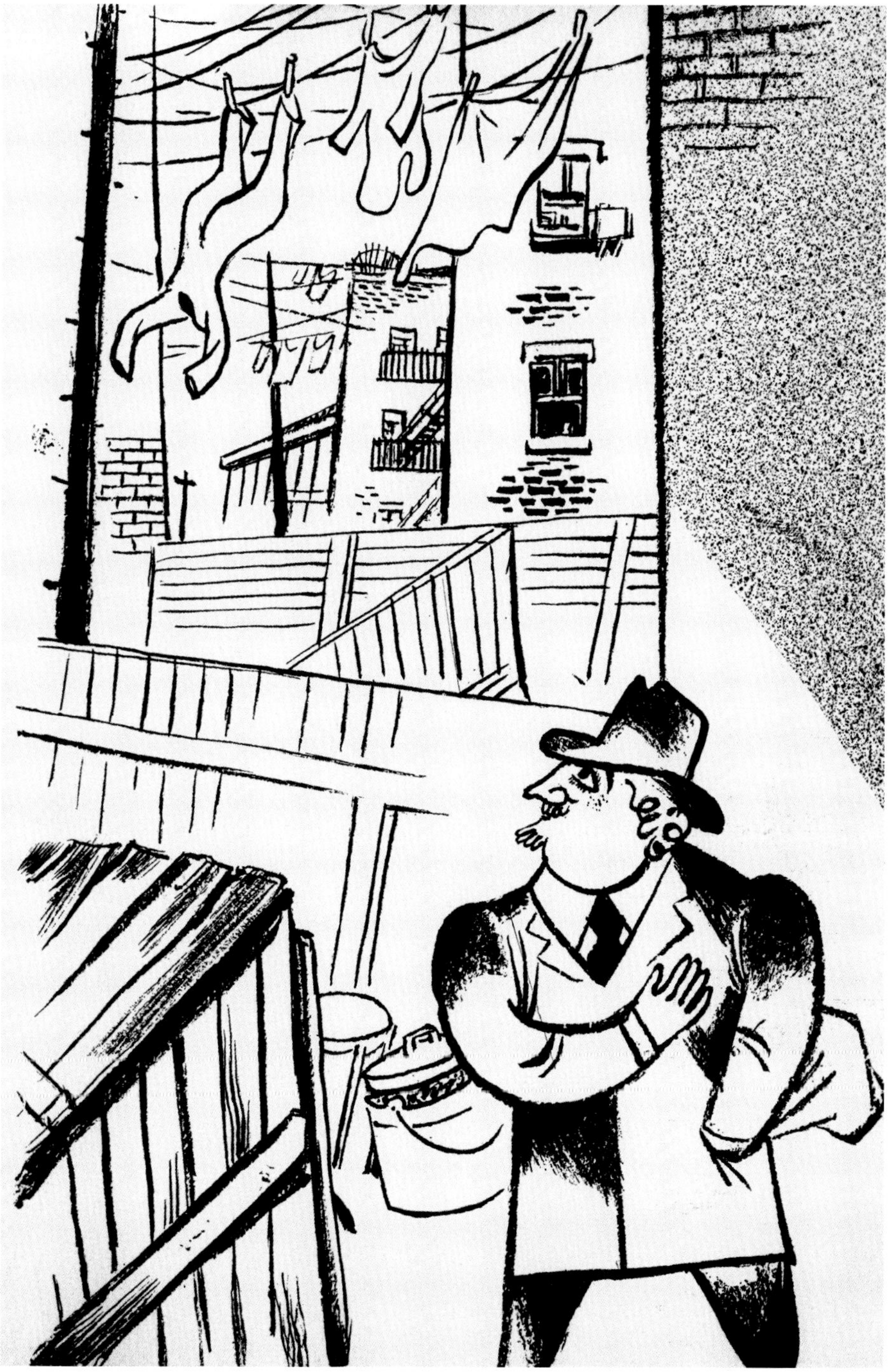

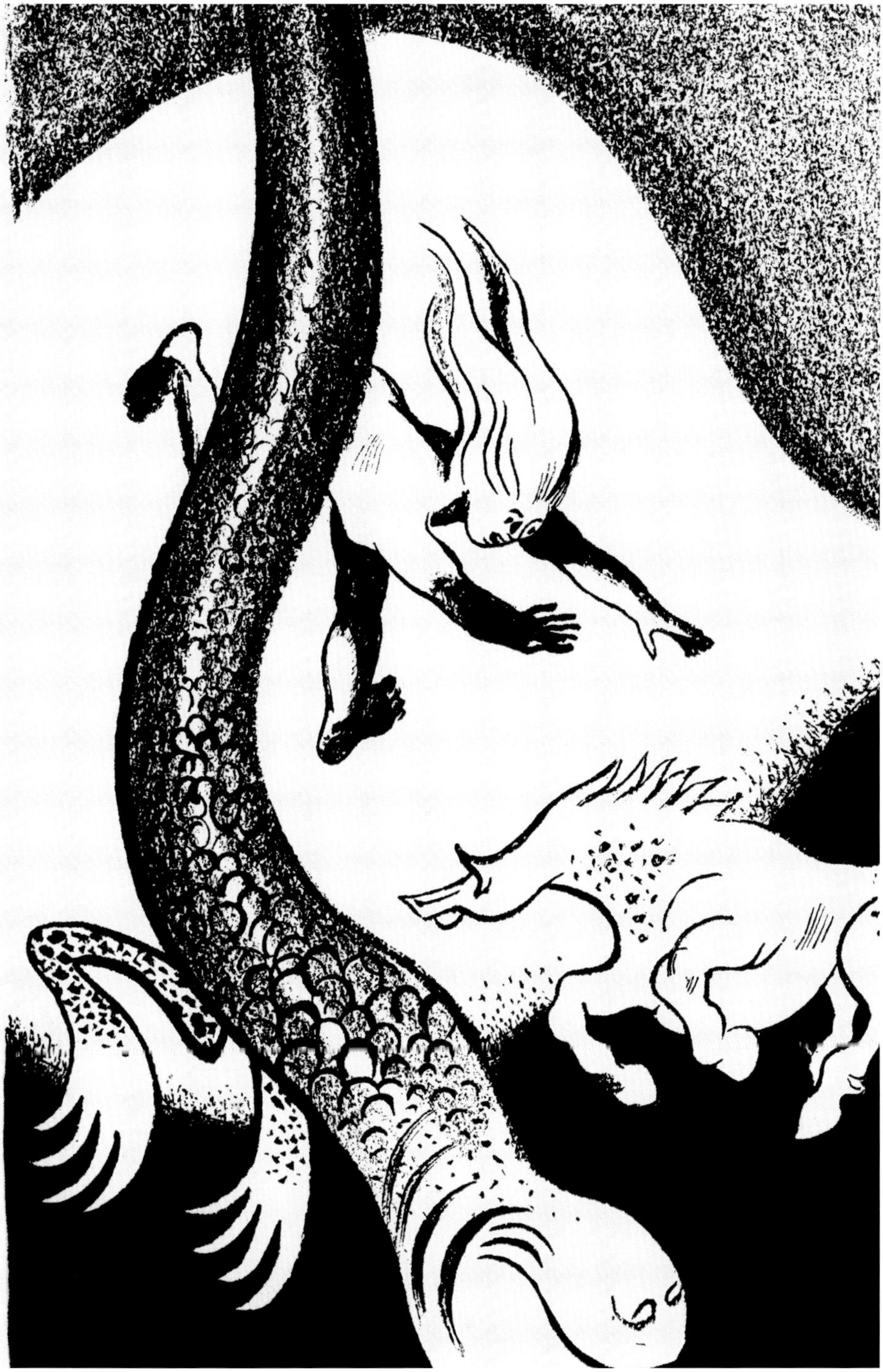

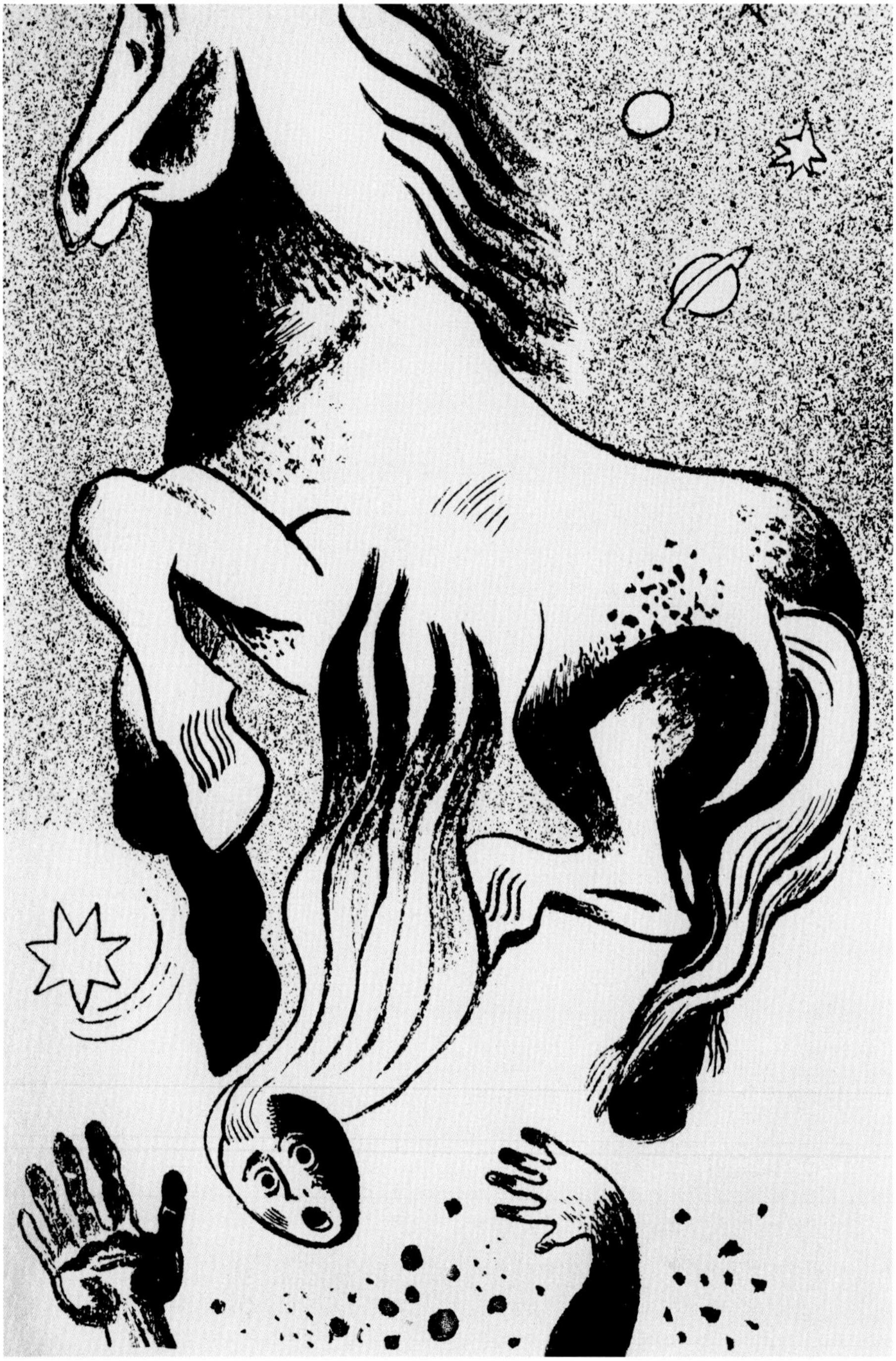

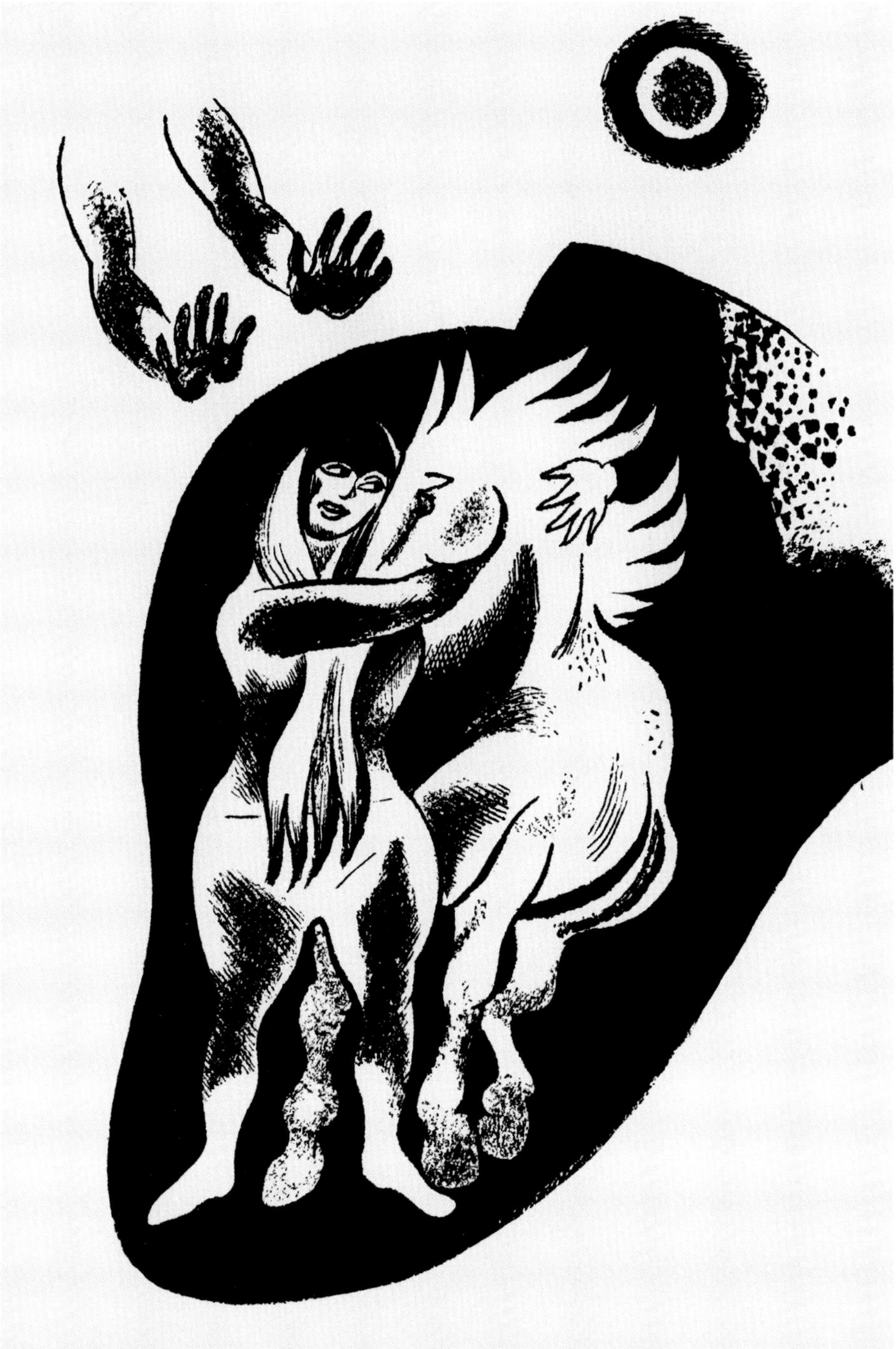

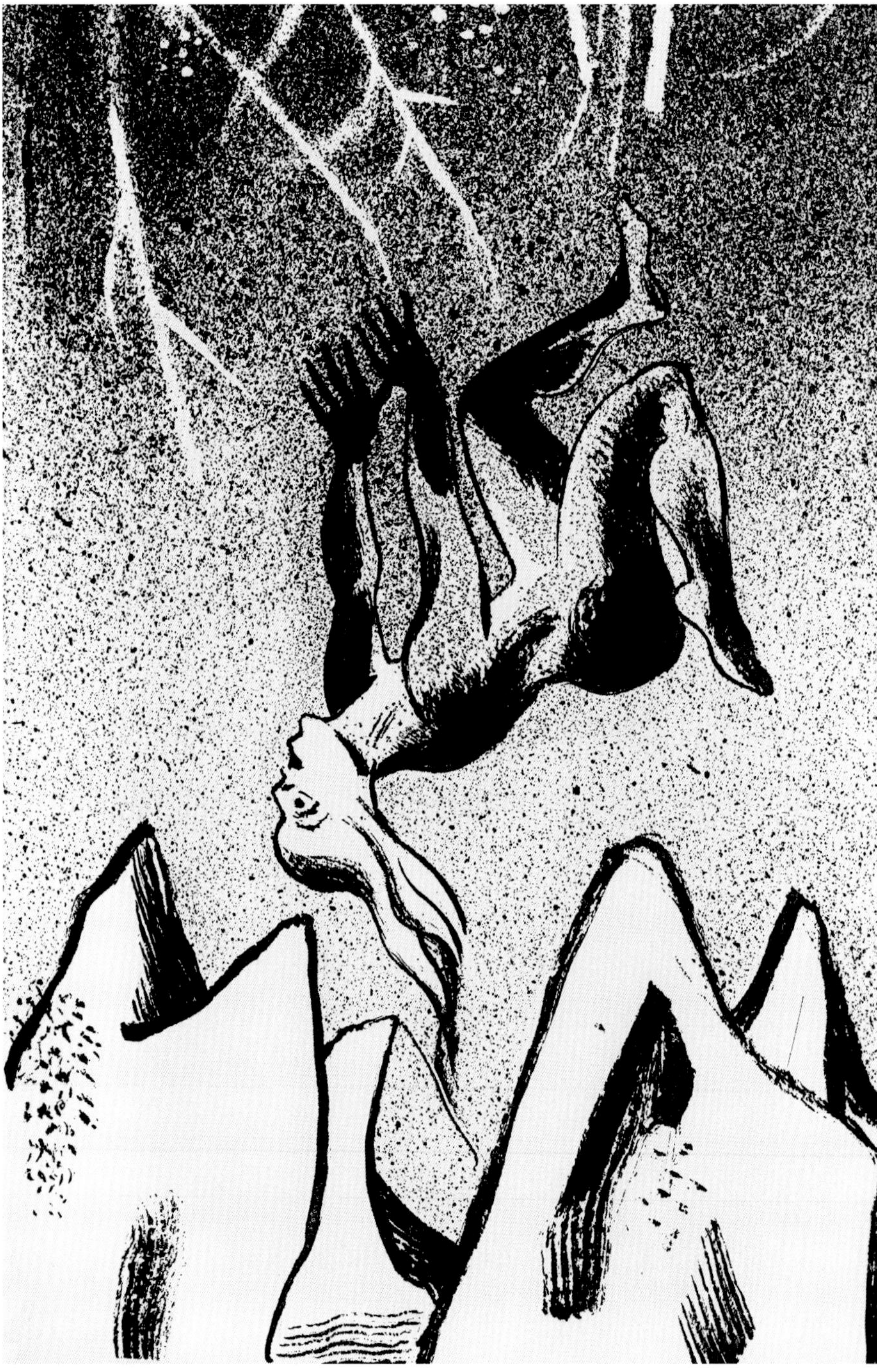

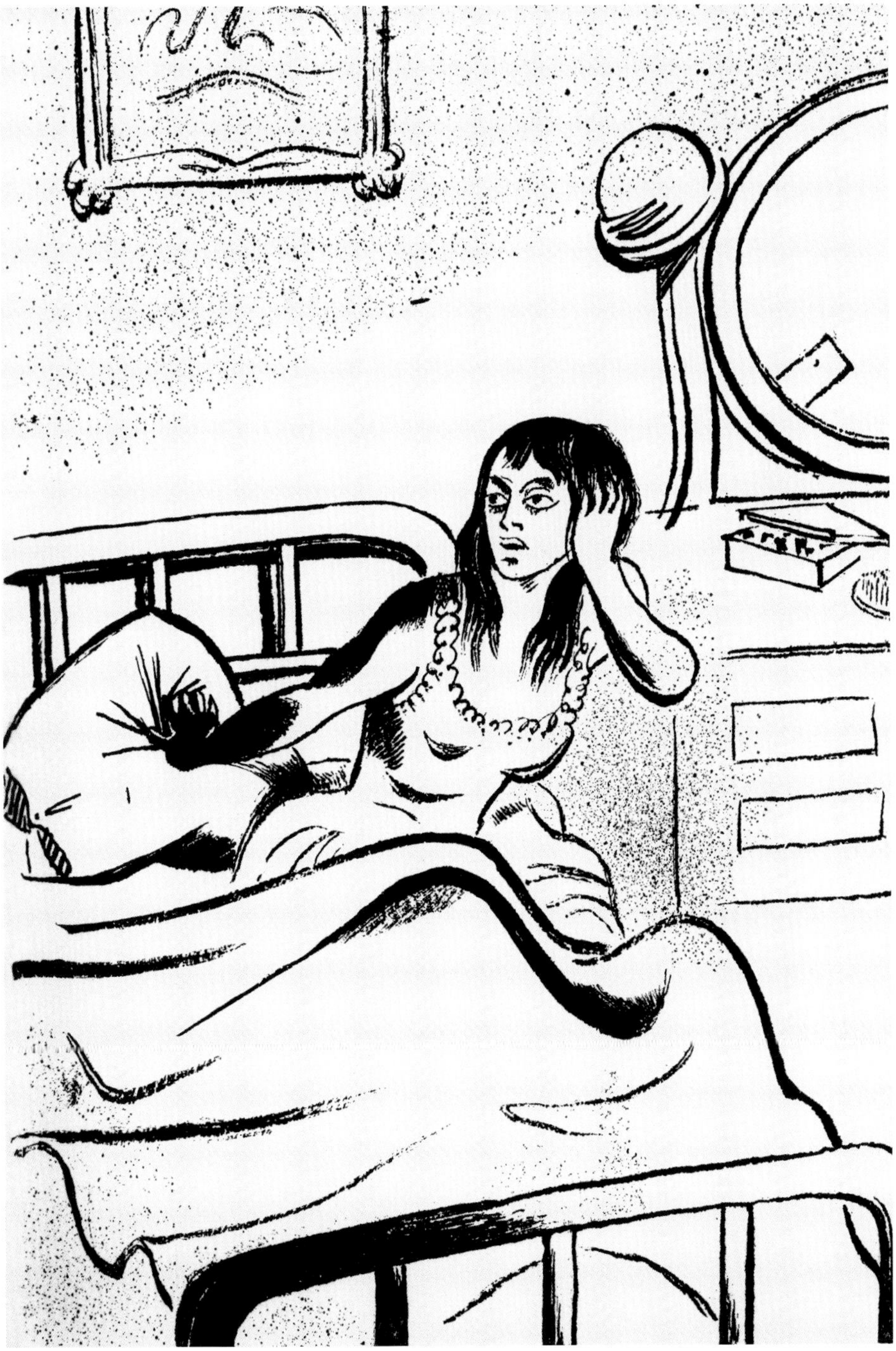

Chapter Seven

Cartoon Books

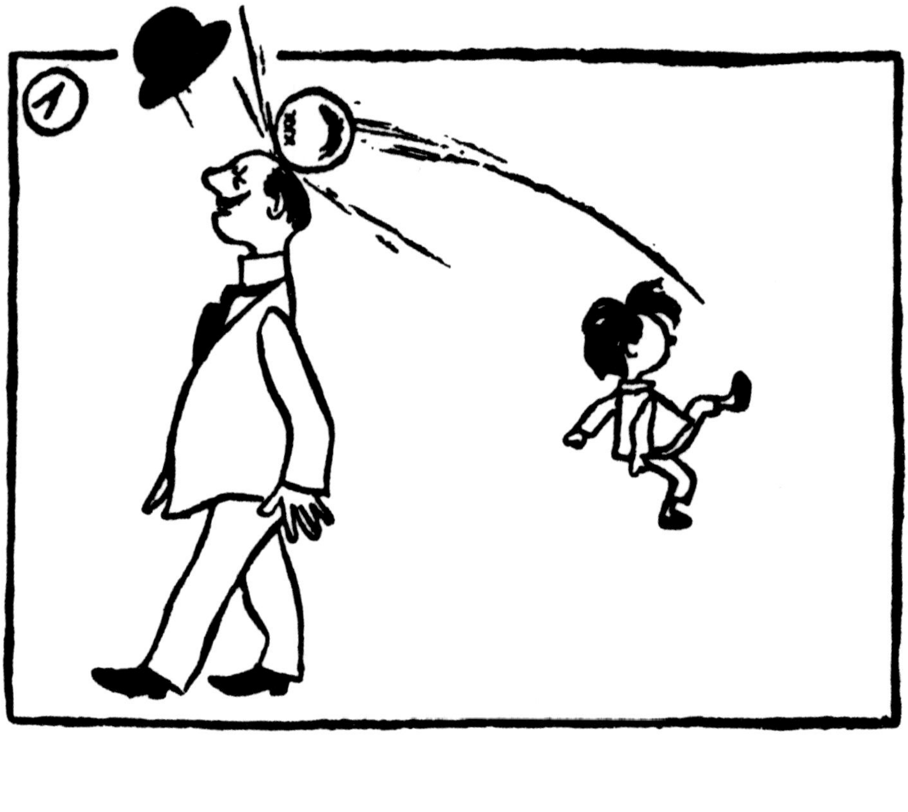

Another avenue of wordless books from this era first appeared as popular newspaper comic strips, which had a proven readership and displayed a lighter focus on the human condition. These books came from long-running strips by Americans Otto Soglow (*The Little King*) and Carl Anderson (*Henry*), and the Danish cartoonist Henning Dahl Mikkelsen (*Ferd'nand*), all of which were based on humorous gags and themes that have never gone out of style. Beyond the humorous gags, these cartoons created a bond between characters and readers that reflected a cultural sense of values.

One example of this cultural affiliation was the German cartoon *Vater und Sohn* by e.o. plauen.

e.o. plauen (1903–1944)

Erich Ohser's pen name, e.o. plauen, was taken from the initials of his name and the town where he was born, Plauen. He moved to Leipzig in 1920, where he studied art and married a fellow student, Marigard Bantzer, in 1930. Their son, Christian, was born in 1931 and was the model for his cartoon.

Ohser was a cartoonist for various German newspapers throughout his twenties before creating his wordless strip, *Vater und Sohn (Father and Son)*, for the *Berliner Illustrirte* in 1934. *Vater und Sohn* enjoyed an immediate success and was later published in three volumes and reprinted in numerous countries.

Vater und Sohn (1936)

The wordless gag strips in *Vater und Sohn* presented the heartfelt relationship and strong bond between a father and his son. The father is a balding and middle-aged man with a mustache and a hefty paunch. He smokes a pipe and dresses in a suit, sleeveless sweater, and a tie. His son, spontaneous and precocious and with a wild mop of hair, inevitably irritates his father—who then reacts without thinking before he exhibits a heartfelt moment of contrition, protection, or understanding (page 154).

The care that the father has for his son is apparent in these strips. Generally, there is a one- or two-panel sequence that creates a simple action, followed by subsequent panels that create conflict, and a final panel of resolution. Ohser provided a father-and-son role model, commenting on the importance of certain activities—at any age—such as reading (page 155). The shared excitement that reading brings to both father and son is humorously indicated in this strip, especially in the swinging of the father's two feet in the last panel. As in the work of Milt Gross and other cartoonists who wrote and illustrated wordless strips, street signs and symbols are used successfully to cleverly provide content (note the use of the question mark in the vacant seat that represents a spoken question).

Vater und Sohn was published, ironically, in Nazi Germany during the years when the German nation followed the war-mongering madness of a father figure named Adolf Hitler. Maurice Horn, in his comprehensive survey *The World Encyclopedia of Comics* (1976), reported that Ohser, despite his popularity, was arrested by the Gestapo for making "defeatist remarks in an air-raid shelter." He committed suicide in his cell on April 6, 1944, the day before his public trial.

Two additional examples of the wordless cartoon book, though not based on any popular comic strip, are by the celebrated cartoonist Milt Gross, and the artist and animator Myron Waldman.

MILT GROSS (1895–1953)

The success of the wordless novel brought a 1930 lampoon of the genre by cartoonist Milt Gross, whose comic strips appeared regularly in newspapers. Gross introduced his brand of Yiddish-dialect humor in his column, "Gross Exaggerations," for the *New York World*. His first book, *Nize Baby* (1926), was based on these columns and became a best seller. Gross followed this with more successful humor books that featured Yiddish dialect, as well as with scriptwriting in Hollywood.

It was during this period of time when Gross was living in California and working on a screenplay based on *Nize Baby* that he had the idea for a novel without words—one that would capture all the melodrama of a silent adventure film. *He Done Her Wrong* never reached the success of his previous books, and through the 1940s Gross continued working tirelessly on other strips like *Count Screwloose of Tooloose* and *Otto and Blotto*.

Following his success, Gross, overworked, suffered his first heart attack in 1945. Although he cut down on his workload in his remaining years, Milt Gross died from a second heart attack in 1953.

He Done Her Wrong (1930)

In *He Done Her Wrong,* Milt Gross presents as slapstick comedy a lighthearted look at romance. In a wild series of panels, Gross tells the story of a roughneck bumpkin wearing a coonskin cap who falls in love with a petite barroom singer (below). A short, conniving villain deceives the couple and takes the woman to New York (opposite and page 158). Ultimately, after a series of burlesquelike events, the villain is foiled. The hero, who is discovered to be the son of a wealthy industrialist (page 159), marries the heroine and together they raise a large family. The villain finds himself looking down the gun barrels of five accusing fathers, demanding that he marry one of their daughters (page 160) who have given birth to the villain's many children.

Whether intentional or not, Gross's lampoon takes jabs at Ward's idealistic picture of the hero in *Gods' Man*. The critics saw Gross's wordless novel as entertaining without the pretentious overtones, ambiguous plots, or obscure symbolism in Ward's woodcut novels. For example, the handsome artist in *Gods' Man* (page 40) braves a storm with threatening waves in a small sailboat before he arrives safely and confidently on shore.

In contrast, Gross's bumpkin is anything but handsome and paddles on a log into New York harbor (page 161). With an expression of self-assurance, he faces the city, where he hopes to find his true love. His confidence dissolves quickly in a series of gags (pages 162–164): A painter drops a bucket on his head; a vehicle strikes the bumpkin as he crosses the street and spins him around like a top; a horse steps on his foot; and a mechanical hand-signal on a truck slams down on the top of his head. Ironically, the sign on the side of the vehicle reads "Safety Truck."

Gross uses words to spin his comedy, as in the scene where both the hero and the heroine are walking to the same corner from different directions (page 165, top). They are likely to bump right into each other and reunite happily (which would spoil the plot). Instead, a sign advertising a show called *Fate* drops down between the couple, interrupting their reunion (page 165, bottom).

Gross devotes a creative effort in the layout for each page in this book. He not only uses the single page as a formal background to his pictures, but moves objects and characters around on the page in an innovative manner that keeps the narrative animated. In some instances, the narrative is enclosed in a traditional square panel (page 166). In other instances, Gross varies this standard approach and displays the action outside the borders of the panels. Sequences of events on pages without panels flow horizontally, vertically, or diagonally so that the reader's vision pleasantly covers each page as quickly as the action of the narrative unfolds. Since the plot is a sequence of burlesquelike events, with the bumpkin in hot pursuit of his true love, this creative layout of the action is an effective addition to the fast-paced narrative.

During this era, stereotypes were used more frequently in gags in both silent film and comics. One example that was dropped from later editions of *He Done Her Wrong* is the scene where the bumpkin falls down a coal chute (page 167, top). He is chasing the villain and thinks he has him by the throat (page 167, bottom). When the bumpkin rinses the coal dust off the man's face, he is surprised to find he is holding an African-American man and not the villain.

Gross's use of picture balloons (page 168) not only enhances the narrative but also entertains readers with its cleverness. In one example, a trader describes the true nature of the villain with a pictorial equation. Inside the balloon are pictures of a skunk, a snake, and the villain, suggesting that all three objects are one and the same (page 169).

This truly entertaining silent film on paper was aptly implied by Gross in the book's extended subtitle, ". . . *Not a Word in It—No Music, Too*," suggesting the absence of the traditional piano often played in theaters accompanying silent films.

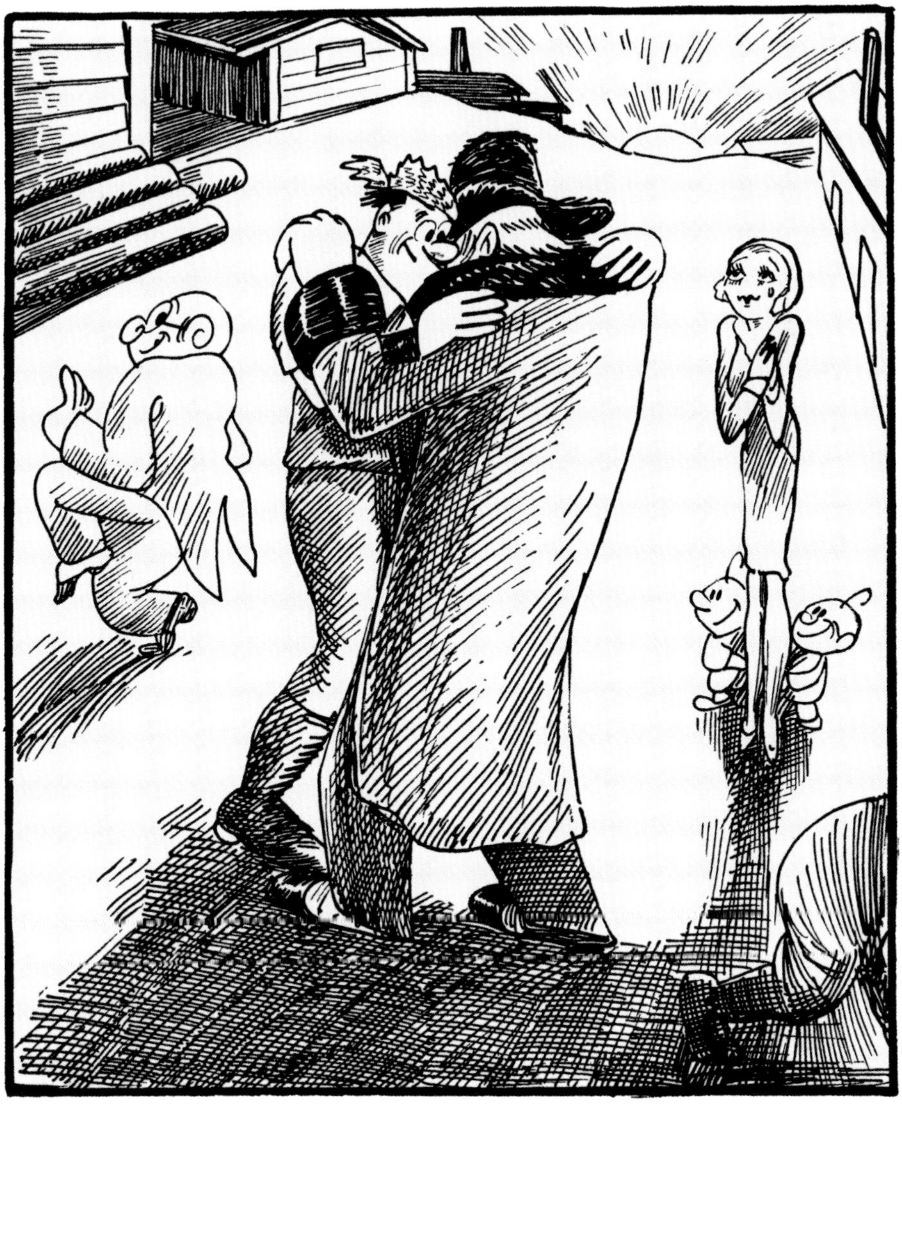

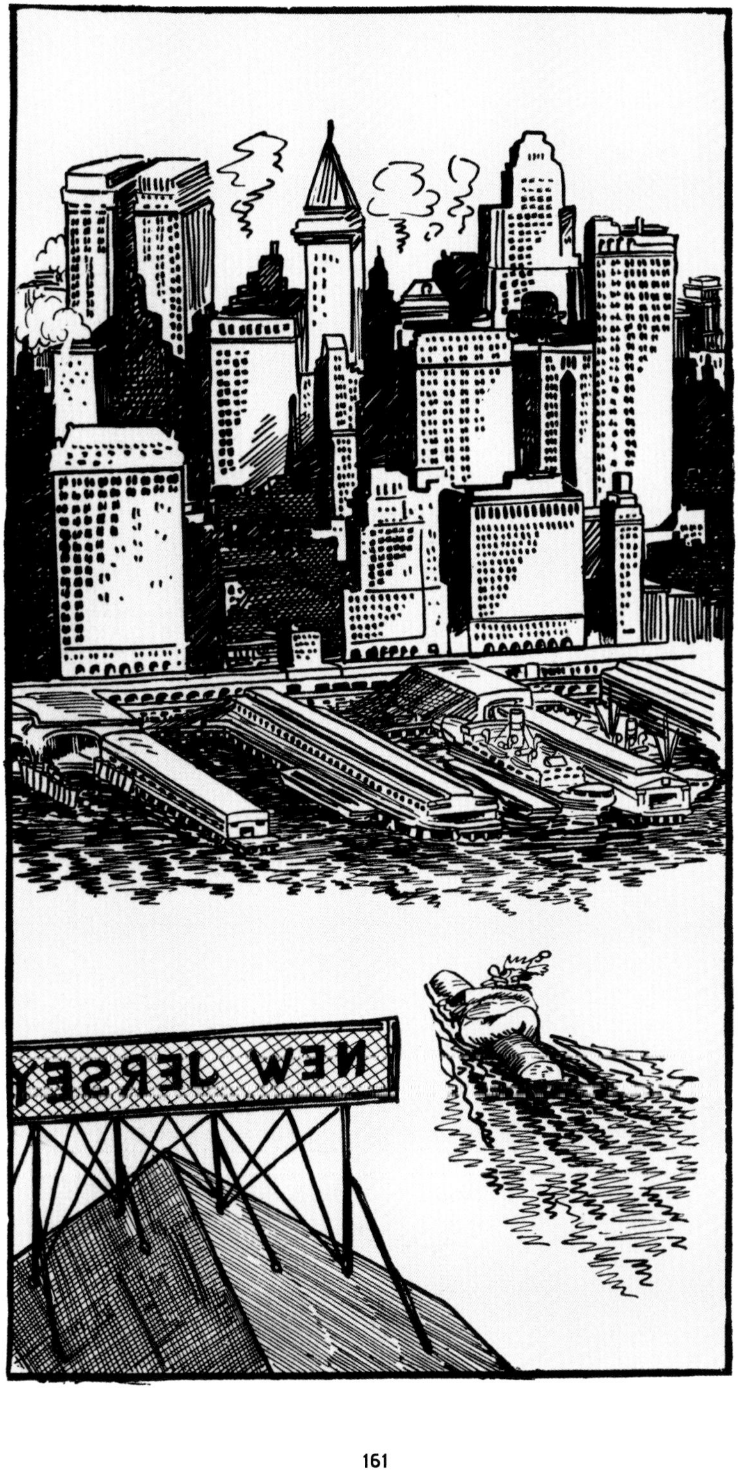
NEW JERSE

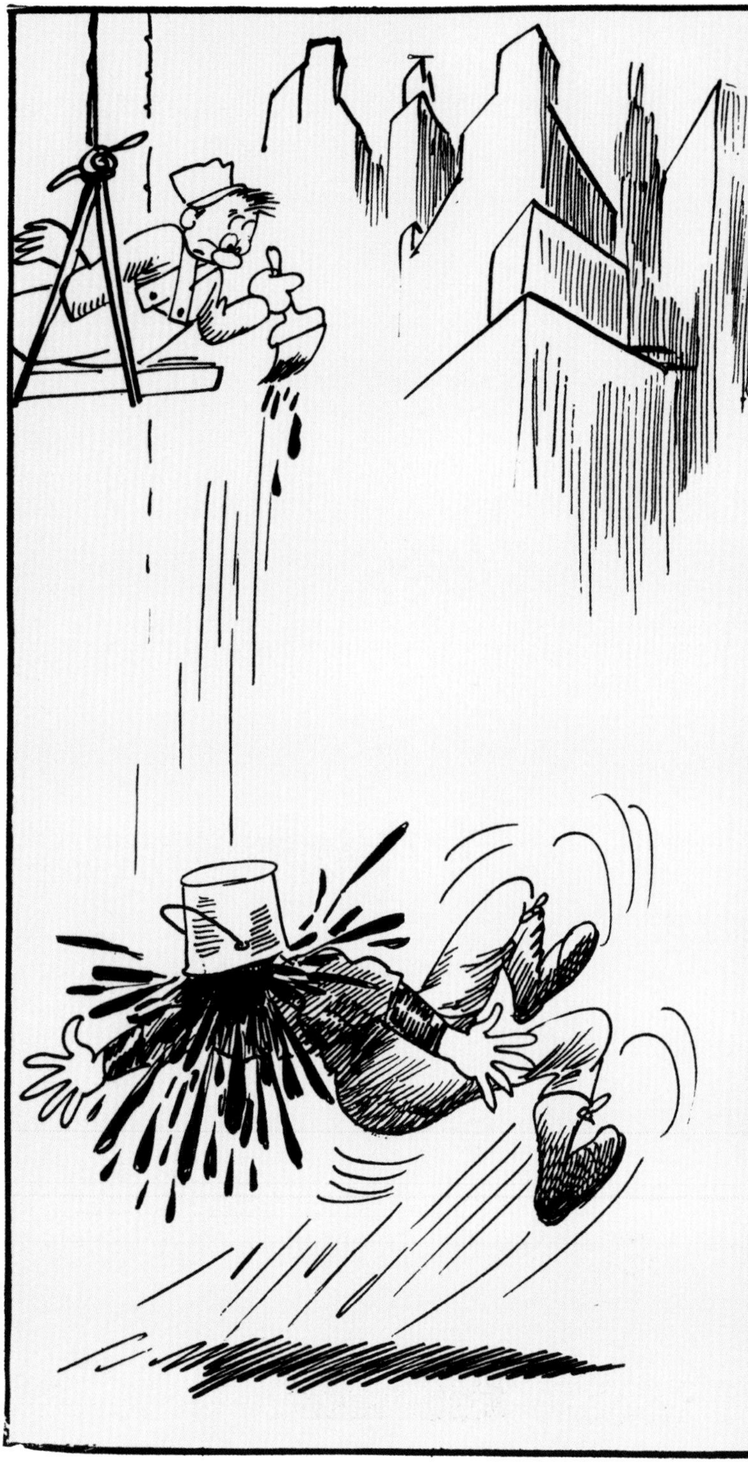

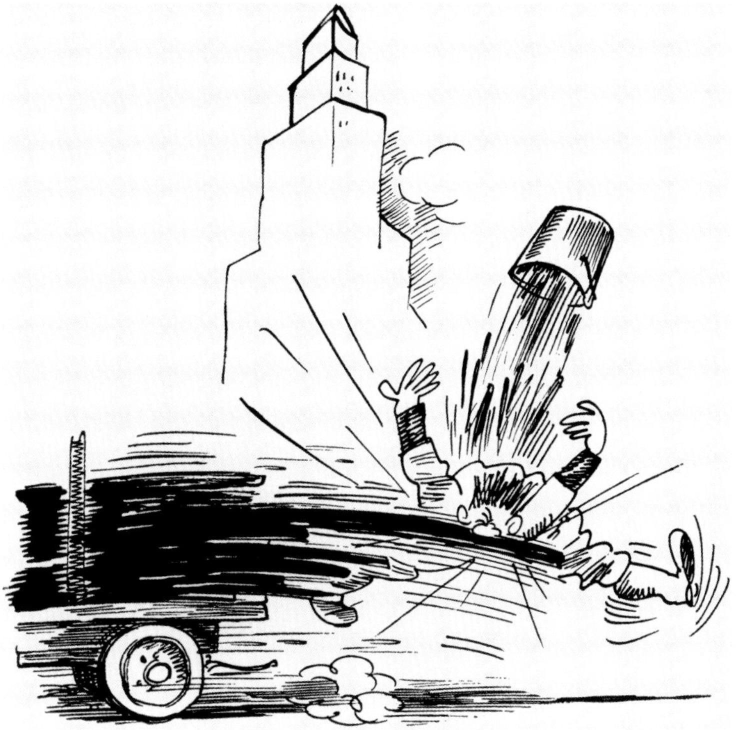

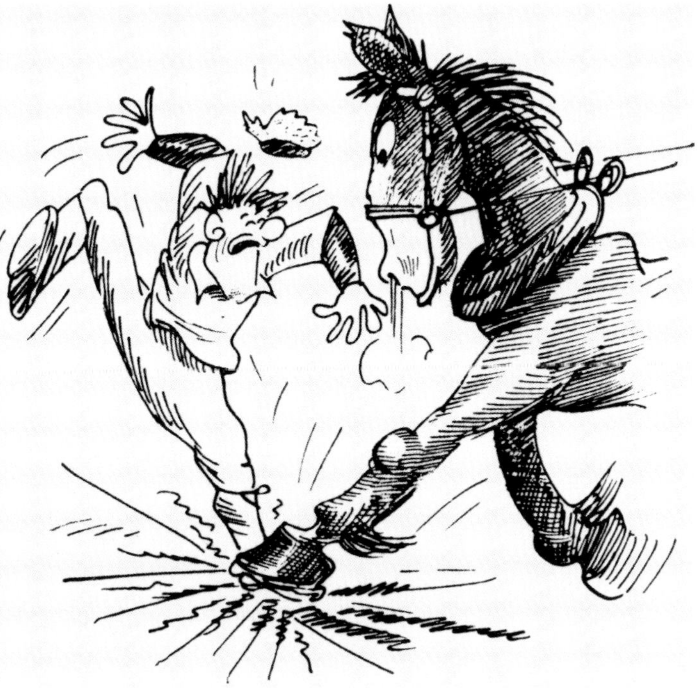

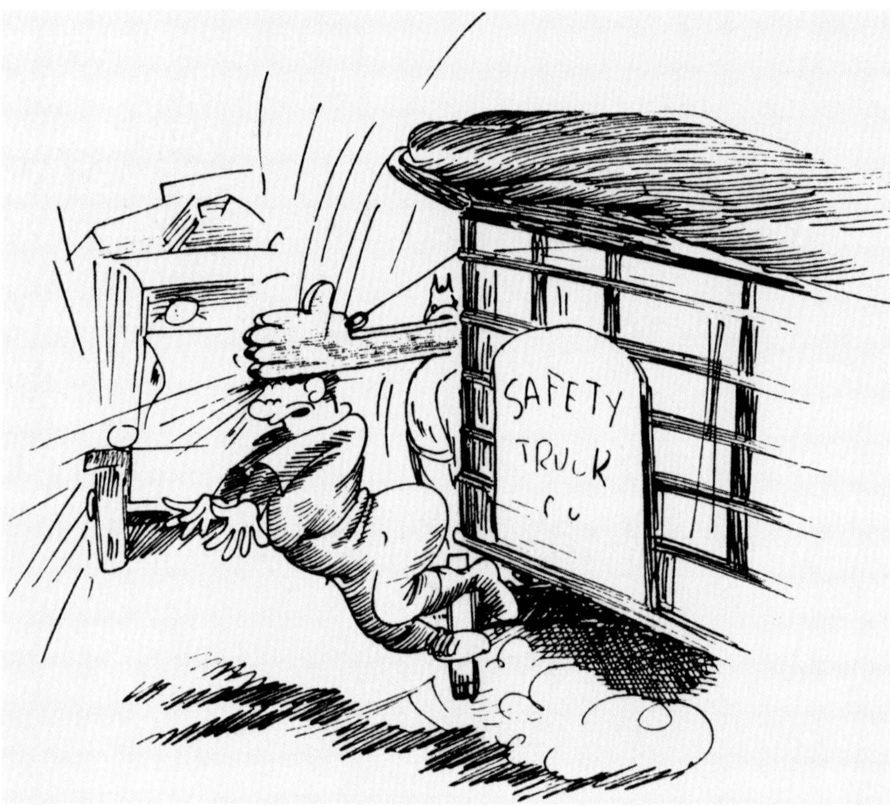
SAFETY
TRUCK
CO

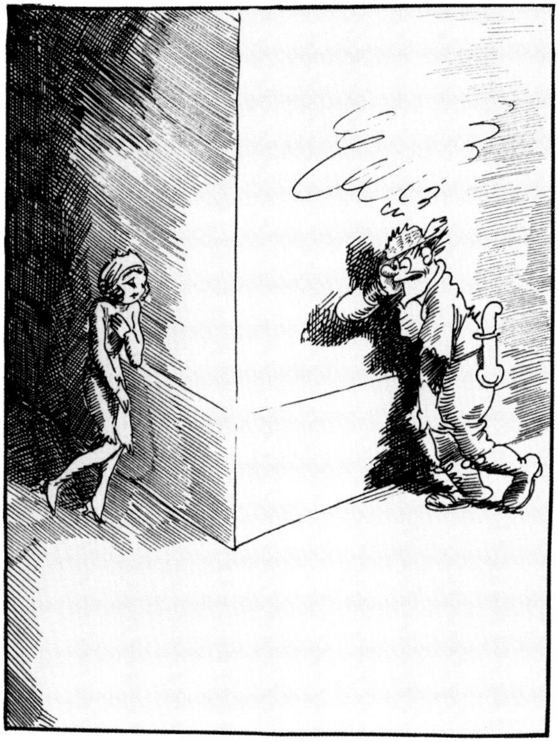

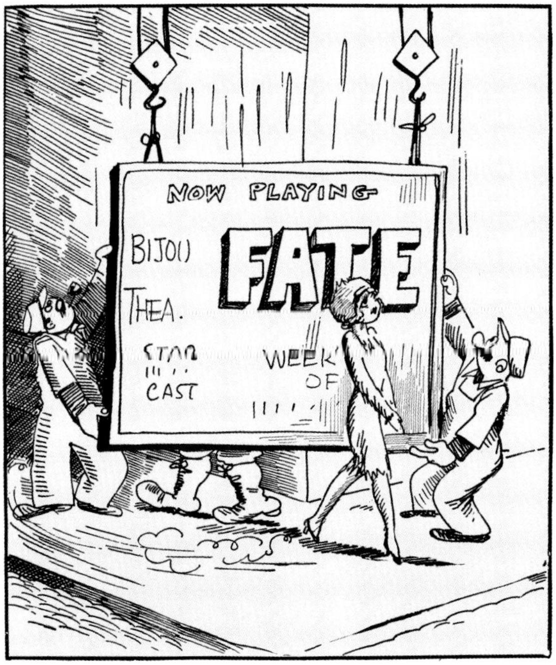
NOW PLAYING
BIJOU
THEA.
FATE
STAR
CAST
WEEK OF

SILENCE

REGISTER HERE

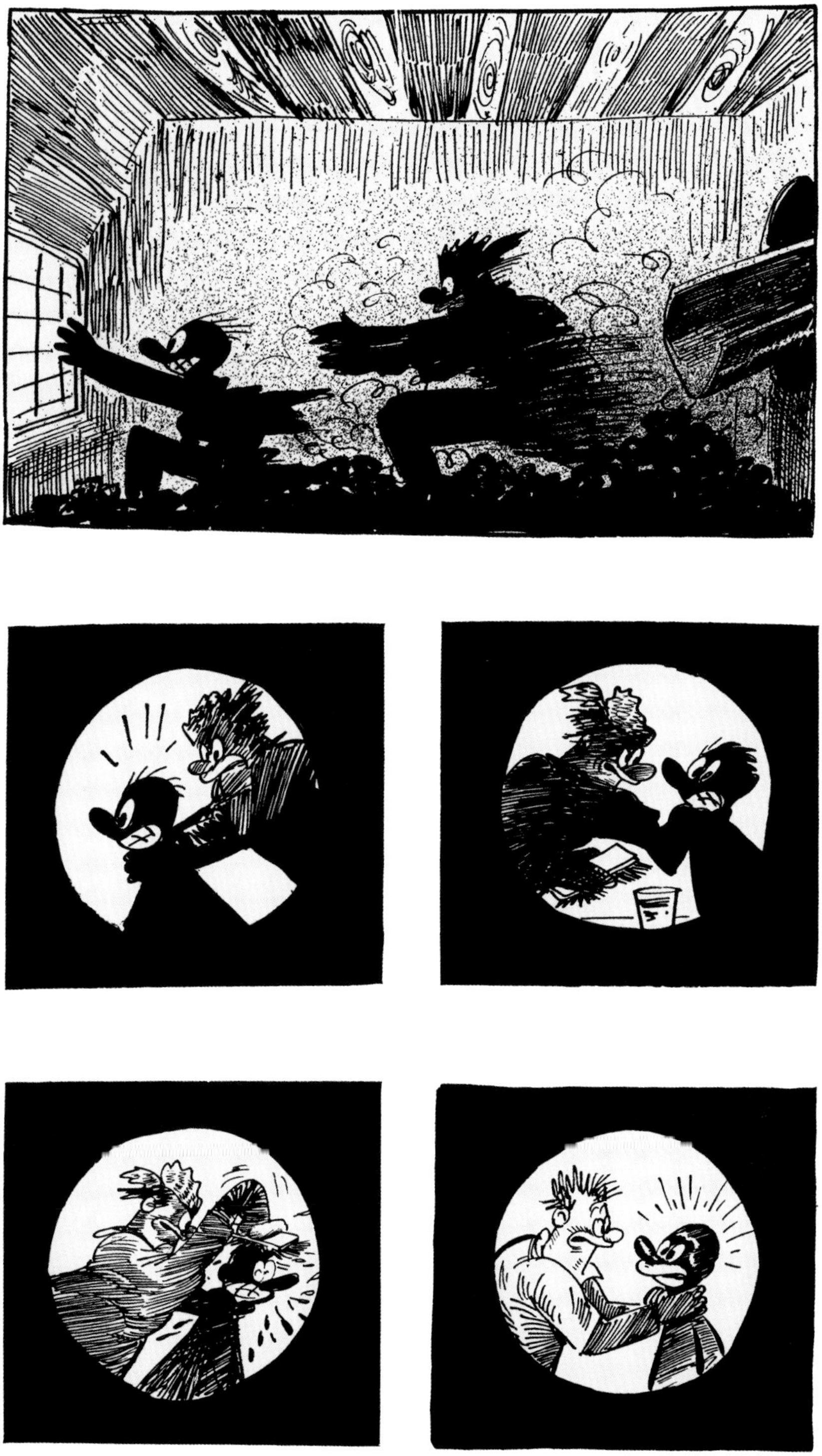

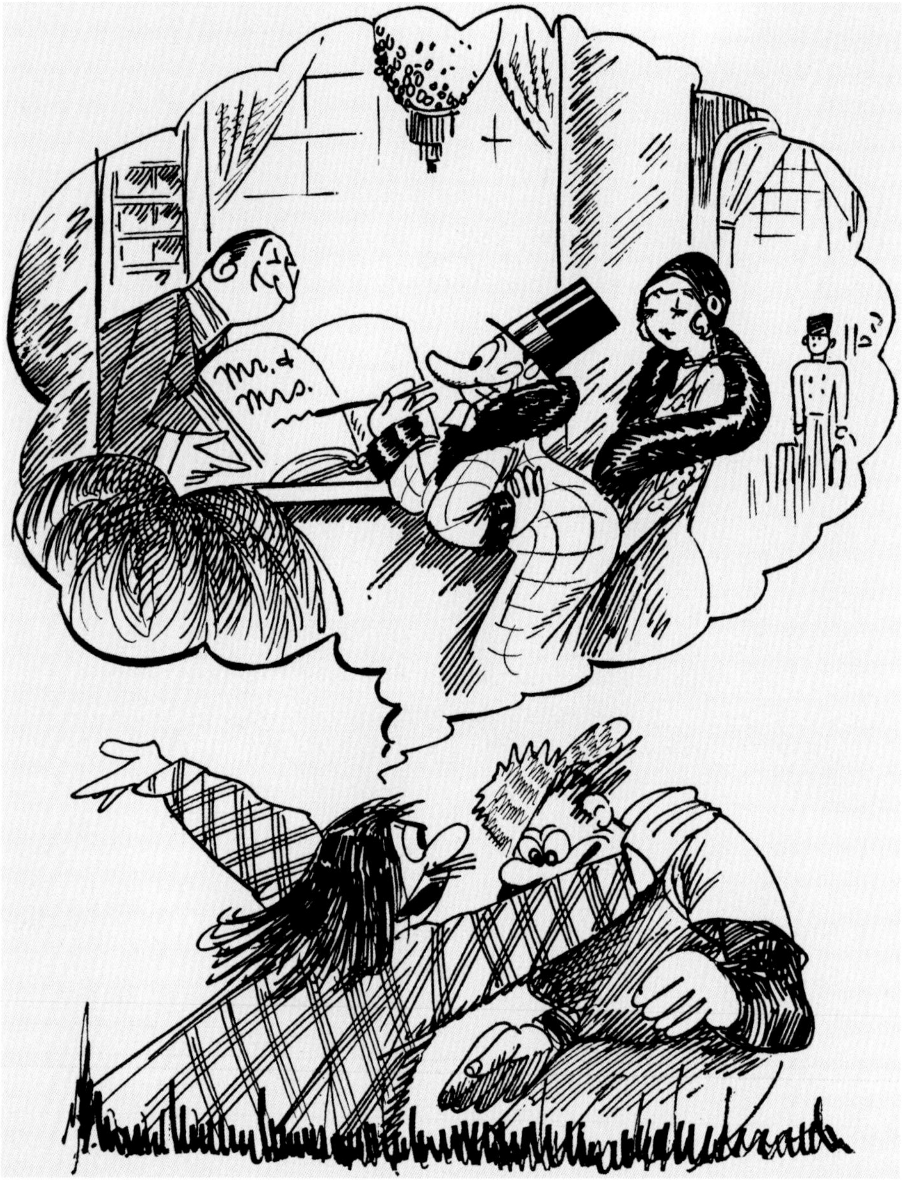
Mr. &
Mrs.

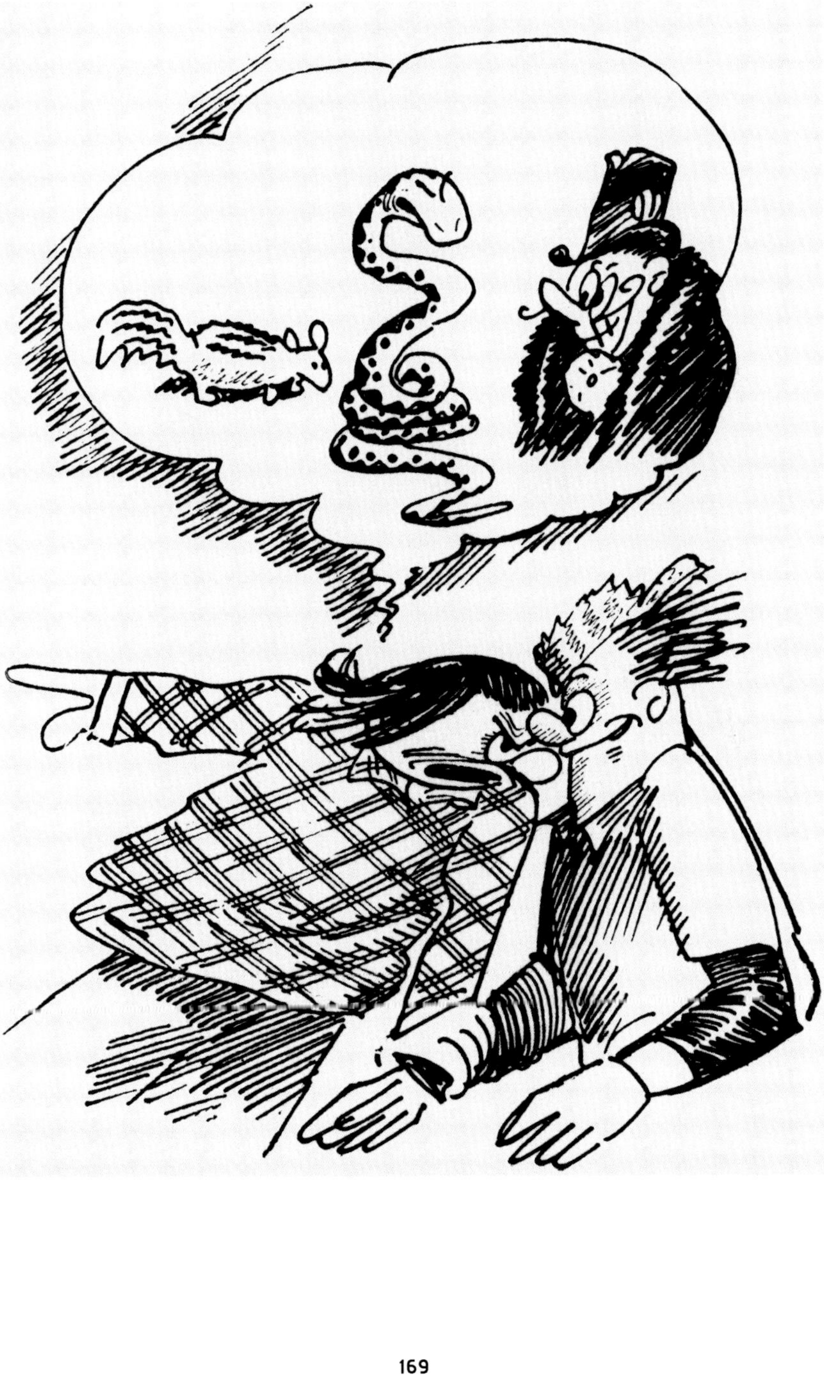

MYRON WALDMAN (1908–2006)

Myron Waldman was born in Brooklyn, New York, and attended Pratt Institute. Waldman worked for Fleischer Studios, a major animation workshop in Hollywood, California, first as a fill-in artist and then as an inker before he was promoted to animator.

Waldman's first animation, *By the Light of the Silvery Moon* (1931), was one in the famous series of "Screen Songs." It was noted for its sing-along device "follow the bouncing ball," which allowed the audience to sing along to the lyrics of songs sung by artists like Cab Calloway and Rudy Vallee. Waldman later worked on the animation for the cartoon characters Betty Boop, Popeye, and Superman, and was most noted for his animation on *Casper the Friendly Ghost.* He also originated Betty Boop's sidekick, a dog named Pudgy. Waldman received an Academy Award nomination in 1939 for the cartoon *Hunky and Spunky*, and worked on animation for commercials, including the chubby-faced Campbell's Soup kids.

Eve (1943)

What has been overlooked in Myron Waldman's career is his single wordless book called *Eve*, which tells the story of a frumpy young woman who works as a secretary and spends her evenings fantasizing about marrying a handsome movie star (opposite). She passes a travel agency and takes a vacation to Miami, where she falls in love with a plain-looking young man (page 172) who shares all her interests (page 173, top). She writes postcards to her friends and family about falling in love (page 173, bottom), but when she returns home, she discovers that the man she has fallen in love with in Miami is the mailman in her office. She feels brokenhearted, and her dream of marriage seems to dissolve until the mailman rushes to her side and announces his undying love for her (page 174).

Waldman's use of picture balloons (page 175, top) skillfully replaces traditional word balloons, and his use of facial motion (page 175, bottom) reflects not only the cartoonist's device of displaying time but also points to his skill as an animator.

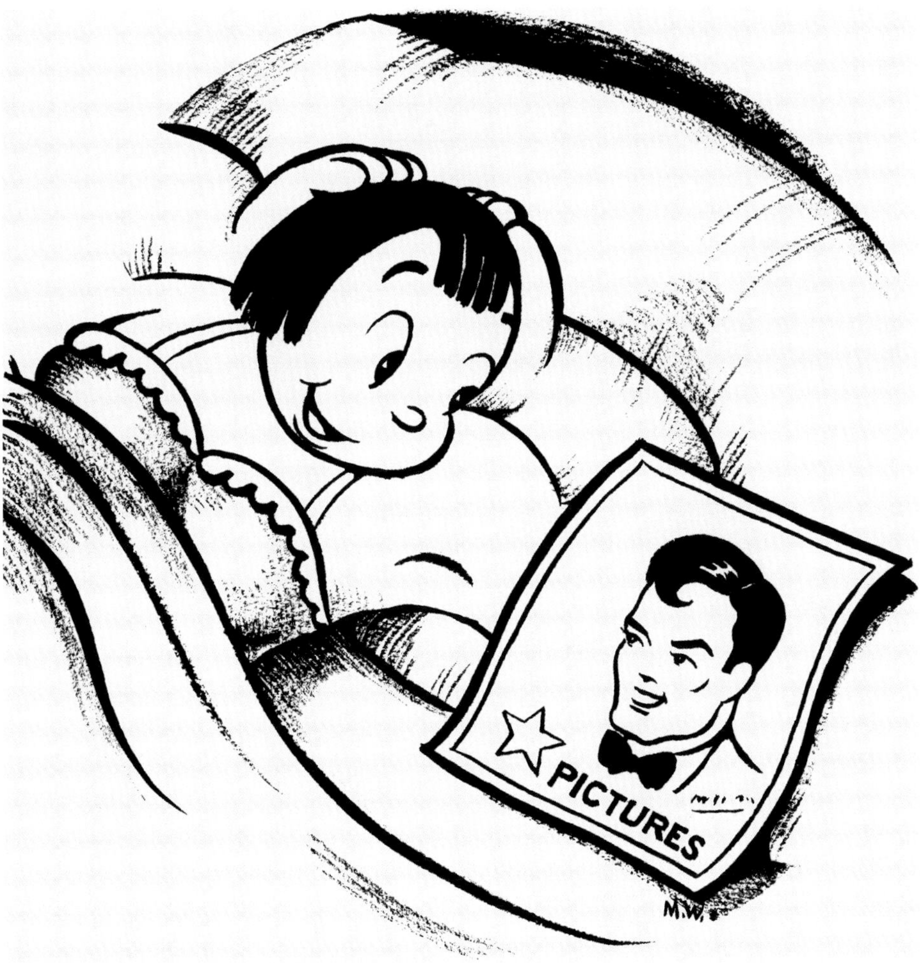
PICTURES
M.W.

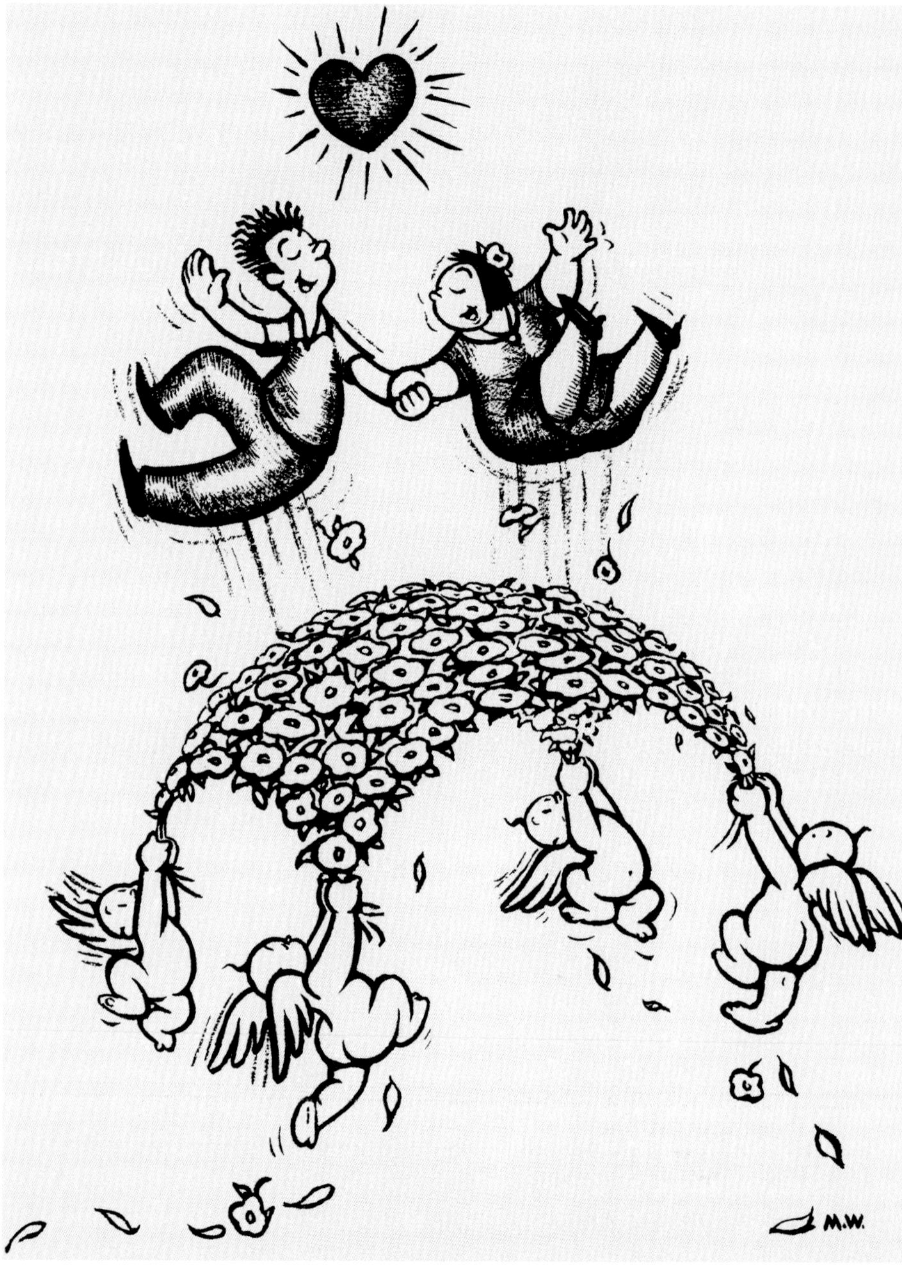
M.W.

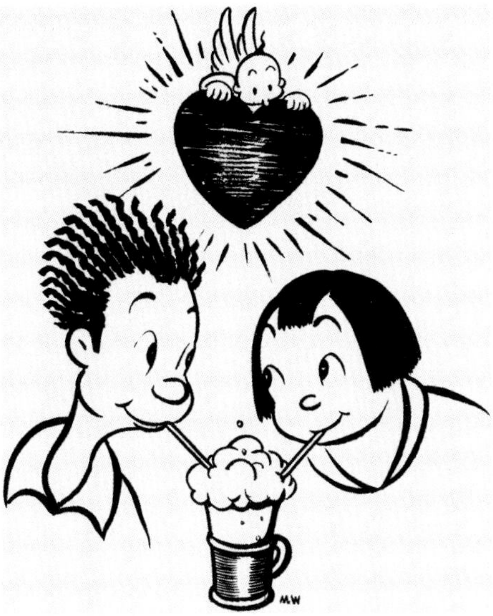
MW

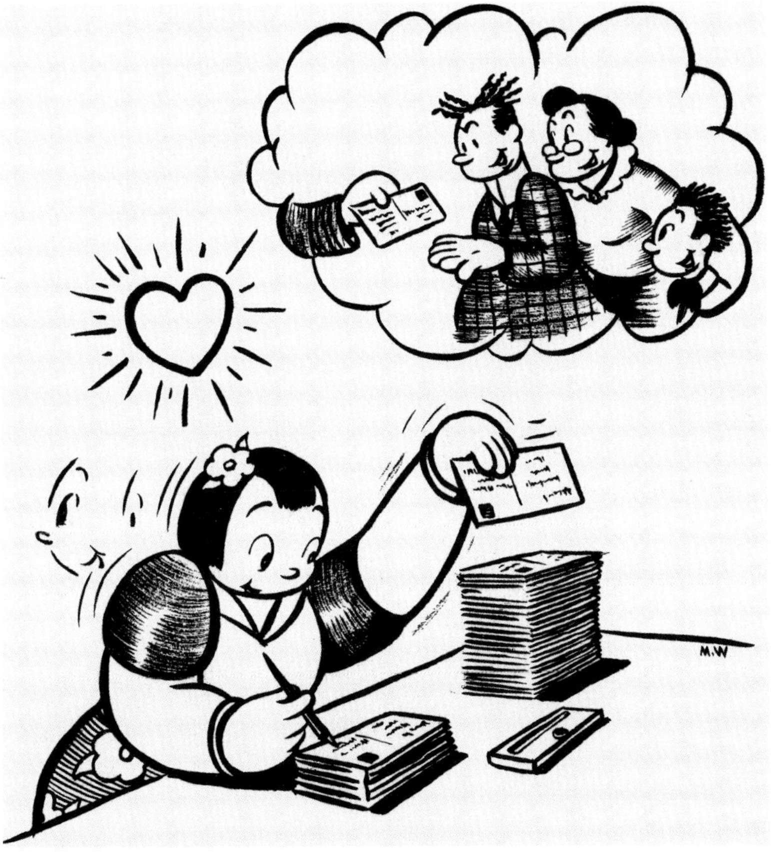
M.W

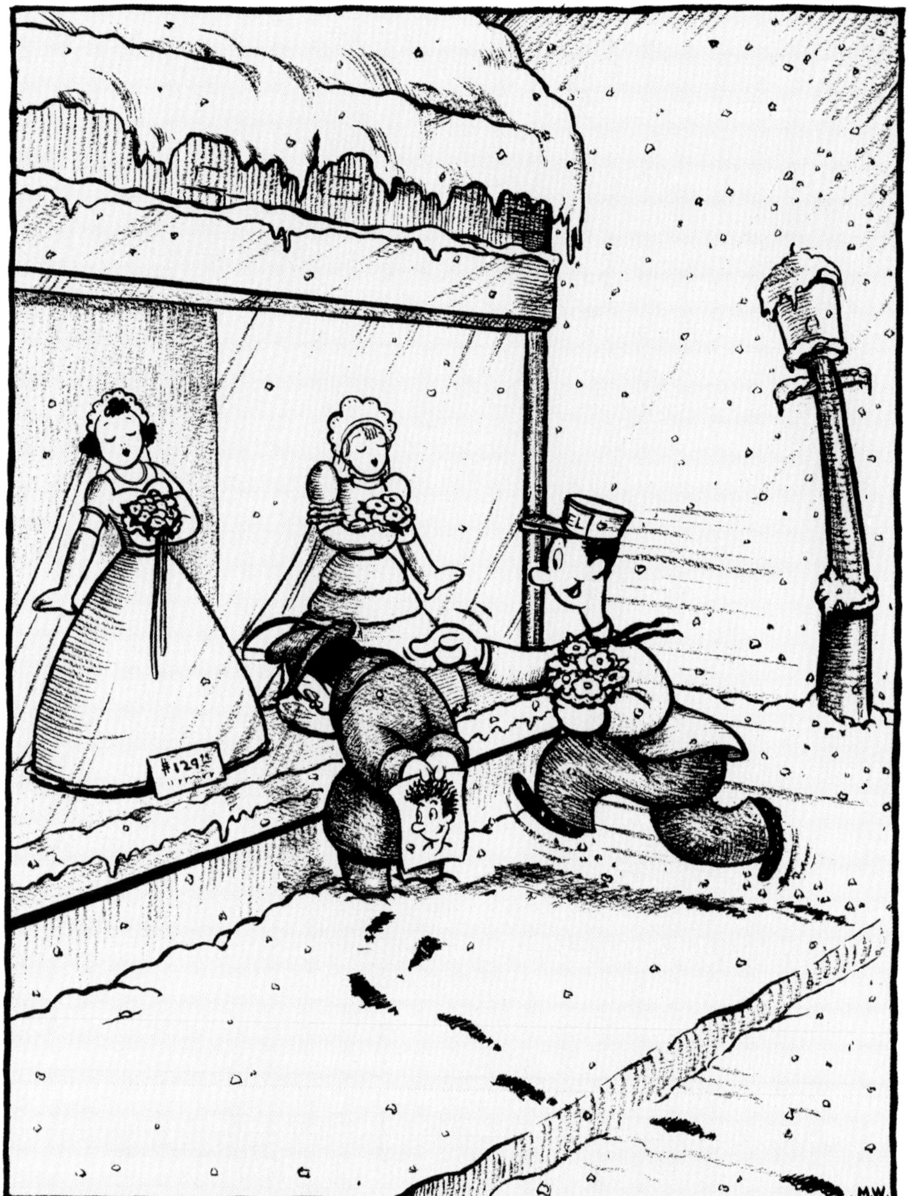
EL
M.W.

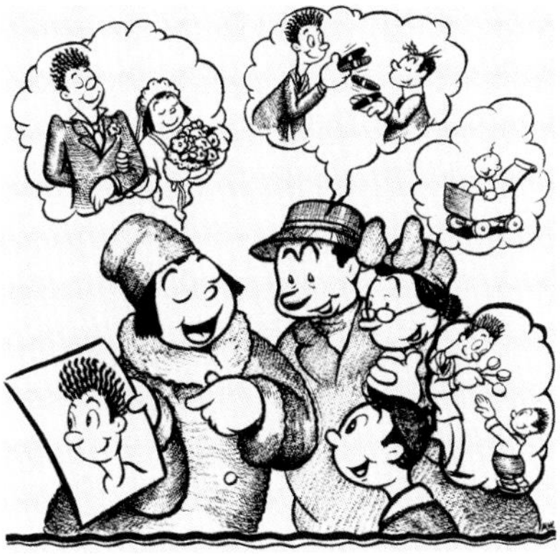

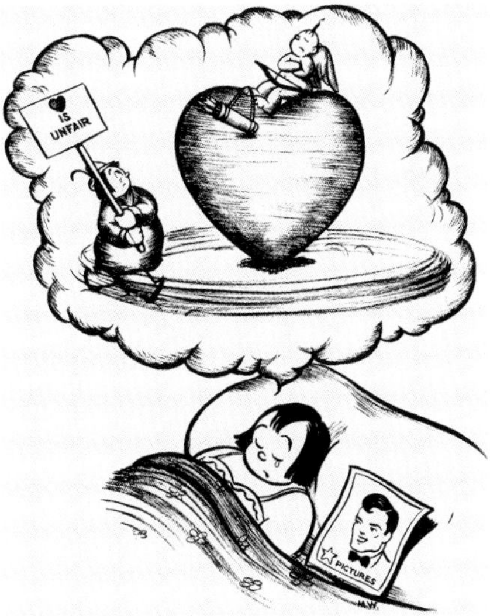
IS UNFAIR
PICTURES
MW

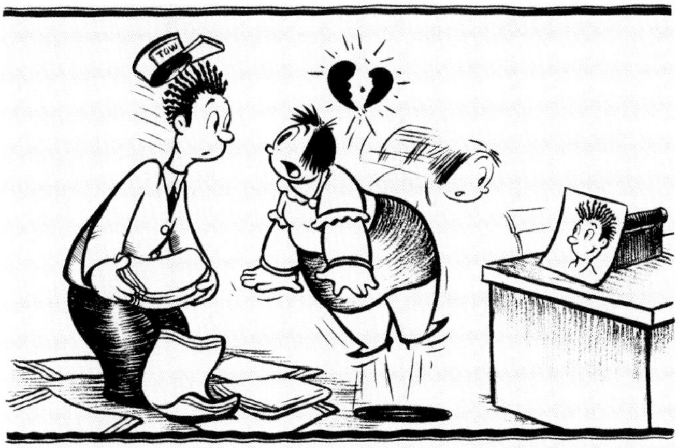
TOW

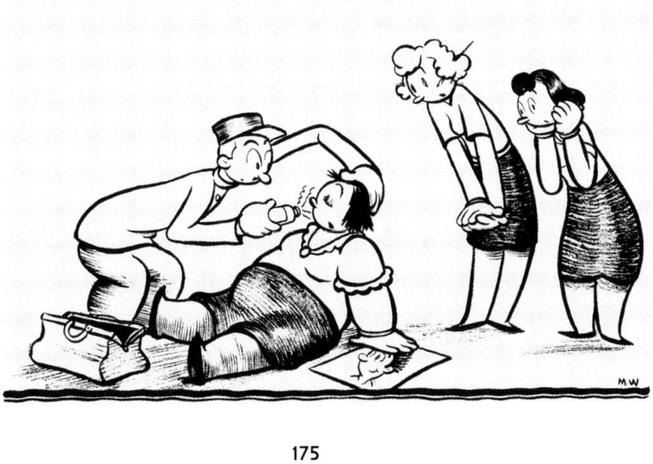
MW

Chapter Eight

István Szegedi Szüts

(1892–1939)

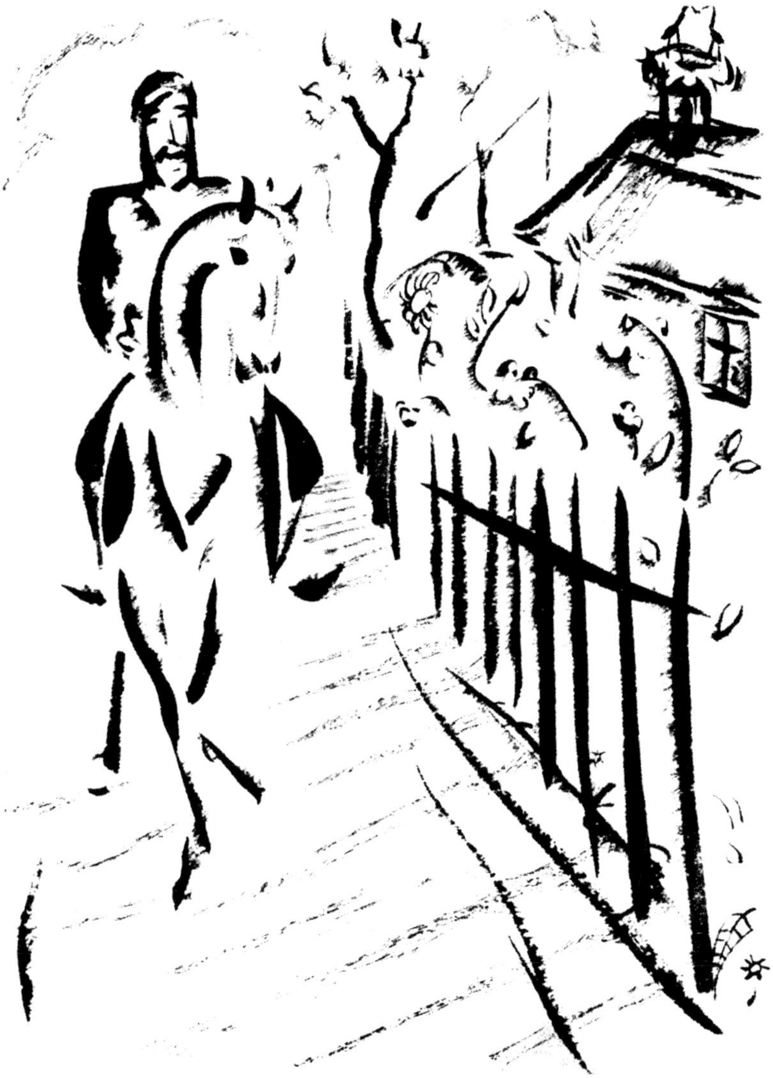

István Szegedi Szüts was born in Budapest and immigrated to England in 1929, where he published his only wordless book composed of pen-and-ink drawings. Little is known about this artist, other than that he settled in Cornwall on the Lizard and exhibited with the Newlyn Society of Artists.

My War (1931)

This story of 200 ink and brushwork drawings is a display of the atrocities of war as seen through the eyes of a Hussar, or cavalryman, named Isikos. In the table of contents, each page is given a title that provides necessary clarification to a narrative that would otherwise be difficult to understand.

These drawings are similar to Japanese ink-and-brush work with a lighter, simpler wave of the brush. There is a simple motion in Szüts's strokes, and the lack of any intricate detail gives this book a feeling of an artist's war journal, quickly capturing a passing moment or event. In his introduction, R.H. Mottram states that Szüts is "one of the chroniclers of a fundamental change in human nature."

In this book, Szüts provides a glimpse of the joys of living before World War I and Isikos's close bond with his horse after he enlists (pages 176, 178, 179). The realities of war on the front become quickly apparent, and the romantic notion that he had of war (pages 180–82) dissolves soon after his first artillery shelling, his injury, and the resulting human carnage (page 183). Szüts uses a dream sequence to display Isikos's psychological state after he is wounded and is awakened to the horrors of war (page 184).

While recuperating in a hospital (page 185), Isikos learns of the pillage of his town by the enemy and the rape of his girlfriend (page 186). He returns home to discover the devastation and squalor of the survivors (page 187). There he voices his feelings about the inequity of the generals and the politicians who are protected from battle, and who glorify patriotism at the expense of the common soldier in the trenches, and about the humble civilians who suffer the brunt of the destruction (pages 188–189). Isikos is imprisoned, tried, and executed for his antiwar sentiments (pages 190–191).

What is truly remarkable about this work is the powerful emotions that Szüts exhibits with only a few lines, as well as his use of white space to accentuate this sentiment. One example is in the haunting page "Stop the War!" from Isikos's dream, that shows the supplication of women and children (page 192).

Another powerful sequence is the rape of Isikos's girlfriend. After the assault, the enemy soldiers gather close to one another in what appears to be a photograph, with the ravaged girlfriend at their feet (page 193) like a hunted animal that has just been shot and displayed like a trophy.

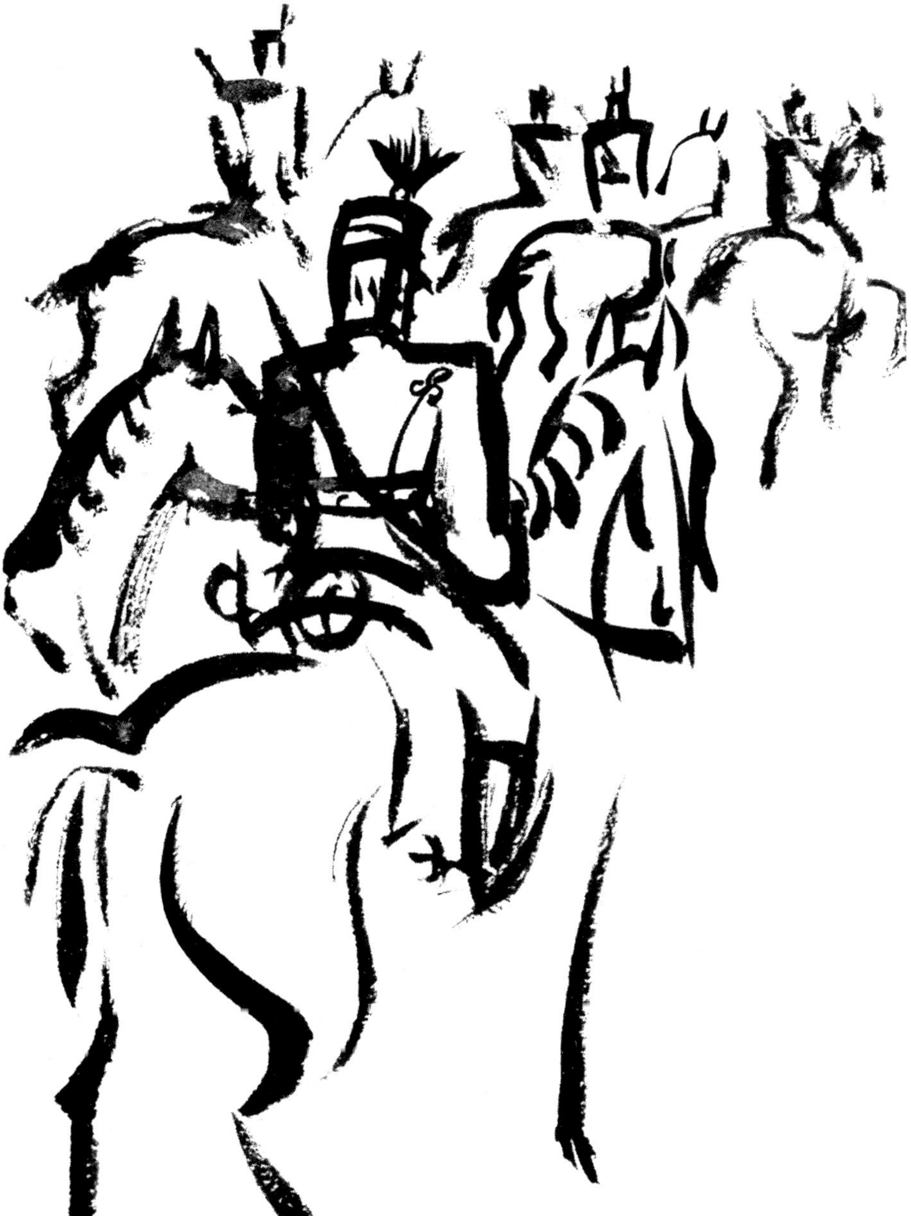

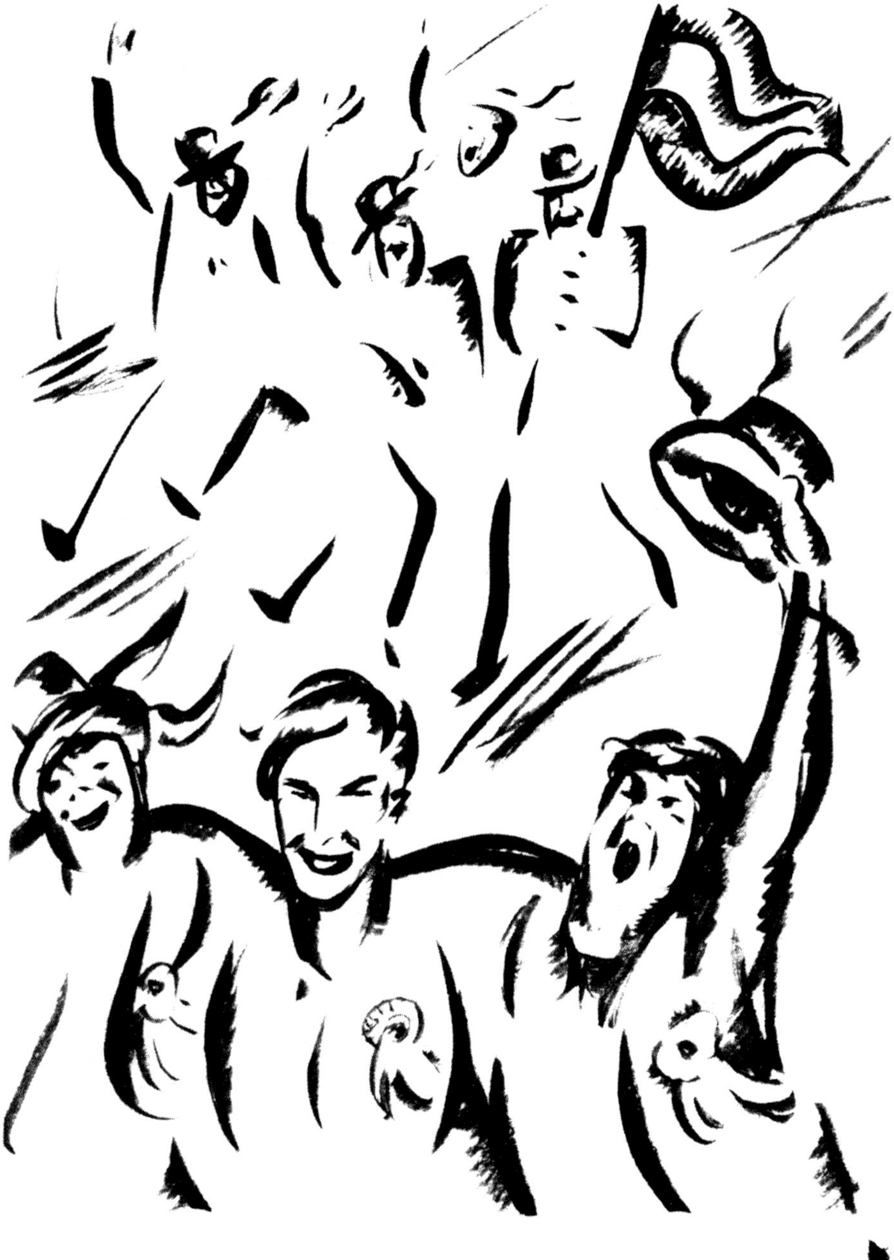

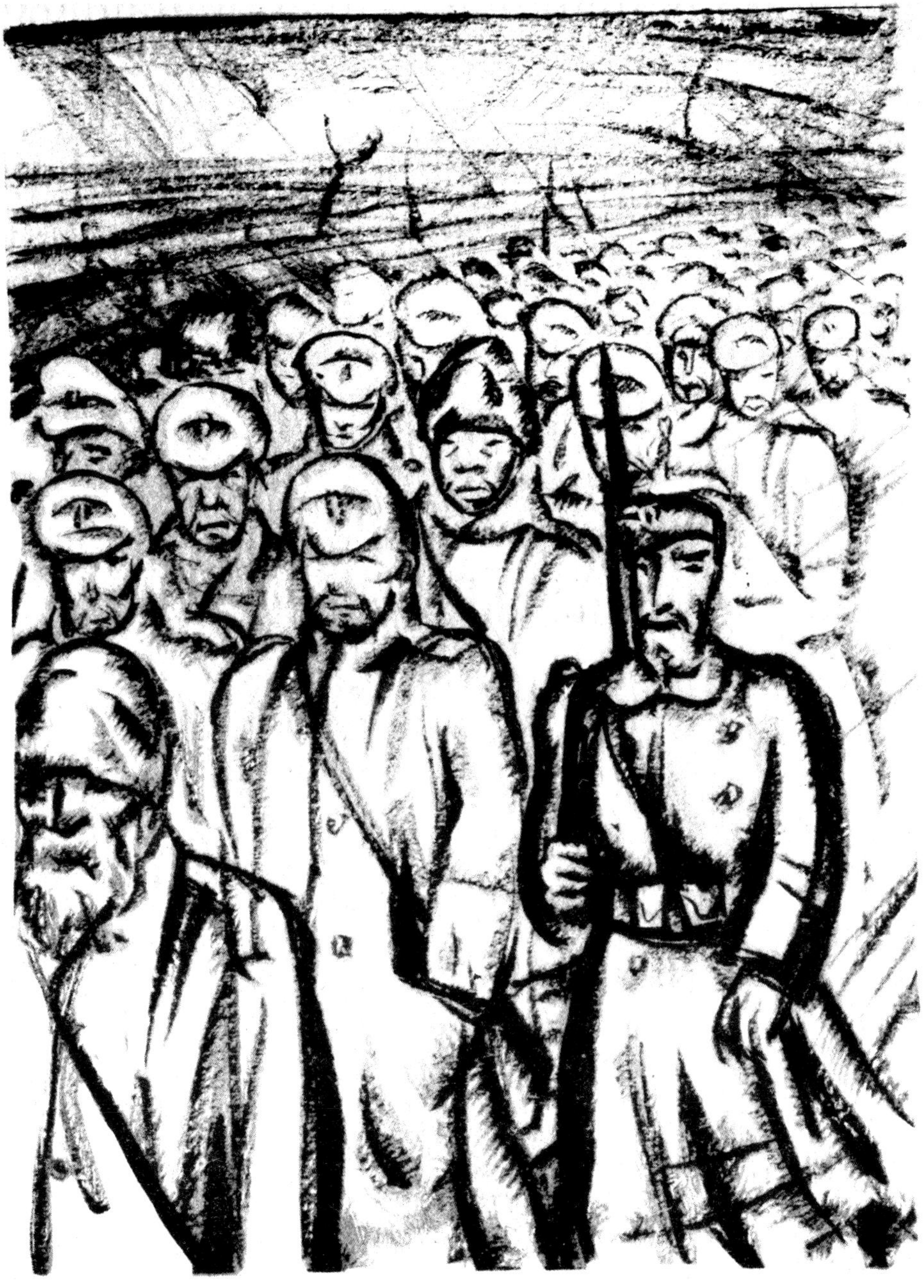

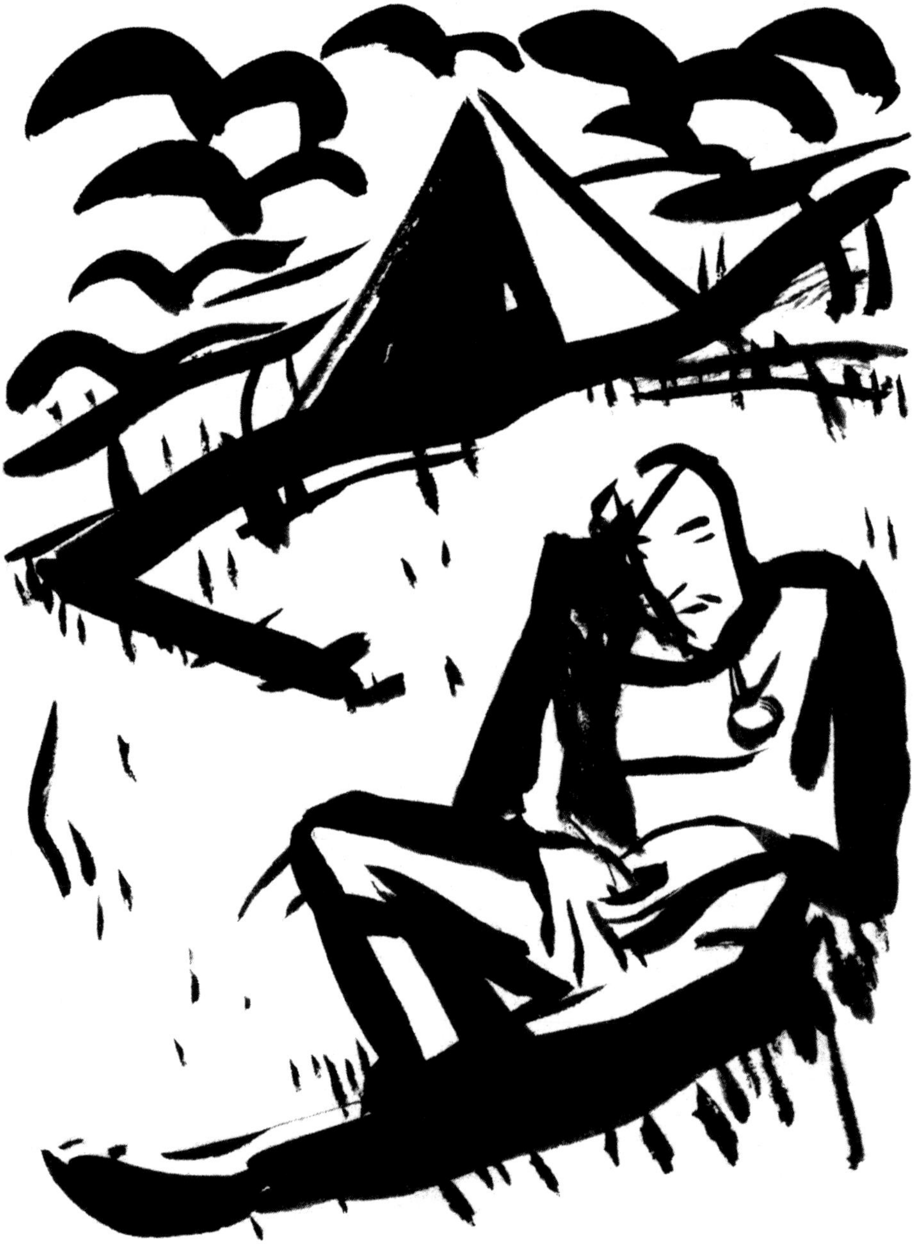

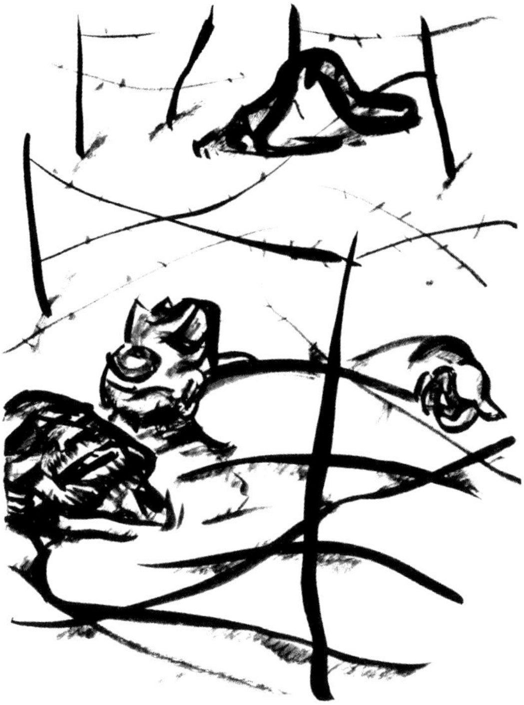

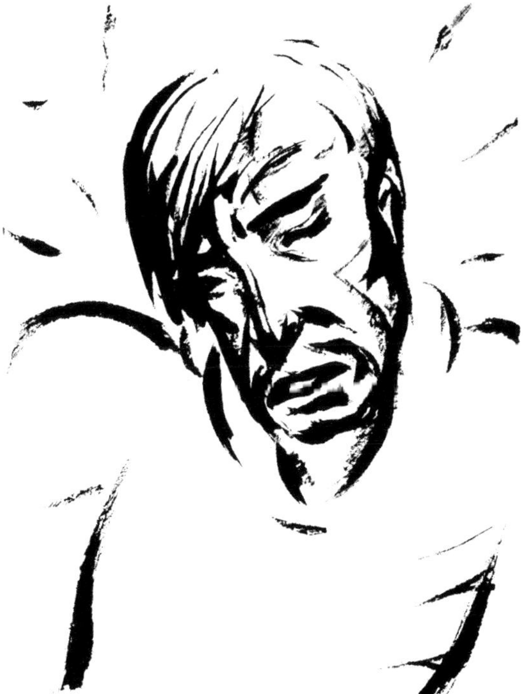

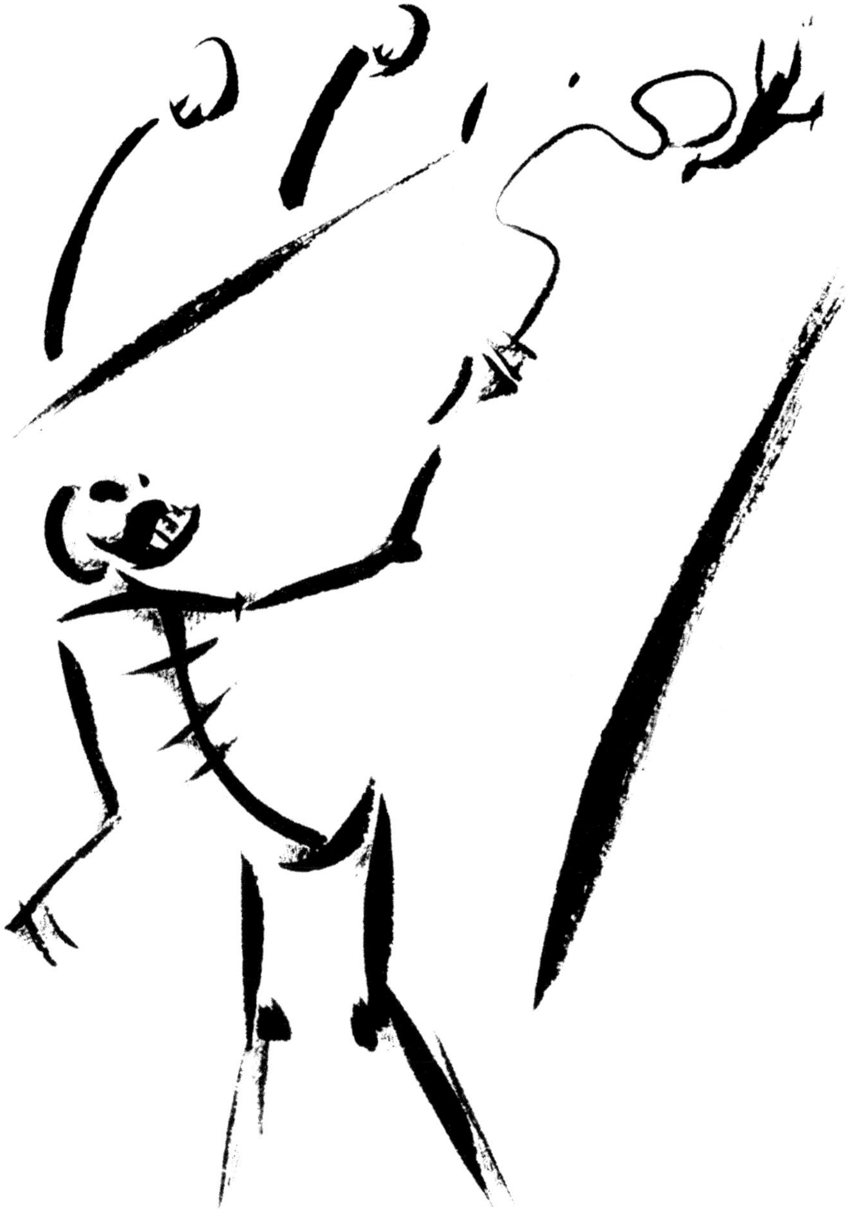

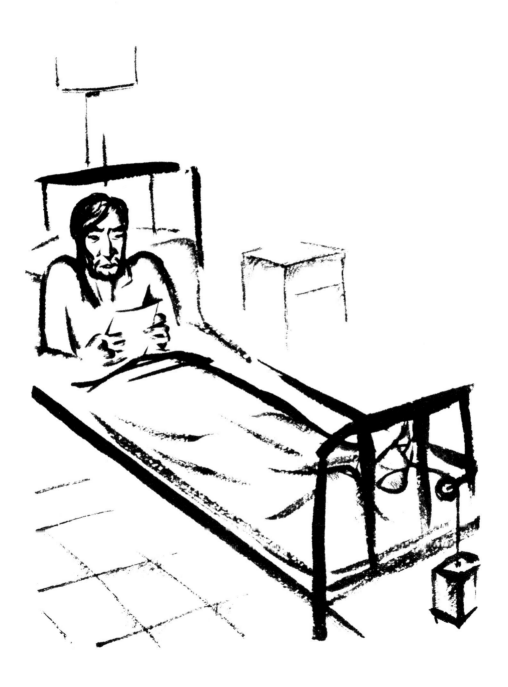

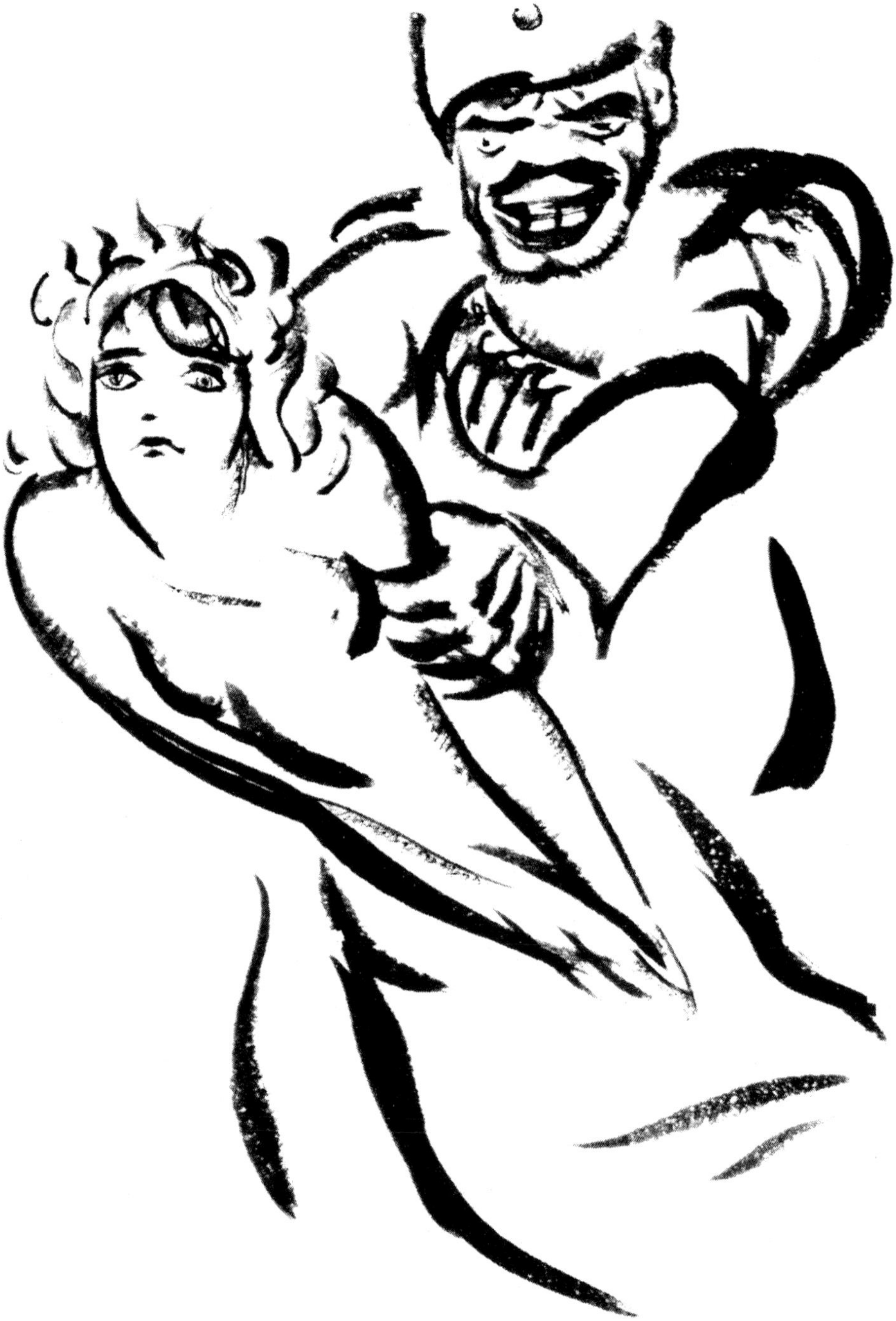

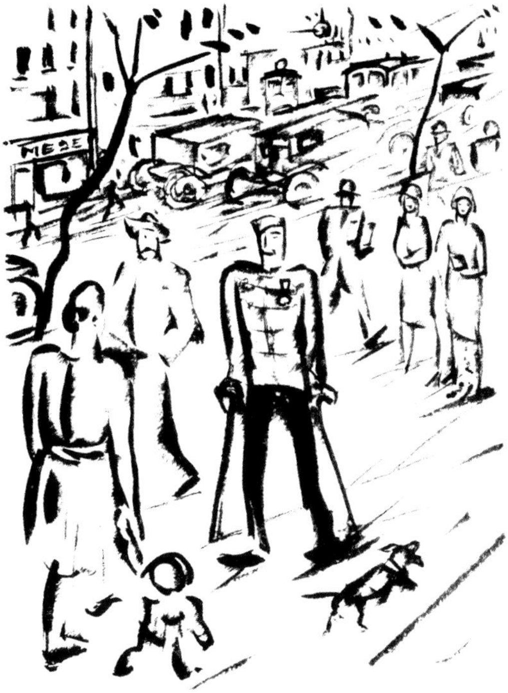

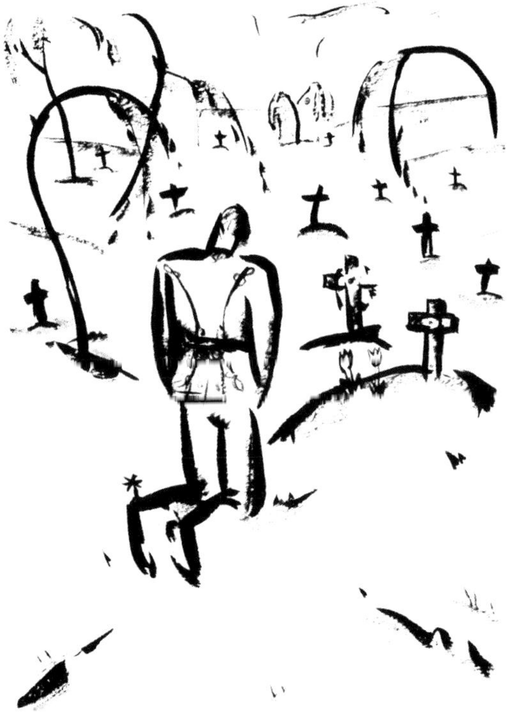

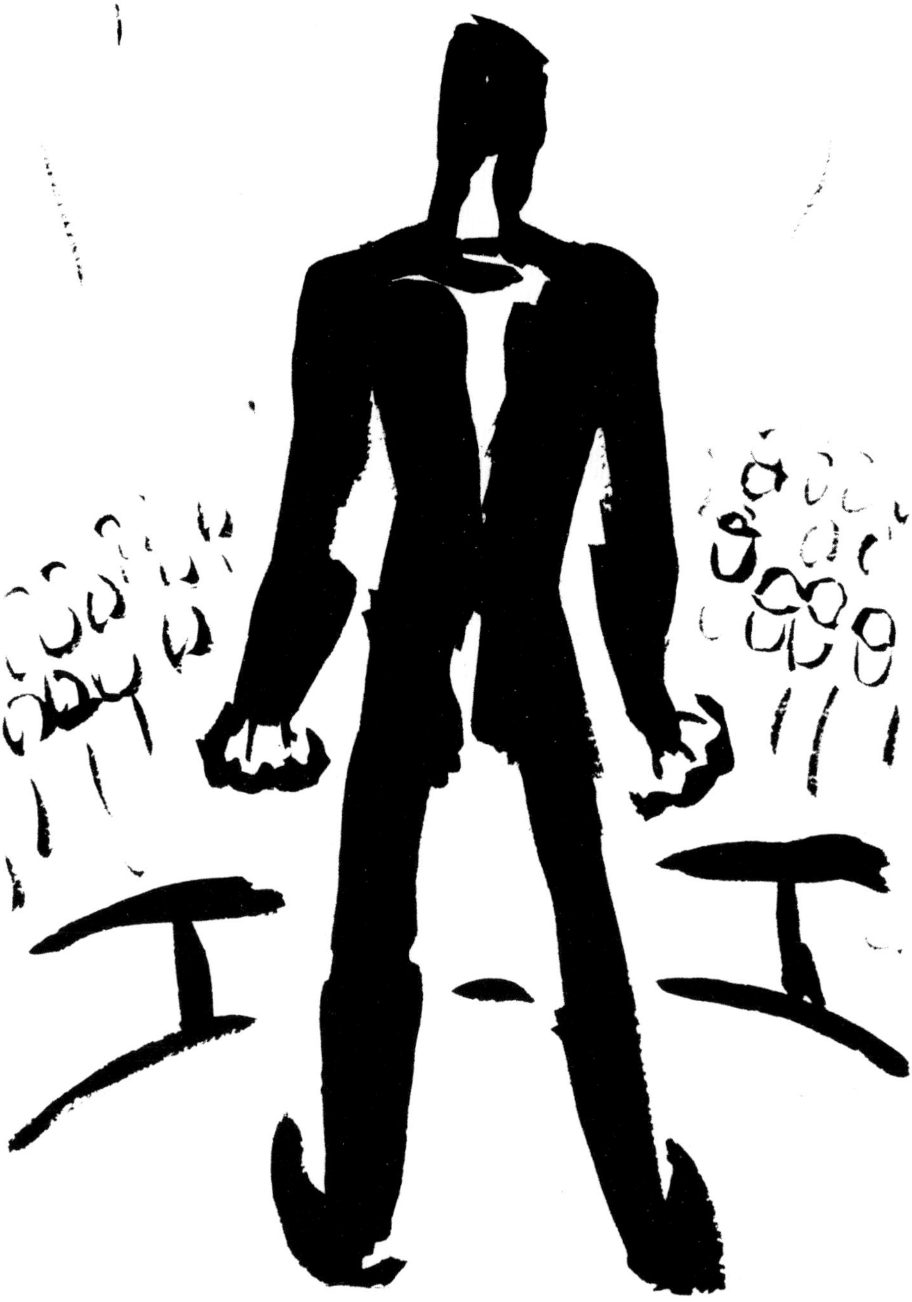

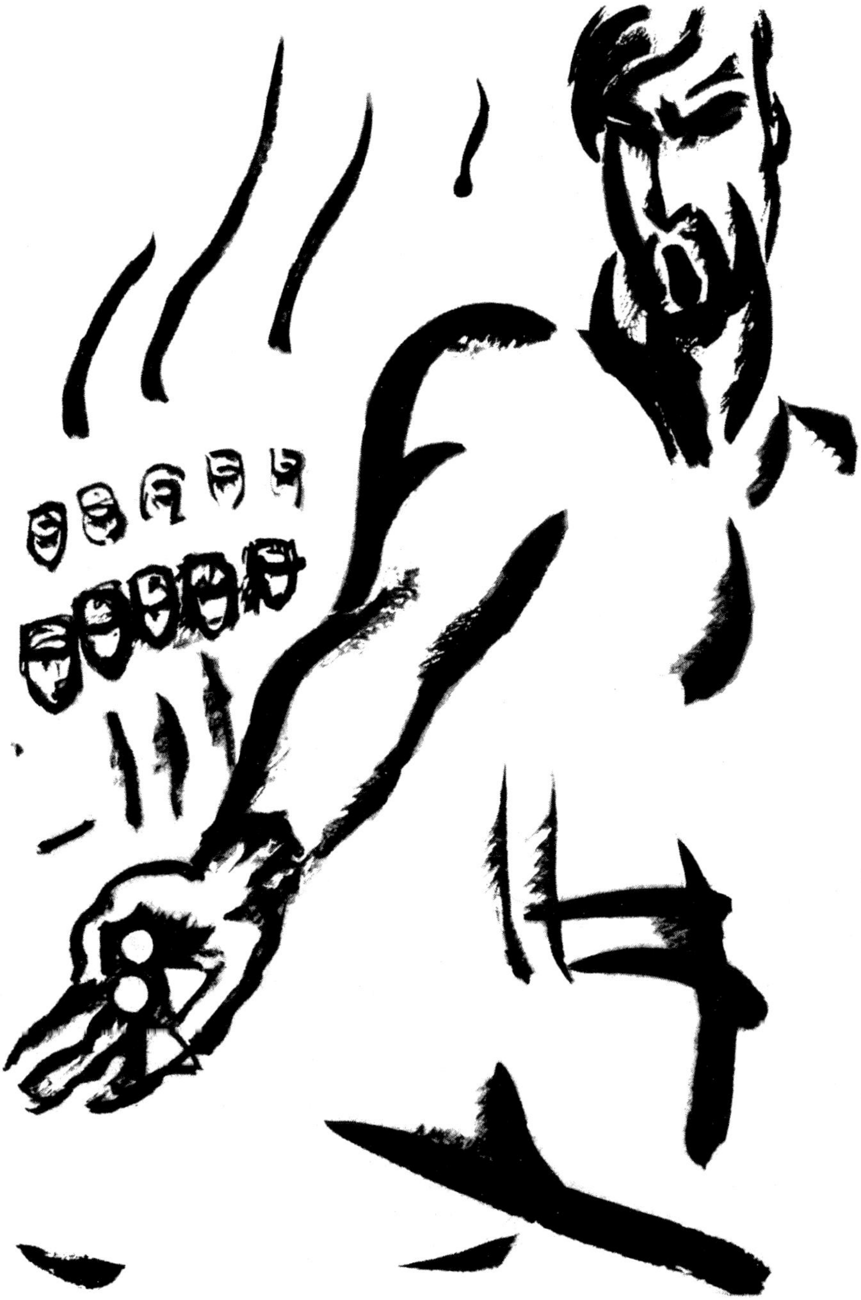

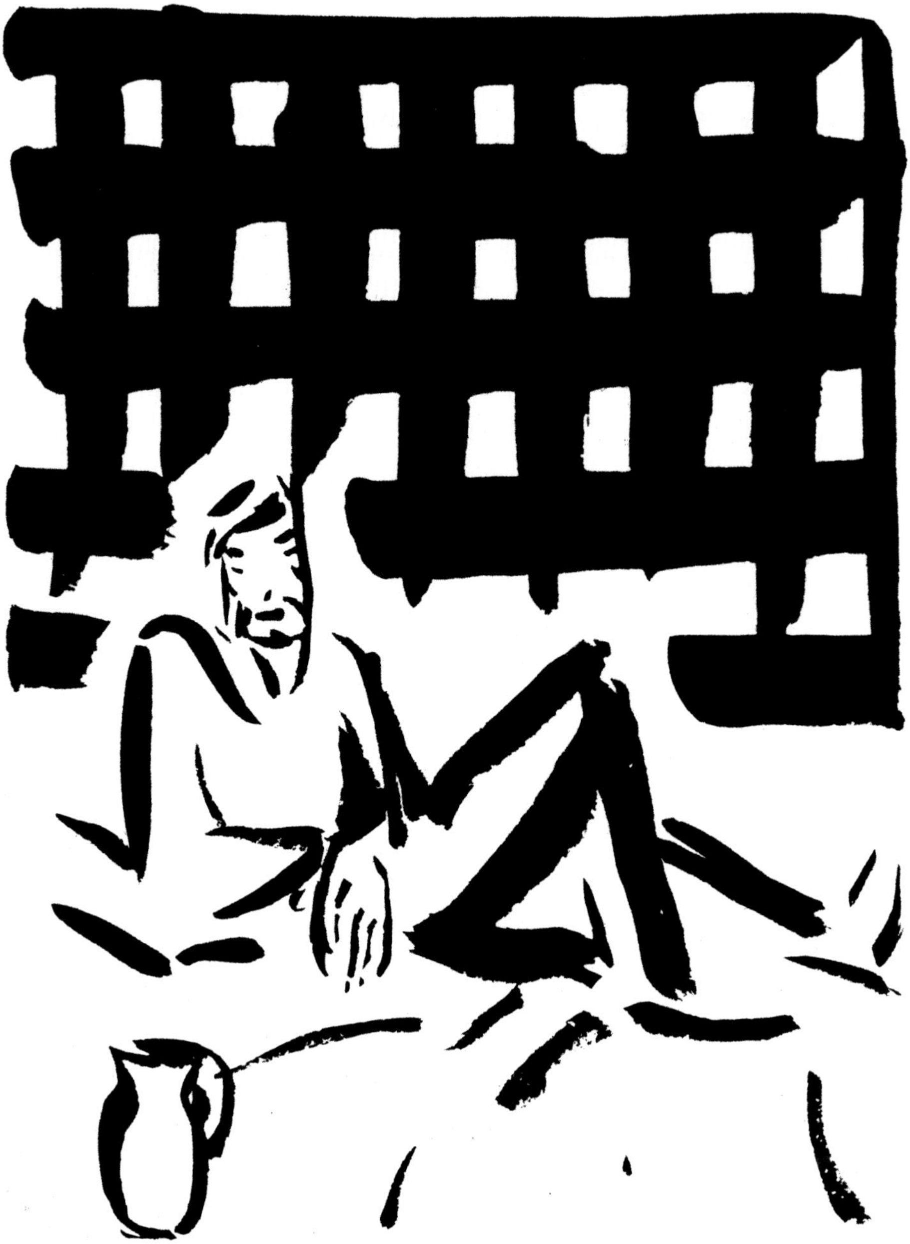

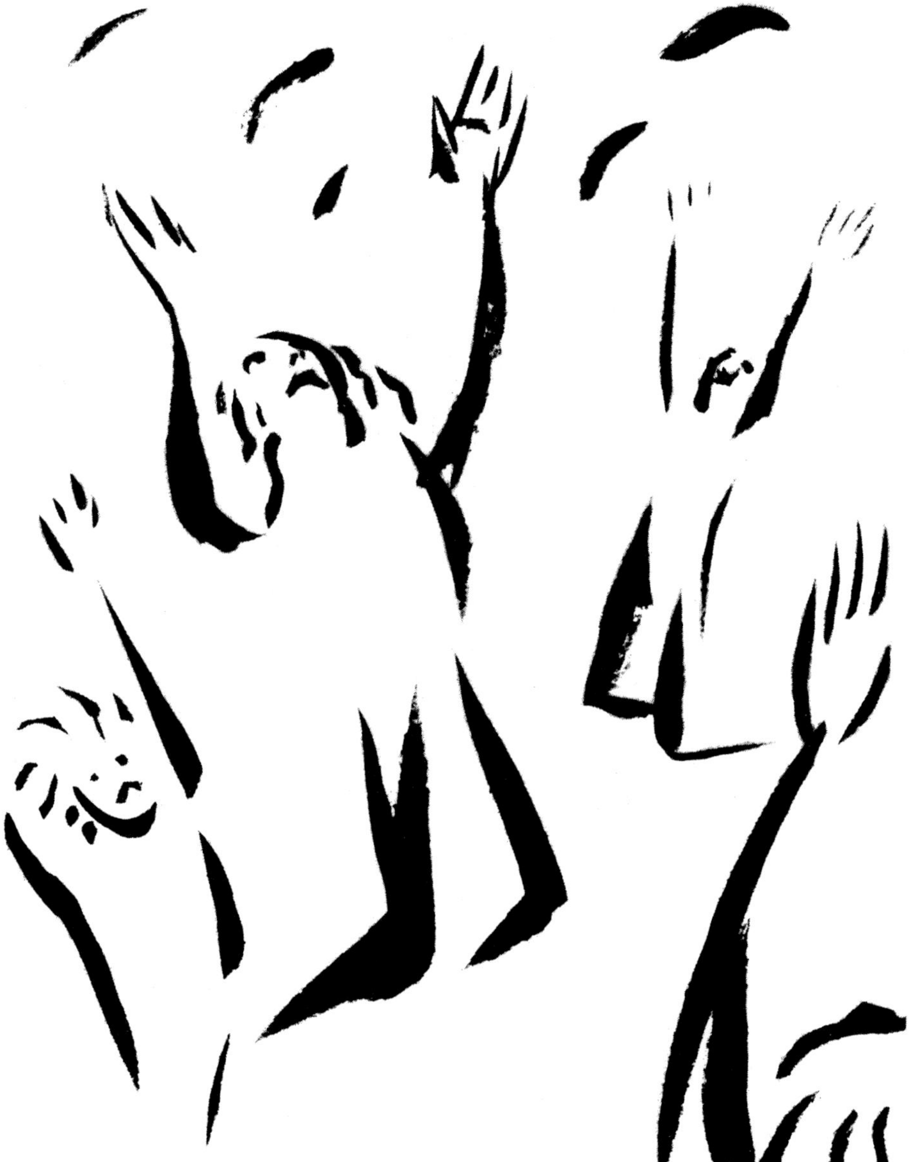

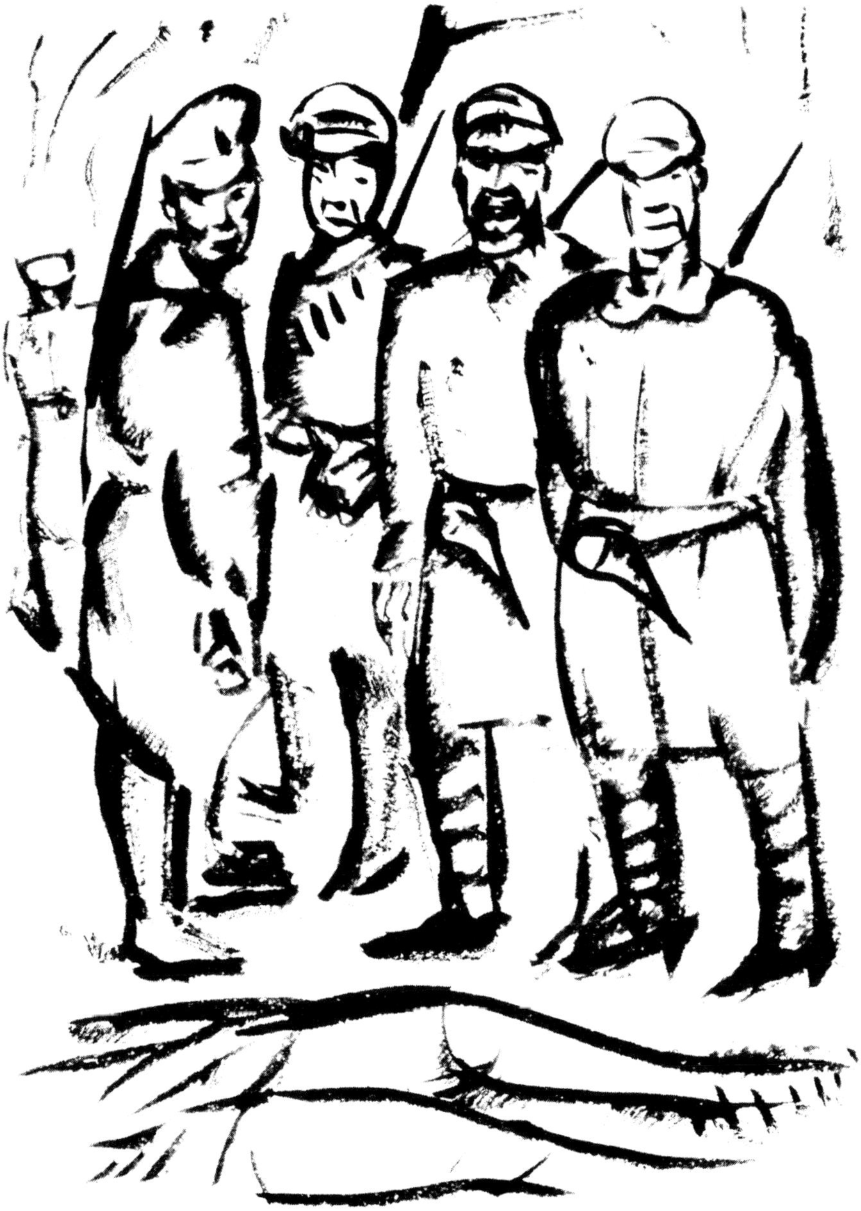

Chapter Nine

Giacomo Patri

(1898–1978)

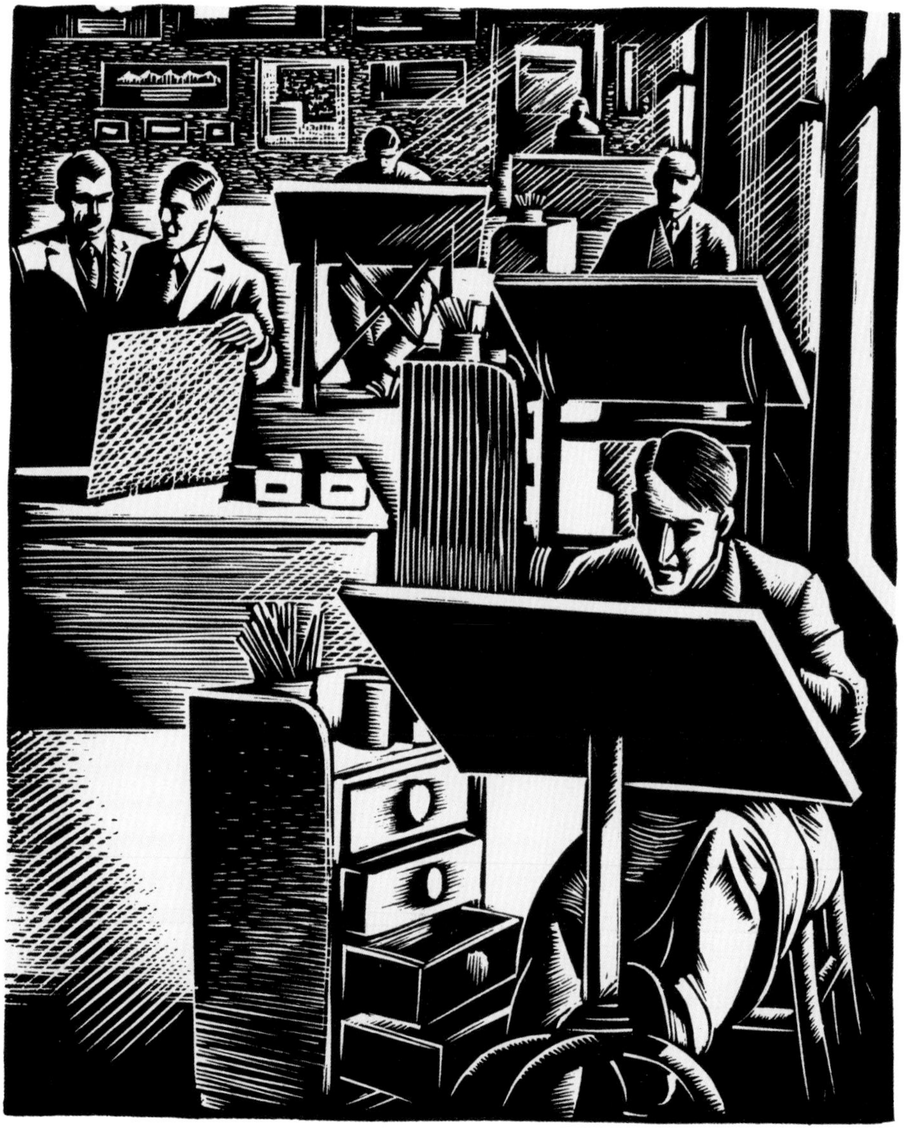

Giacomo Giuseppe Patri emigrated from Italy to San Francisco in 1916. He attended the California School of Fine Arts and worked many years as a commercial artist and illustrator for various newspapers including the *San Francisco Chronicle*. His allegiance with leftist ideology and the growing labor movement encouraged Patri to illustrate various trade pamphlets during the 1930s before he published *White Collar*—his memorable work on the Depression.

Patri taught at the California Labor School before it was closed during the communist scare tactics of the McCarthy era, as well as the innovative Presidio Open-Air School. In 1948 Patri opened his own art school for the working people called the Patri School of Art Fundamentals, and taught until its demise in 1968. He continued his artwork and published a new edition of *White Collar* in 1974. Giacomo Patri died of liver cancer in 1978, which his stepson Georges Rey reports was "attributed by his doctor to his habit of using his tongue to fashion the point of his brushes, full of carcinogenic inks."

White Collar (1940)

Giacomo Patri's major effort, which followed the spirit of the labor movement during the Depression, was *White Collar: A Novel in Linocuts*. Rockwell Kent, in his introduction, describes the power of this book:

> A million novels could be founded on that crash, all different in plot and characters yet all alike in common tragic theme of sudden poverty, disrupted homes, of broken lives, of final and irrevocable hopelessness. A thousand lifetimes would be spent in reading them. One story might epitomize them all: this story does.

Patri's novel reflects the economic despair that white-collar workers shared with blue-collar workers during the Depression Era. In this socialistic call to arms endorsed by the American Labor Movement, Patri tells the story of a white-collar worker from an advertising agency (opposite) as he innocently assumes he can climb the ladder of success by determination alone. The worker enjoys a traditional family life (page 196) with a wife, two children, and even a picket fence (page 197). As he loses job after job, his economic condition becomes bleak. His family suffers the loss of materials and is unable to afford the simplest of services like gas and water. They move from home to apartment to shelter, until they finally are forced into homelessness. At this time the worker accepts the full disillusionment of the system. His belief in capitalism is shattered, and in the last page, he accepts the goals and fellowship of the labor union.

There are four important aspects of *White Collar* that deserve attention. These features include the creative use of text, innovative page design, use of icons and dream symbols, and the display of controversial themes.

Patri, more than any other artist in this wordless genre, employs the unobtrusive and, at times, blatant use of words on buildings, display windows, doors, bills, and flags to contribute to his pictorial narrative.

At the beginning of the story we discover an important aspect of the white-collar worker from the title of the book—*The Climb to Success*—that he reads on a train (page 199). This immediately identifies him as an enterprising, young entrepreneur. Another example of text is the print (page 200, top) with protest signs proclaiming, "Unfair to Labor." The white-collar worker passes unemployed men and women who raise these signs on the street, but he dismisses them because his world is unaffected by the ills of the Depression. We also learn from office signs and window displays that the worker is an advertising artist (page 200, bottom). This clever use of text without employing word balloons provides information that is essential to understanding the narrative.

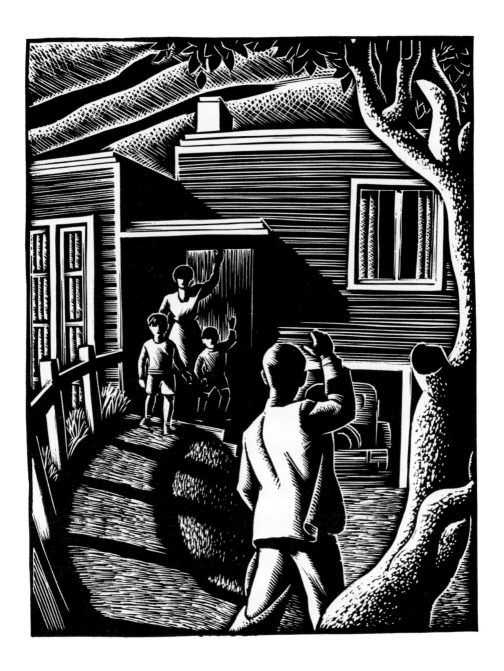

In one of the more heartfelt series of panels, words are used prominently on many of the pages to convey the action. For example, the worker and his wife are burdened with bills (page 201), which are labeled or are given enough letters to decipher the words easily, such as Bank, Milk, Coal, Gas & Electr[ic], Gro[cery], and [Ins]urance. The easily recognizable bills make it easier for readers to identify with the life of this white-collar worker. The couple is additionally burdened during this time with an unexpected pregnancy (page 202). They discuss their dilemma with a doctor, who offers the worker (page 203, top) a book with the title, *Law*. The book is opened in the next panel (page 203, bottom) showing the words "Abortion A Felony." The couple is forced to seek someone who will perform an illegal abortion, in this case directed by a sign on a door to "Dr. A. T. Grab," with obvious connotations in his last name of snatching every cent from the white-collar worker. Dr. A. T. Grab's waiting room is filled with patients, including a dejected woman sitting under a sign that reads "Private." When they enter to speak with Dr. A. T. Grab (page 204, top), behind him hangs a sign that reads "$50°° Pay in Advance," which the white-collar worker cannot afford. They are forced to visit a "Public Clinic" and the "Maternity Ward," where there are "No Vacancies."

The second aspect is Patri's innovative page design, which is represented in a very simple manner. For example, when the worker jumps from one agency to another looking for work after he is forced to take another loan (page 204, bottom), the floor design on the page is like a chessboard (page 205), highlighting the action of the white-collar worker as a pawn in a fruitless system.

Third, the utilization of Christian icons and dream symbols is expressed early in the narrative when a picture of Christ is displayed on a wall directly above the worker. Later, after learning of his wife's pregnancy, the worker prays to this picture for guidance. After his wife delivers the child, whom they cannot financially support, she suffers from a subsequent illness. Her hospitalization forces him to take out another loan and work longer hours for less pay (pages 206, 207, top). In comparison to an earlier scene when the hanging picture was above the man, on this page the picture of Christ is displayed on an equal level with the white-collar worker (page 207, bottom left). The next panel shows that the picture has been removed, leaving the wall barren (page 207, bottom right), emphasizing the lack of sustenance that religion offered the worker and his family during their crisis.

In another image with strong Christian connotations, the white-collar worker preaches the objectives of labor unity to his coworkers. Behind a slightly opened door is a man hidden in the background (page 208). Like Judas, this man betrays the worker to management and, as a result, the worker is fired and the family is evicted from their home (page 209). The worker, shown preaching the gospel of organized labor and being betrayed, evokes comparison to Christ and reflects the model of the hero as a martyr against injustice, established by Masereel in his first woodcut novel, *25 Images de la Passion d'un Homme*.

In his dream symbols, Patri replicates the inner and outer world that Ward created in his wordless novel, *Wild Pilgrimage*. Patri creates short dream sequences within the main story that he sets apart with the use of the color orange. Patri opens his book with a symbolic image of a man walking inside a white collar, pacing as though he were inside a prison (page 246). Patri uses this image again at the end of the book when the white-collar worker gains his freedom from the walls of injustice, opens up the collar, and steps outside to freedom. One of the secondary sequences involves the worker setting out on the road to success, which is presented as an image of a road spiraling up into the clouds to the top of a world where a throne sits (page 239, bottom). As the worker's life and ideas are shattered in the main story, this sequence proceeds with the road shattering, the worker repairing the road, and finally, his resignation when the road crashes down to solid ground.

The white-collar worker, despite his failing economic condition, stands up tall, his facial expression reflecting personal resolution following this internal reconciliation. These dream sequences work well in displaying the worker's inner conflict (page 240). Instead of dreaming impossible dreams of sitting atop a throne in the clouds, he accepts the reality of living in a shanty town (pages 210–211) and, as seen on the last page, working with others and their families toward a plausible dream of a unified force of men and women that extends in fellowship as far as the eye can see (page 239, top).

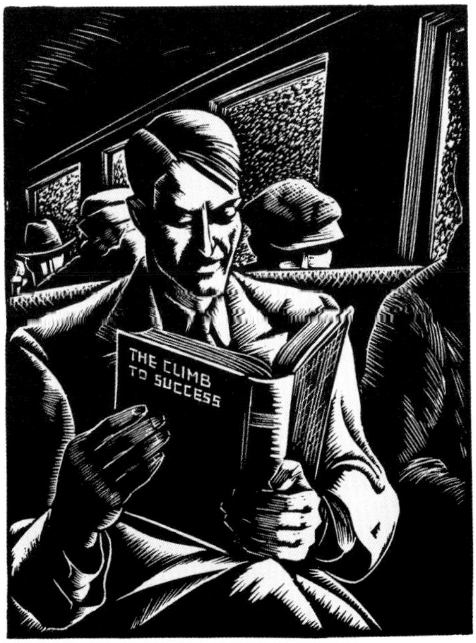
THE CLIMB TO SUCCESS

White Collar is noted for its powerful and controversial themes such as abortion, the cost of health care, and the rejection of Christianity during the white-collar worker's tailspin into the growing unemployment and homelessness. The value of Patri's work is that he exposed the realities of the Depression that forced traditional families to take necessary steps for survival that were contrary to conventional practices and beliefs at the time.

UNFAIR TO LABOR
THIS FIR
UNFAIR
TO LABOR

FRED H. BERRY
ADVERTISING
FRED H. BERRY
ADVERTISING
CLOSED

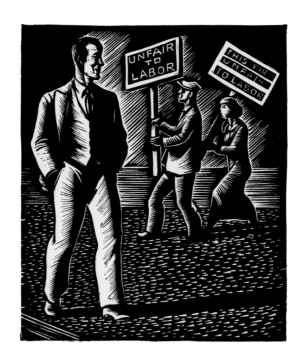

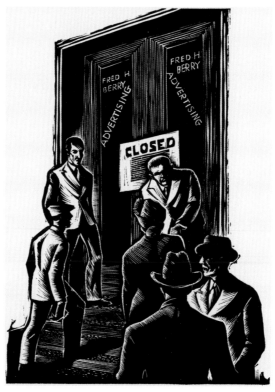

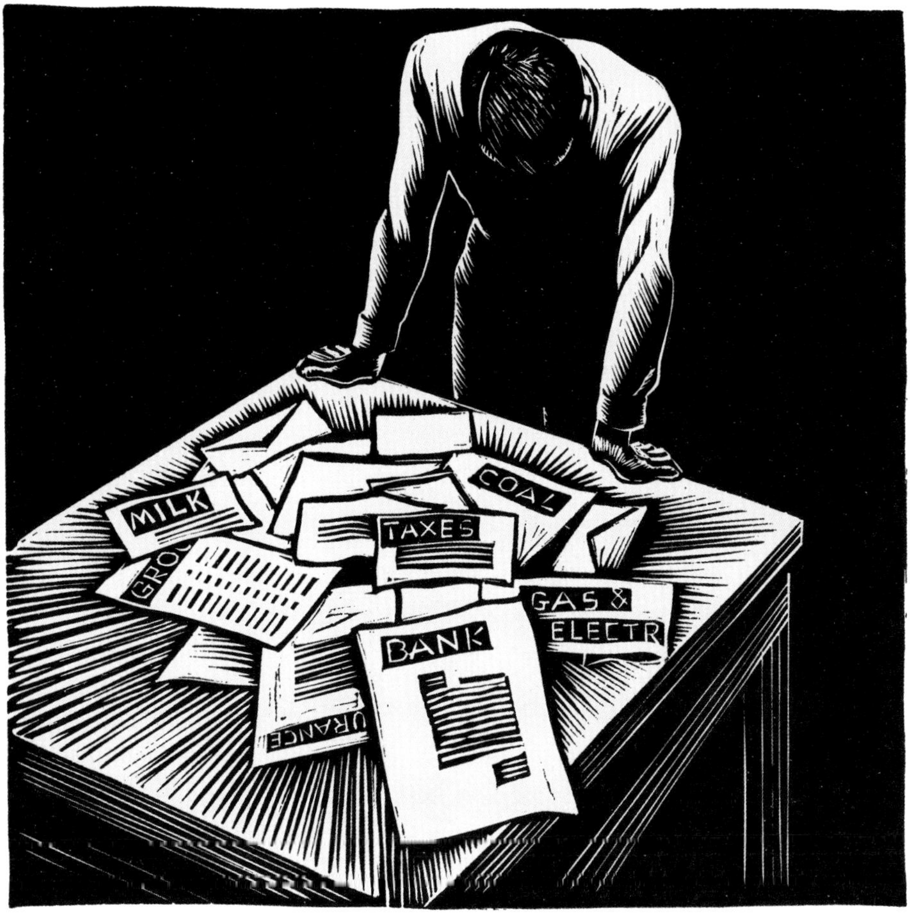
MILK
COAL
TAXES
GROC
GAS &
ELECTR
BANK
URANCE

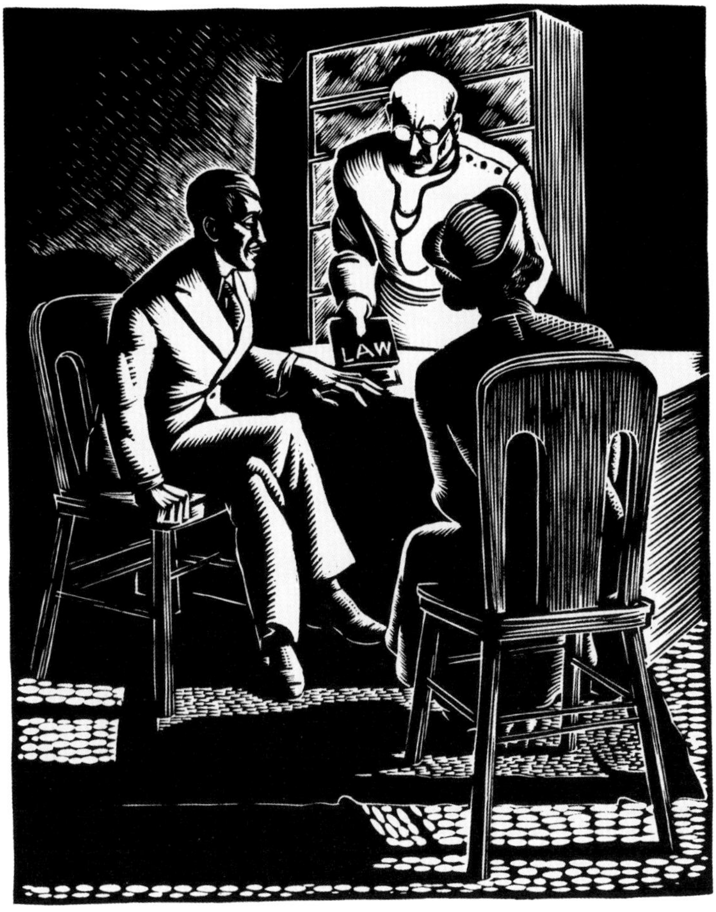
LAW

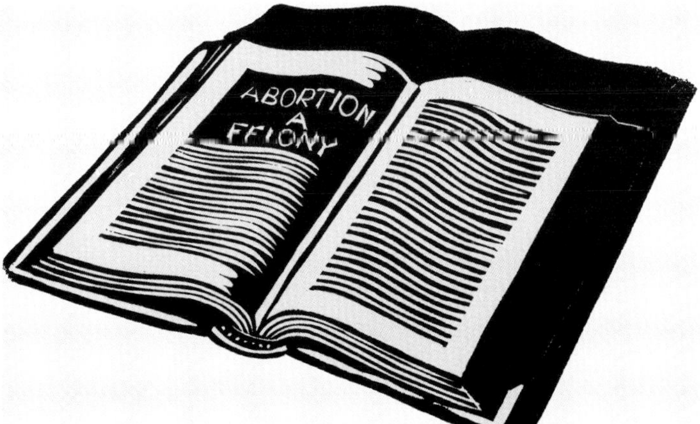
ABORTION
A
FELONY

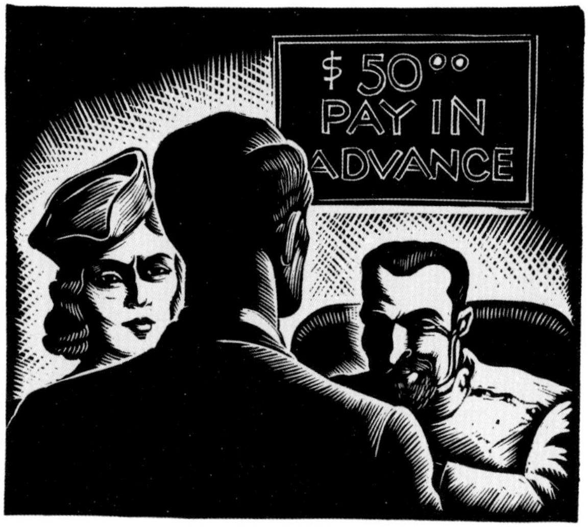
$ 50°°
PAY IN
ADVANCE

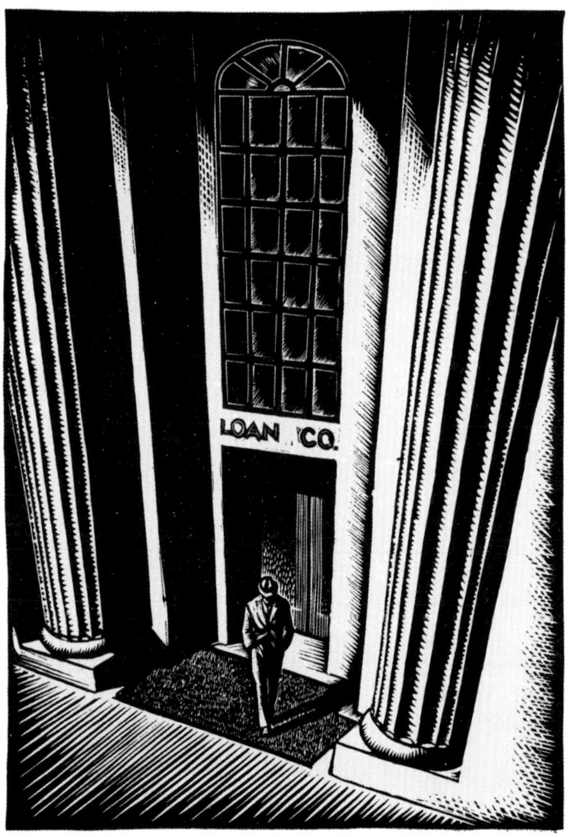
LOAN CO.

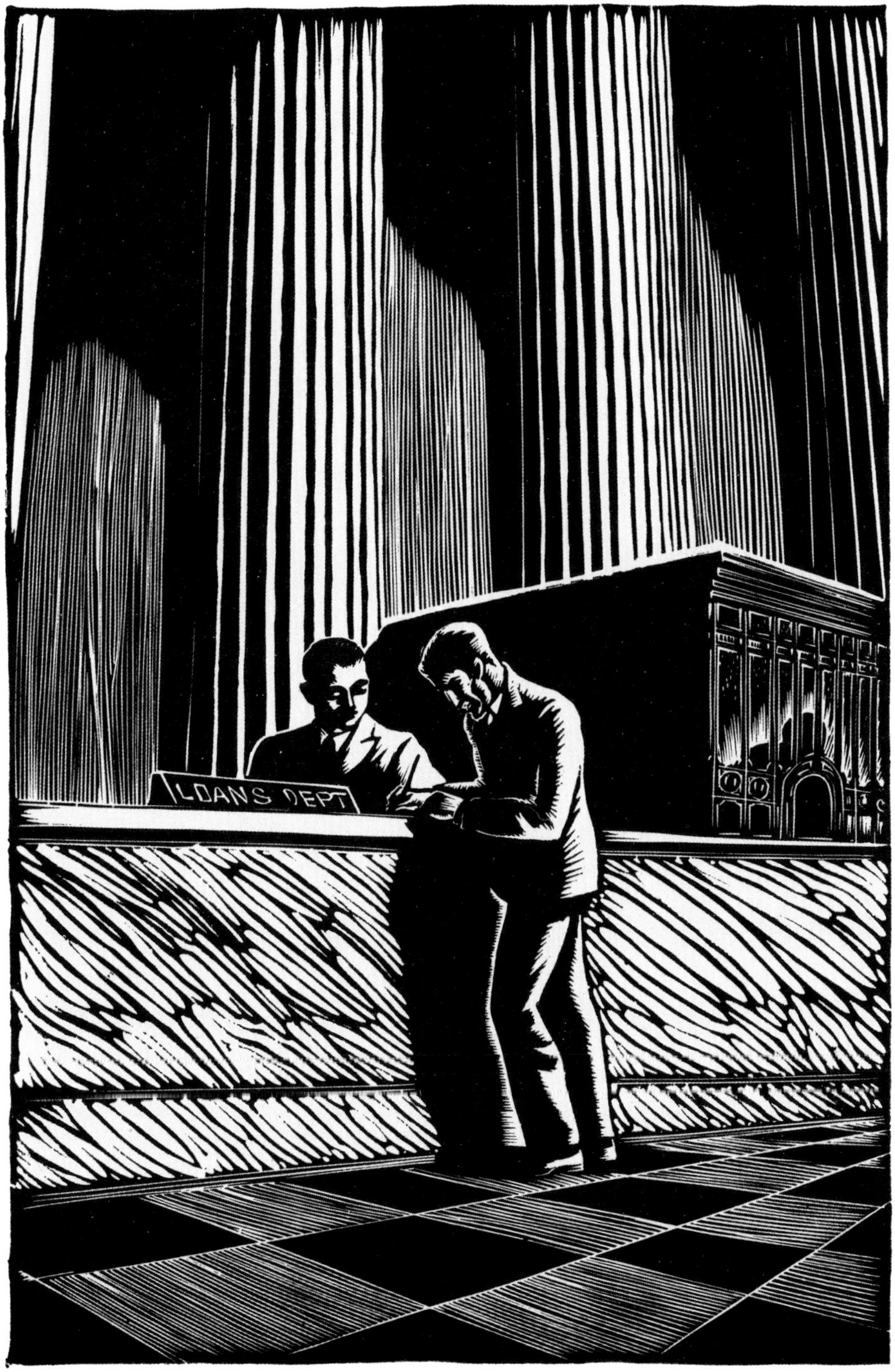
LOANS DEPT

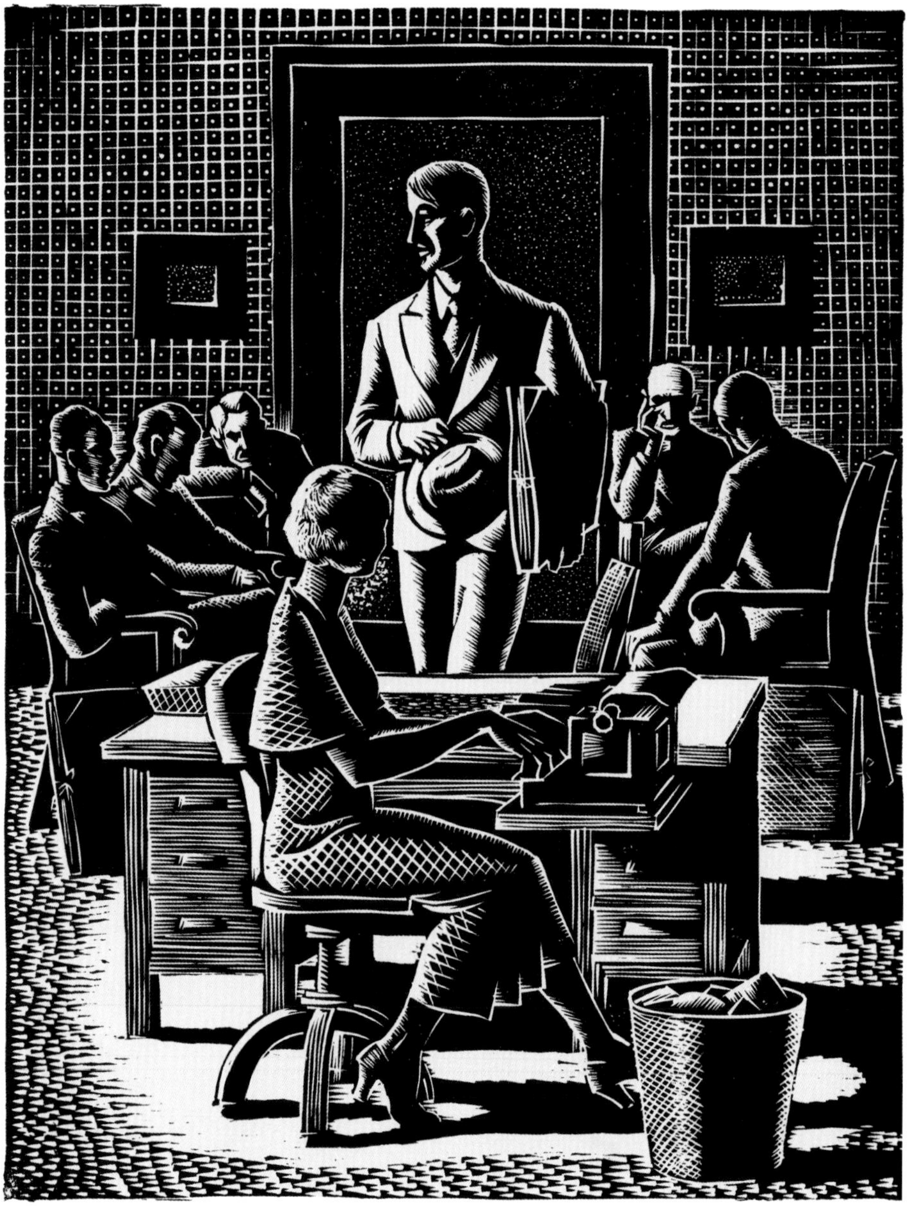

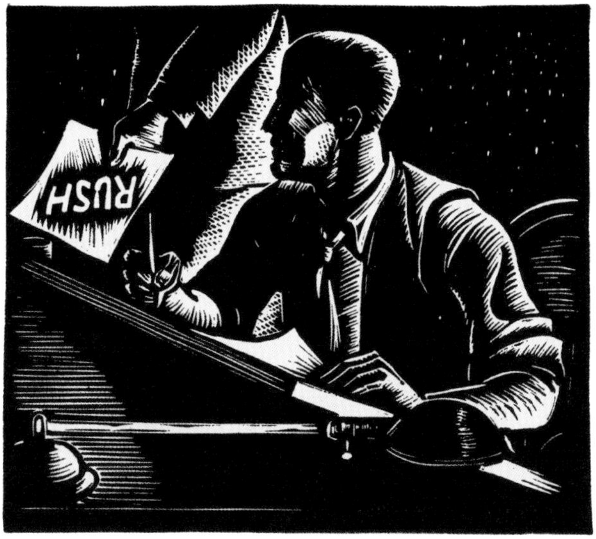
RUSH

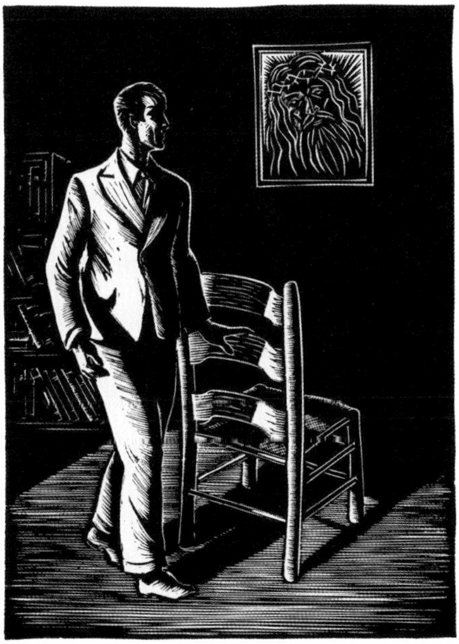

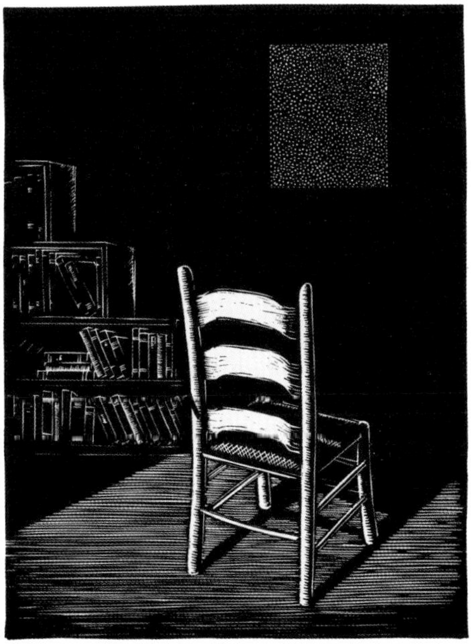

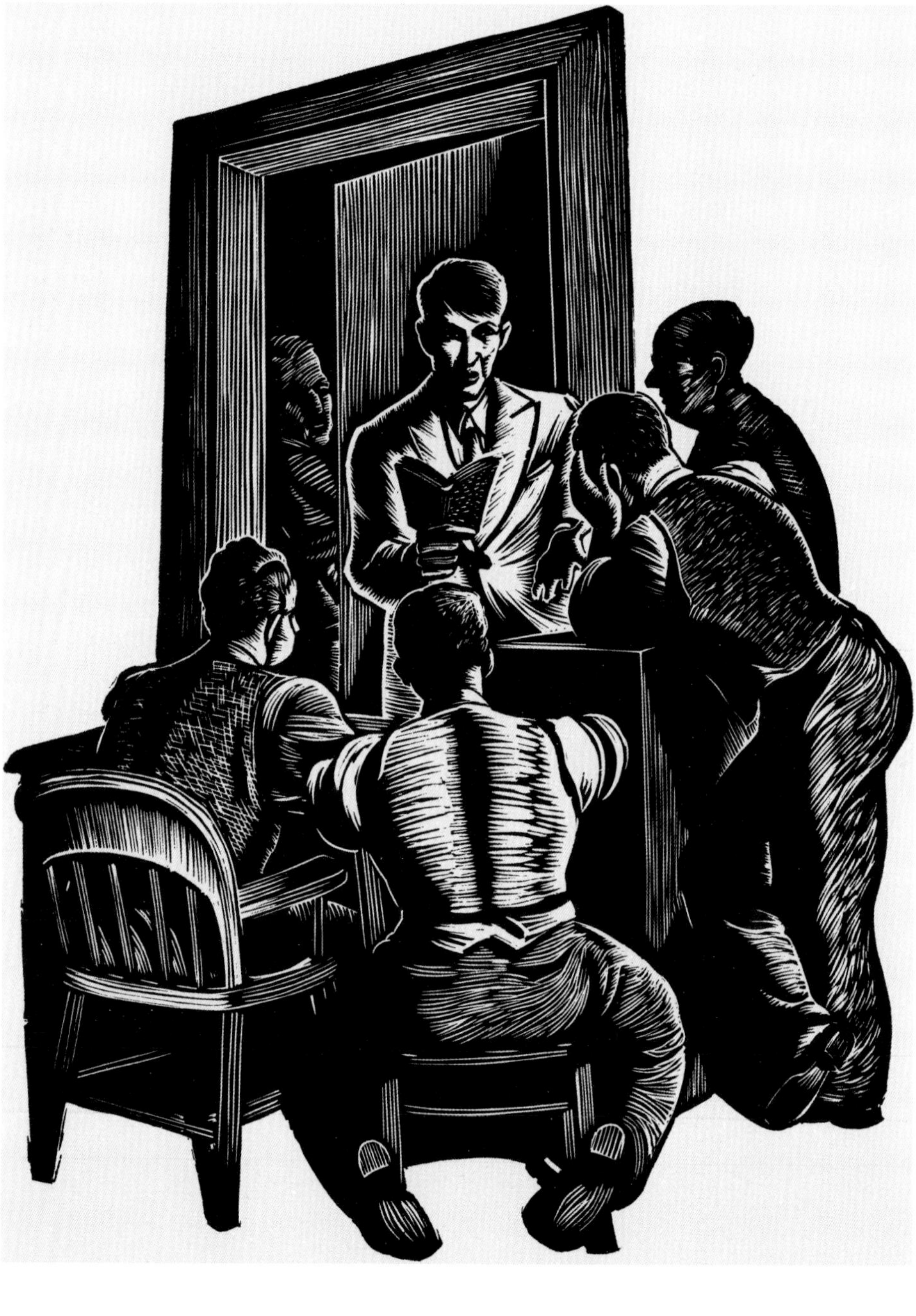

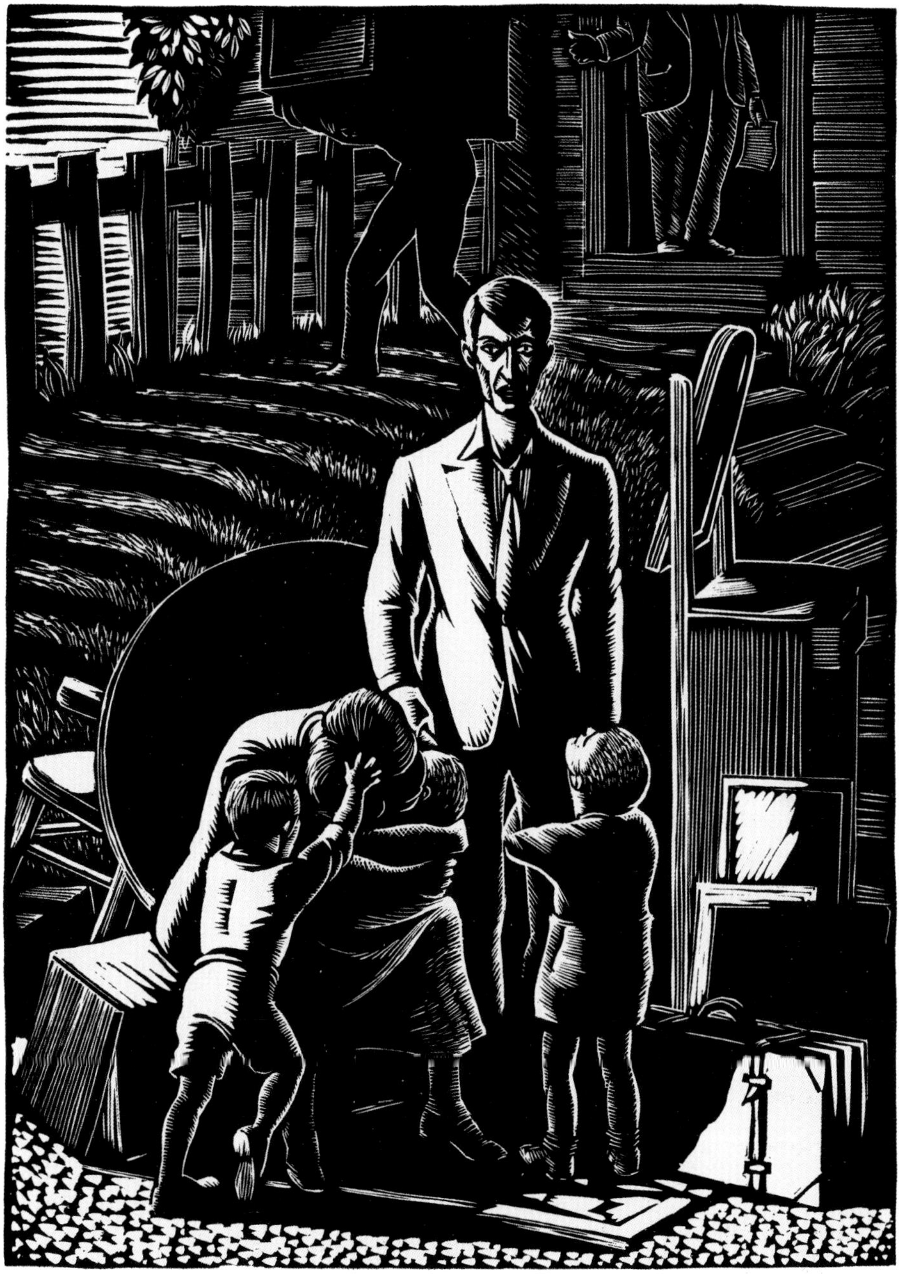

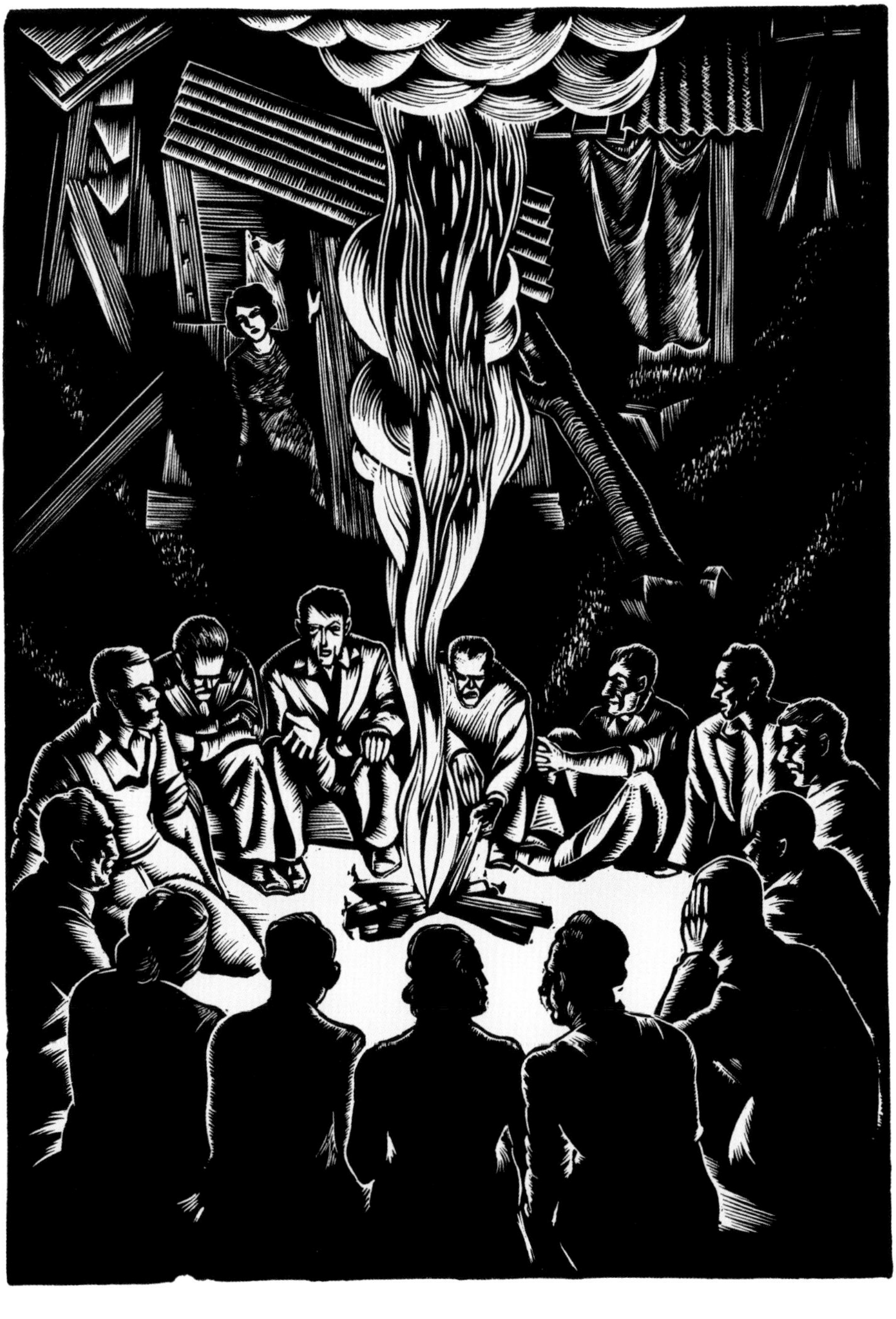

Chapter Ten

Laurence Hyde
(1914—1987)

Laurence Evelyn Hyde was born in Kingston-upon-Thames near London, England. He immigrated with his family to Canada in 1926, and settled in Toronto in 1928. Throughout his life Hyde produced many wood engravings and linocuts for illustrated books and limited-print editions.

Hyde was strongly influenced by the prints of the British artists Paul Nash and Eric Gill, as well as by Rockwell Kent and Lynd Ward, with whom he corresponded. Hyde contributed numerous pen-and-ink illustrations for various publications, including left-wing journals, and started a prosperous freelance business doing scratchboard drawings for advertising firms in the late 1930s. He worked on two unfinished series of prints, *Discovery* and *Macbeth,* before his work on *Southern Cross,* his first and only wordless book. Hyde moved to Ottawa in 1942 to work for the National Film Board of Canada, and he retired in 1972.

His work as a wood engraver was commemorated in an exhibition at the Glenbow Museum, Calgary in 1986. Patricia Ainslie, curator of the exhibit and author of the catalogue, felt that his "engravings attest to the skill and vivid imagination of the artist." She conducted a series of rare interviews with Hyde in 1985, which were later published in two issues of *The Devil's Artisan.*

Southern Cross (1951)

From 1948 to 1951, Laurence Hyde worked on the blocks for *Southern Cross,* which was published in a small edition by Ward Richie Press in 1951. *Southern Cross* is a stunning wordless novel, told in 118 wood engravings, about the atomic-bomb testing by the United States in the South Pacific following World War II. The inspiration behind this book was Laurence Hyde's fury with the United States for continued testing of these bombs in the Bikini Atoll following the mass destruction and unthinkable horrors resulting from the atomic bombs dropped on Hiroshima and Nagasaki in August 1945. Hyde's graphic novel involves a Polynesian island (page 212) and the islanders' idyllic life (pages 213–217, top) which is forever lost after the arrival of American sailors who evacuate the islanders from their homes. During the evacuation, an island fisherman kills a drunken sailor (pages 217, bottom and 218, top) who assaults and attempts to rape his wife. The couple flees with their child into the jungle (page 218, bottom) to avoid capture, unaware of the danger they are risking by keeping themselves hidden. After the other islanders have evacuated, the Americans detonate an atomic bomb (page 219, top) on the ocean floor. After the bomb explodes (page 219, bottom), a powerful gust knocks down the towering trees on the island while the fisherman's wife

holds her child with an expression of fear and incomprehension (page 220, top). The fisherman is immediately charred and deformed from the blast (page 220, bottom). His child's eyes express a look of shock as he gazes on his father's burnt body (page 221, top). Flesh falls off his legs, exposing his bones. A close-up of the wife's eyes, bulging out of her sockets (page 221, bottom), shows the extent of the torment she is experiencing from the impact of the radiation. Birds and fish lie dead at their feet (page 222, top). The wife drops to the ground beside her husband (page 222, bottom). Their child, with tears in his eyes, opened wide in terror (page 223, top), crawls over to his mother's lifeless body. Hyde leaves us with the haunting image of the child who sits utterly alone beside his dead mother under a lone star in the dark heavens (page 223, bottom).

The reality of the bomb and the consequences to the islanders are real horrors. The images of death from the blast and the final picture of the child beside his mother—in stark contrast to their idyllic and simple life—remains evidence of the horrors of the atomic bomb.

The blocks in *Southern Cross* are 4 x 3 inches, except for a full-page bleed measuring 7 x 6 inches, which is inserted after the detonation of the bomb. Hyde opens up white space on many pages wherein he presents the islanders and their happy-go-lucky

manner of working and playing during the day. There is an energy in his lines that flows through his characters. He expresses the islanders and their natural way of life with a warm, free-flowing design in contrast to the highly stylized, cold, symmetrical line construction he associates with the American military. Hyde also restricts the use of white space in many of the scenes with the military, who arrive at night and hide in darkness or in the shadows, suggesting something devious.

The scholar Martin S. Cohen makes an insightful connection about the anti-war feelings of Hyde and Masereel.

> The tradition of the novel in woodcuts had passed across an ocean, a Depression,
> and a World War, but totally ignorant that Masereel had been a pacifist and a Red
> Cross worker. While cutting the blocks for the first of his woodcut books, Hyde
> wrote this dedication to his novel: Dedicated to the International Red Cross
> Societies and to the Society of Friends (Quakers).

This link between Frans Masereel and Laurence Hyde demonstrates strong pacifist sensibilities rooted in these artists and their strong social consciousness displayed in their daring statements against exploitation, genocide, and corruption.

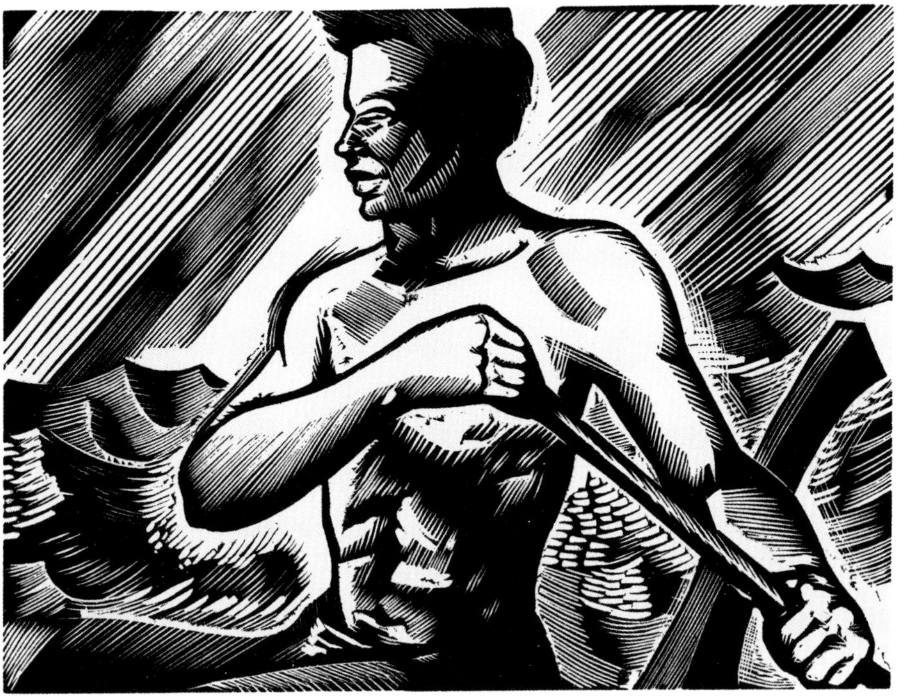

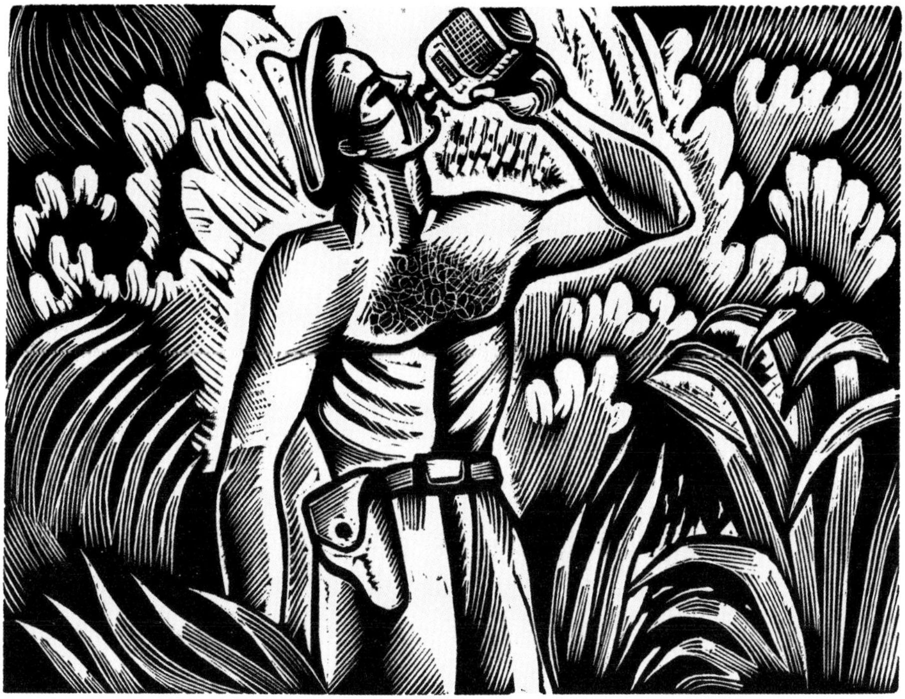

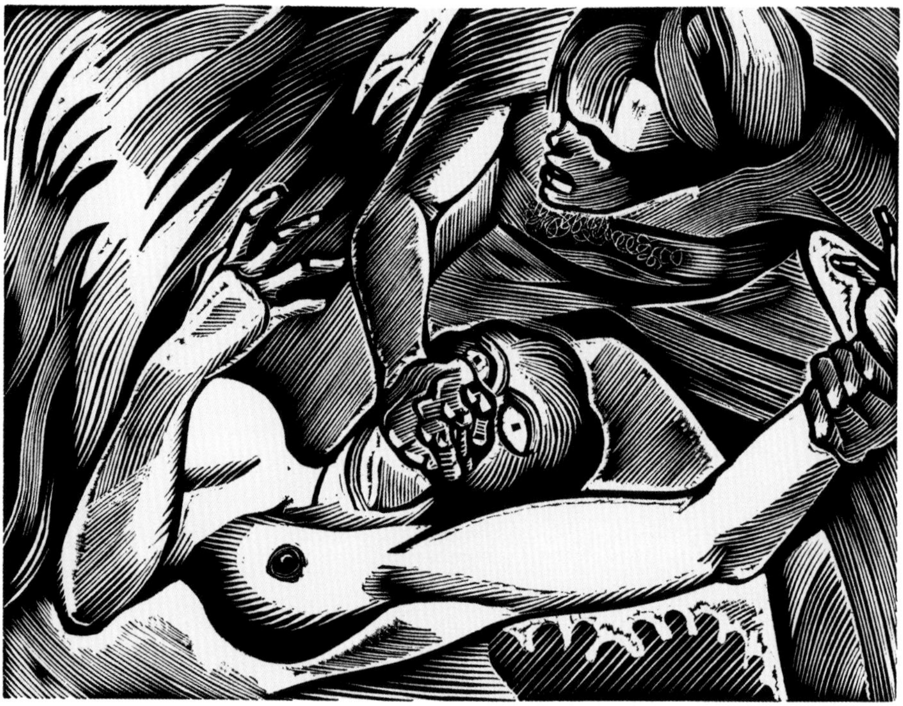

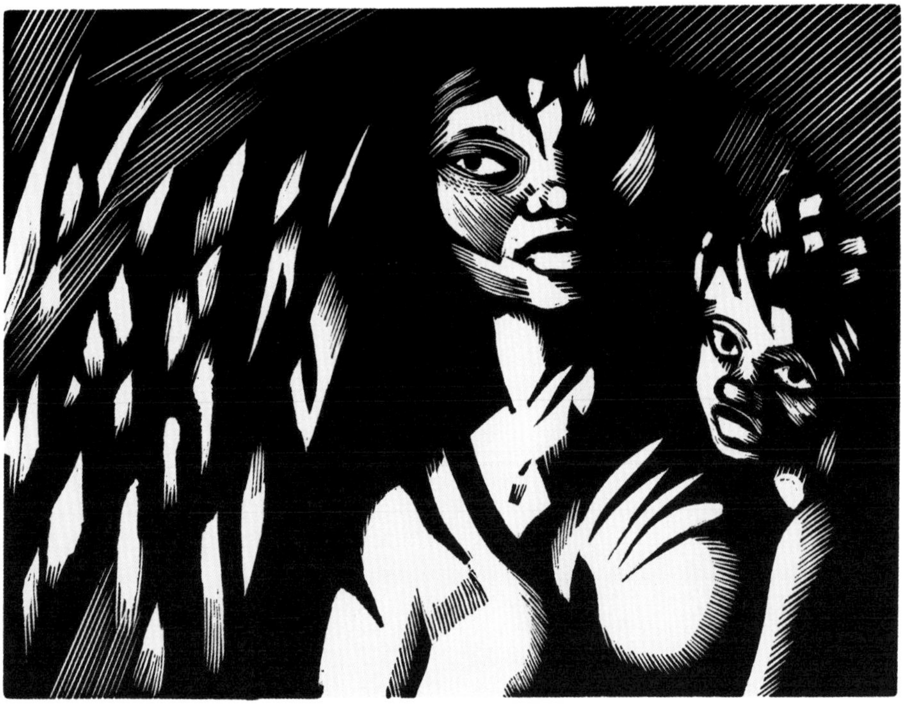

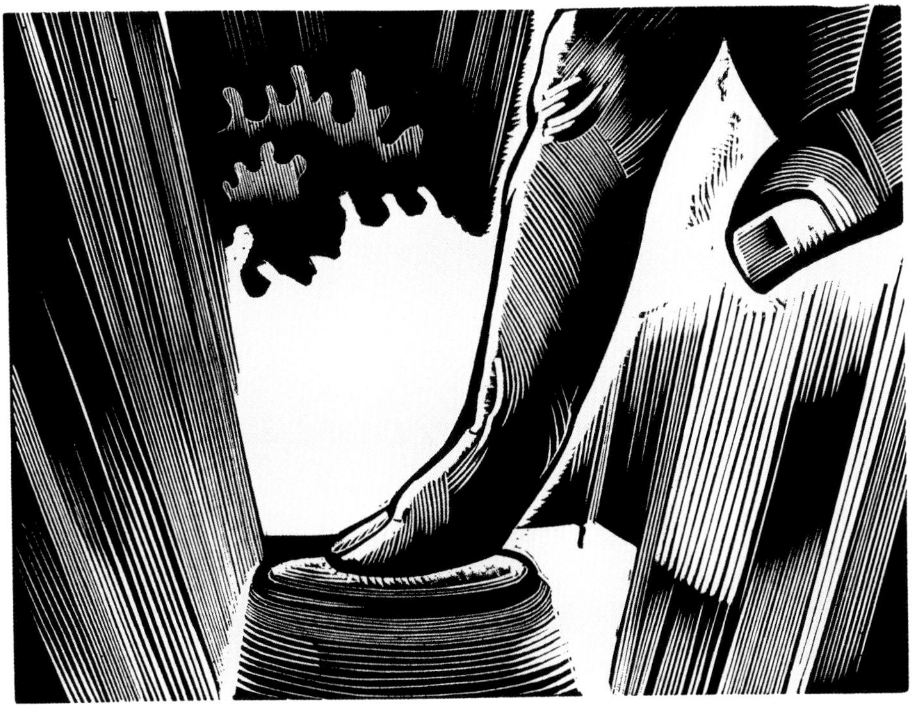

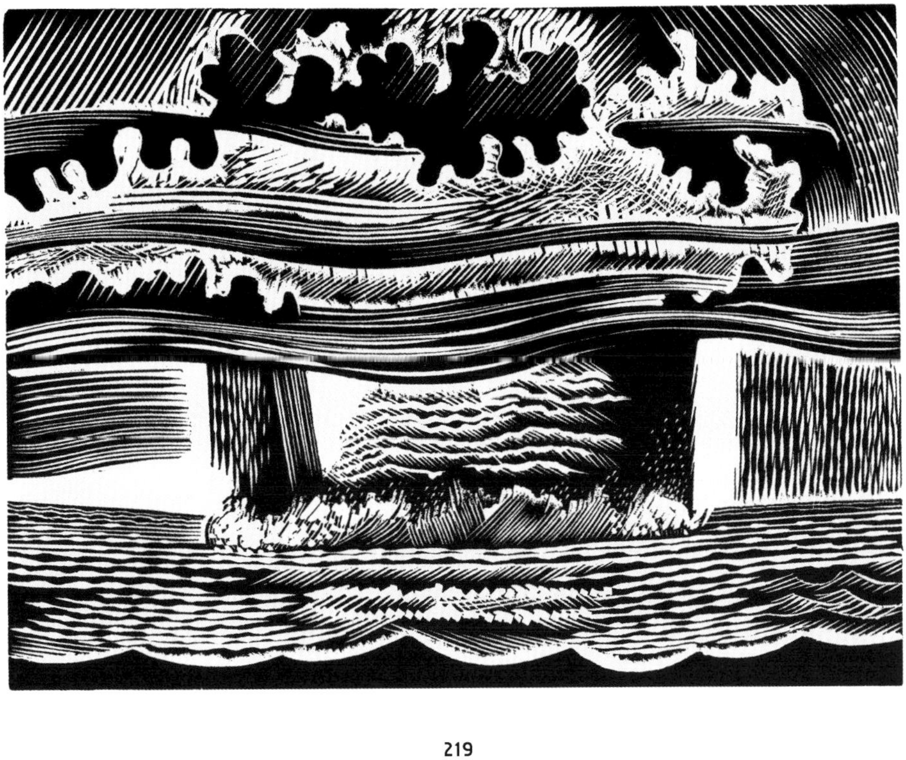

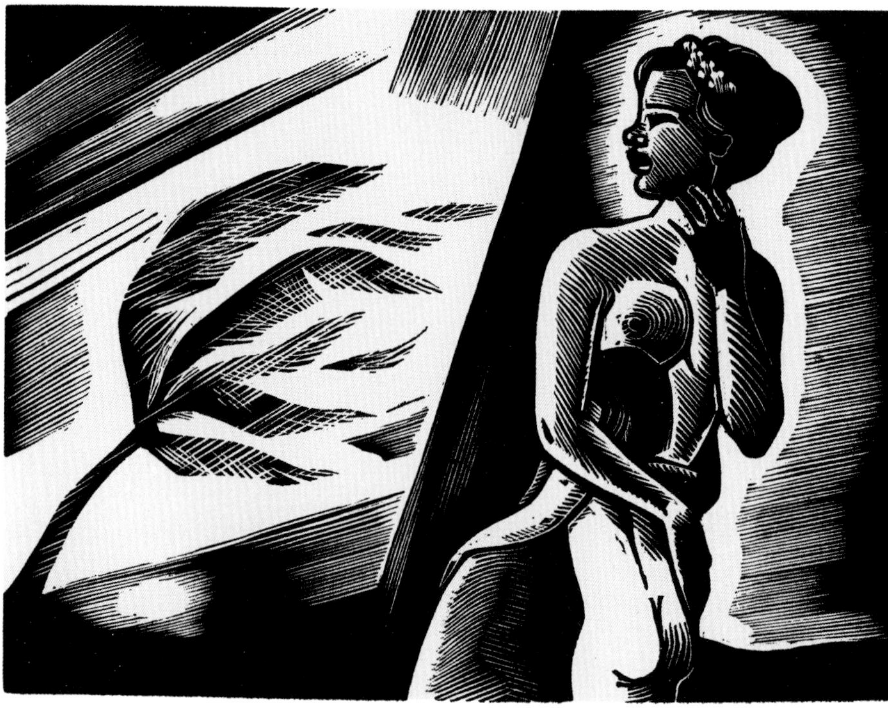

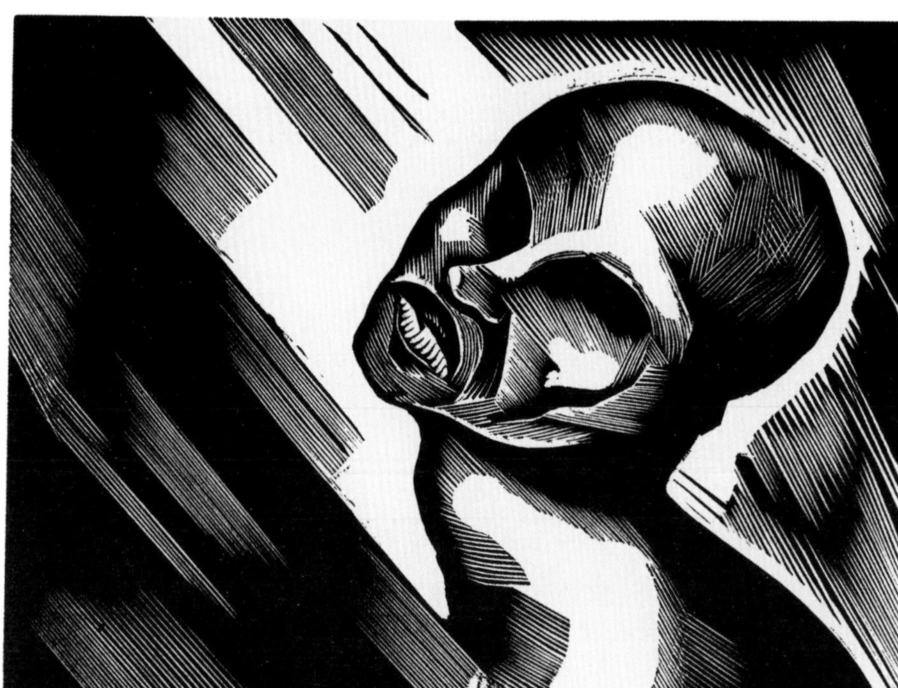

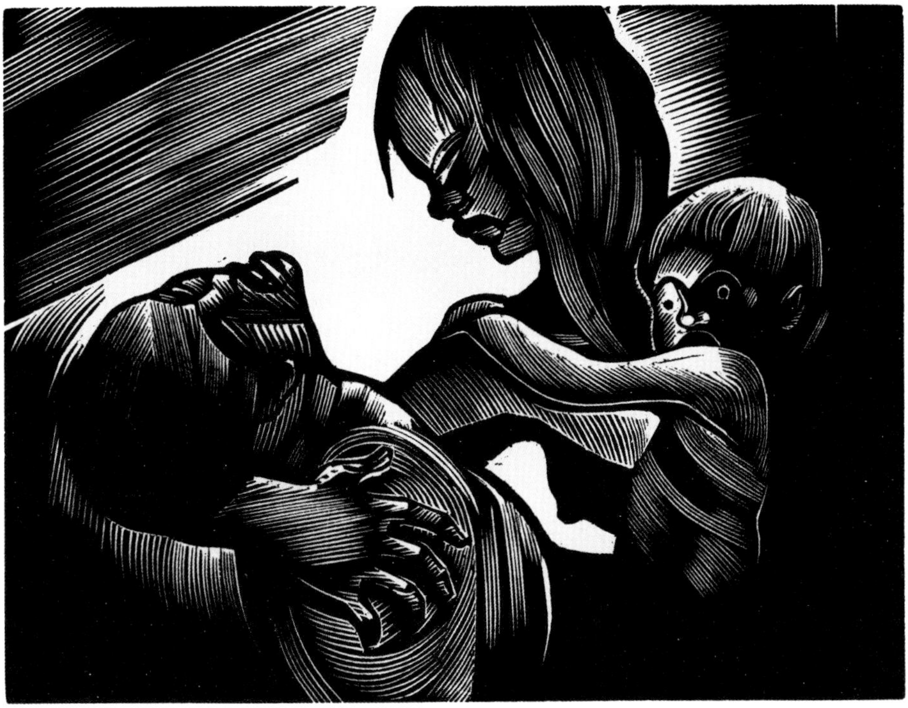

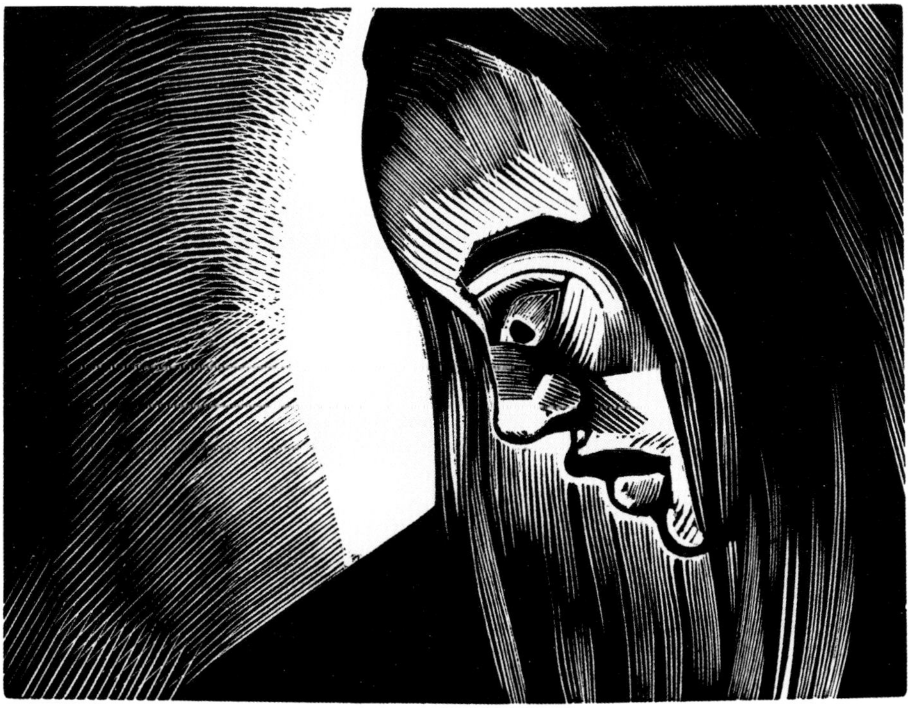

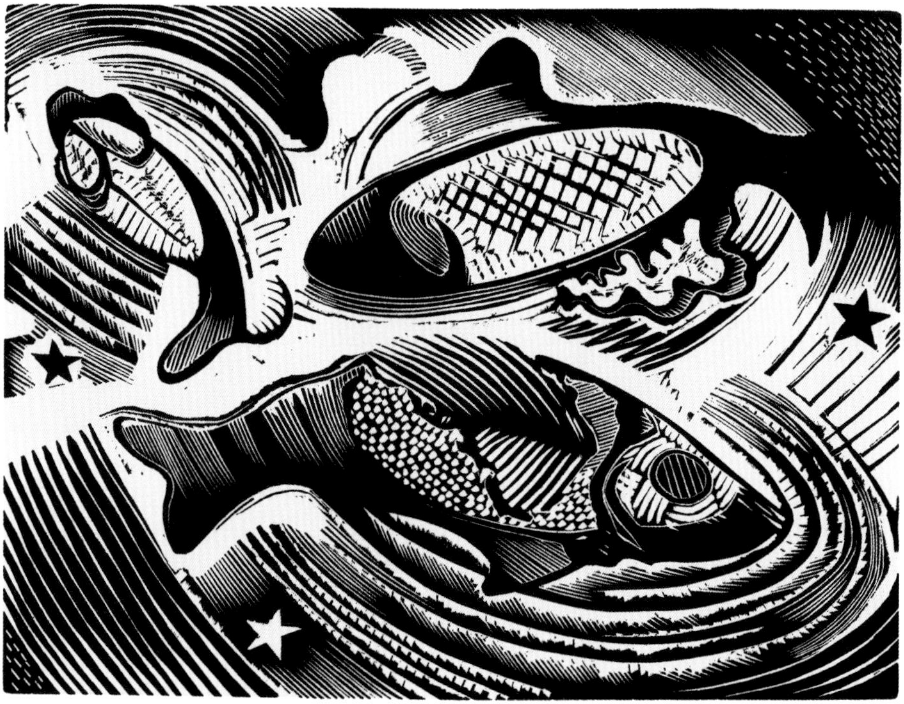

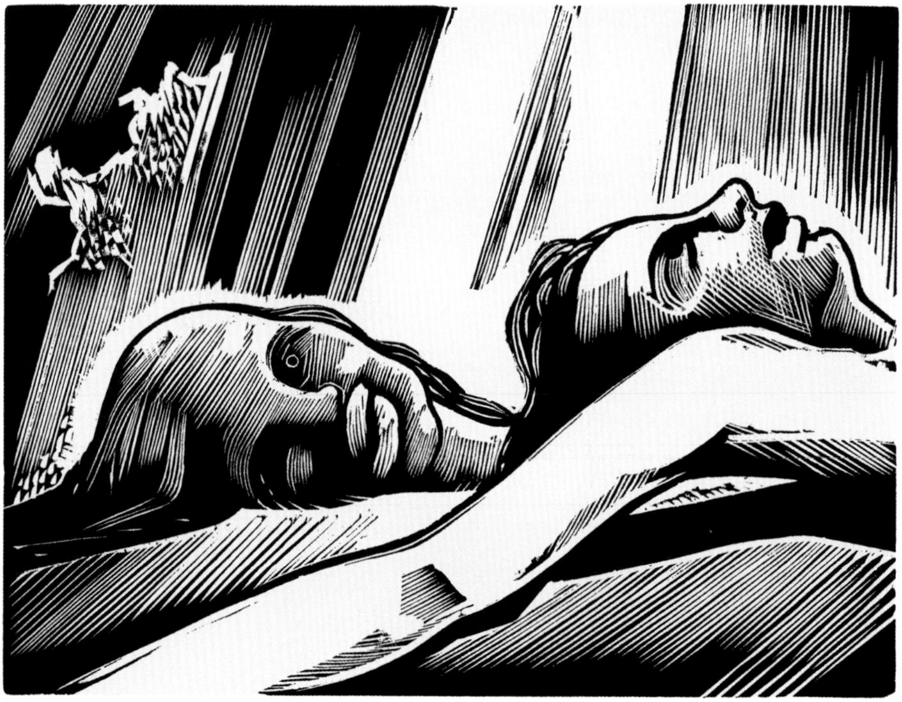

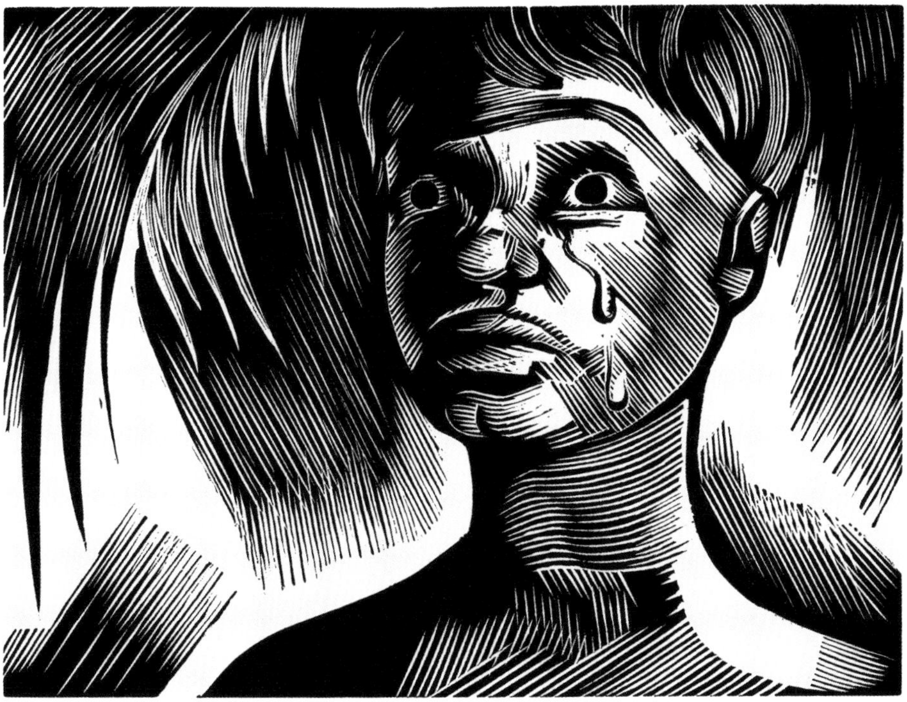

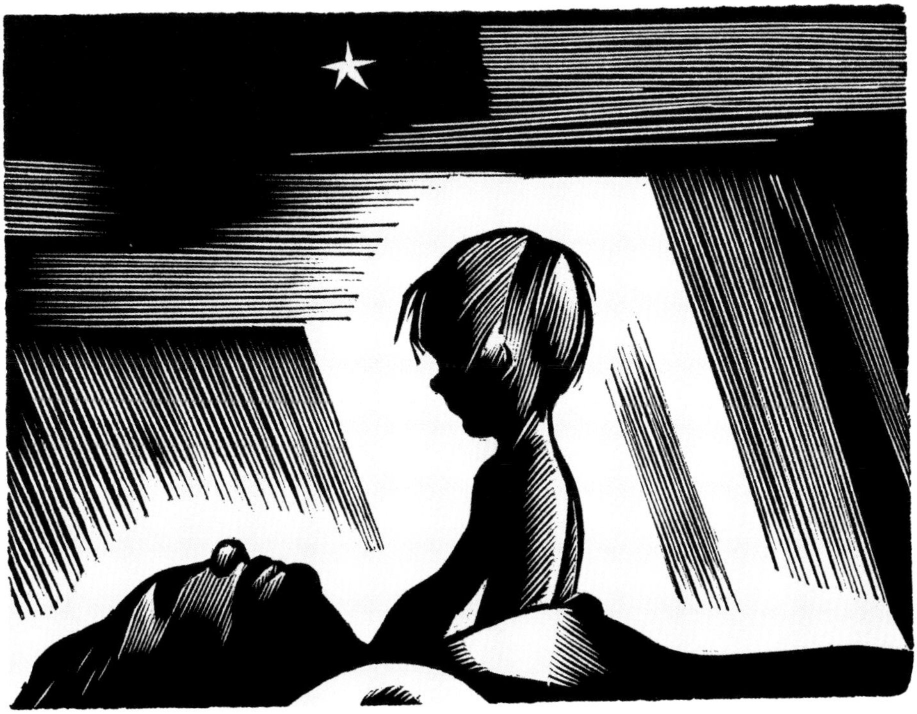

Chapter Eleven
Conclusion

One cannot finish looking at this sampling of woodcut novels and wordless books without recognizing the power in the images and content that creates an indelible impact on our lives. This artwork entertains on a general level with distinct stories and characters. In addition, the black-and-white images have a mystic quality that captivates readers, allowing us to identify with an entire range of human feelings. We smile at the innocence of the hero in Masereel's *Passionate Journey*, the bumbling antics in Gross's *He Done Her Wrong*, and fondly recollect childhood playfulness in Bochořákova's *Childhood*. We are angered at the abuse suffered by Nückel's heroine in *Destiny*, and the injustices endured by the general population exposed by Ward and Patri during the Depression. We are astonished at the surprise ending in Ward's *Gods' Man*, Masereel's allegorical musings in *The Sun*, and Gropper's dream sequence in *Alay-oop*. Who isn't sickened seeing the devastation of war in Szüts's *My War* and Hyde's *Southern Cross*? Even more mysterious are the personal reactions certain pictures or sequences have for individual readers, and the power these reactions have to open the door to self-discovery—a cathartic experience that is the highest achievement of art in any medium.

For decades the works of these visual artists have only been recognized as anomalies in the world of picture books. For example, the genre of the adult wordless book is only briefly acknowledged in the history of book illustration. This has changed with the growing public recognition of the graphic novel and masterpieces like *Kings in Disguise* by James Vance and Dan Burr, *Jimmy Corrigan: The Smartest Kid on Earth* by Chris Ware, *It's a Good Life if You Don't Weaken* by Seth, and the Pulitzer Prize-winning *Maus: A Survivor's Tale* by Art Spiegelman.

The influence of wordless books on graphic novels is noted in personal interviews and statements by the artists. Many have voiced the tremendous effect this early work had on their lives and, in some cases, attribute their career choice to the discovery of the woodcut novels of Masereel and Ward.

The obvious offspring are contemporary wordless novels like Eric Drooker's *Flood! A Novel in Pictures*, and Peter Kuper's *The System*, with their intense focus on social injustices and flare for metaphorical narrative. These books share with today's finest novels the capacity to create page-turning, imaginative stories that touch our lives. It is no coincidence that as the popularity of the contemporary graphic novel has risen, much of the work featured in this book—some long out of print—are currently being reprinted by recognized mainstream publishers.

These early woodcut novels and wordless books of the early twentieth century have now found their proper place in history—they are the original graphic novels.

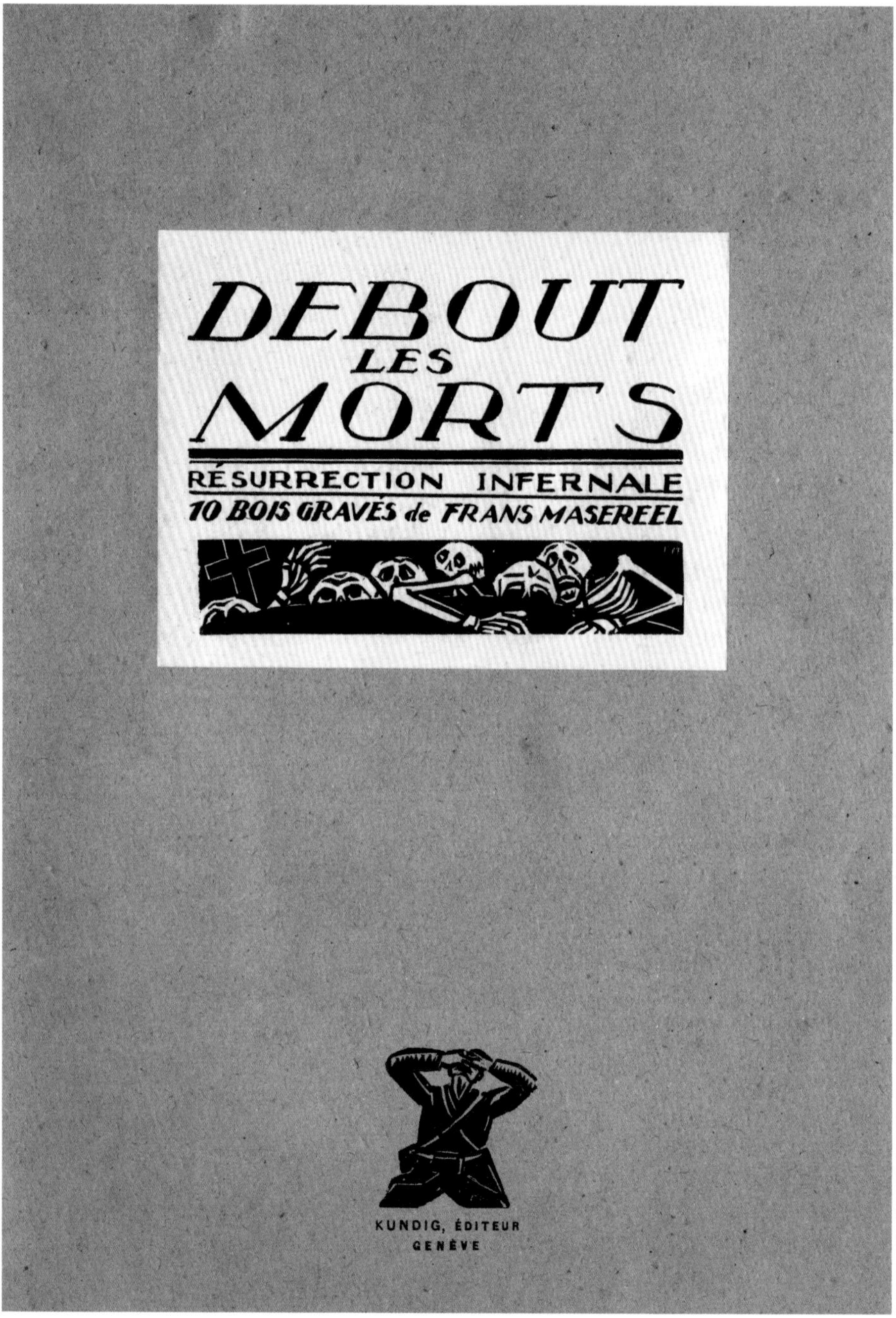
DEBOUT
LES
MORTS
RÉSURRECTION INFERNALE
10 BOIS GRAVÉS de FRANS MASEREEL
KUNDIG, ÉDITEUR
GENÈVE

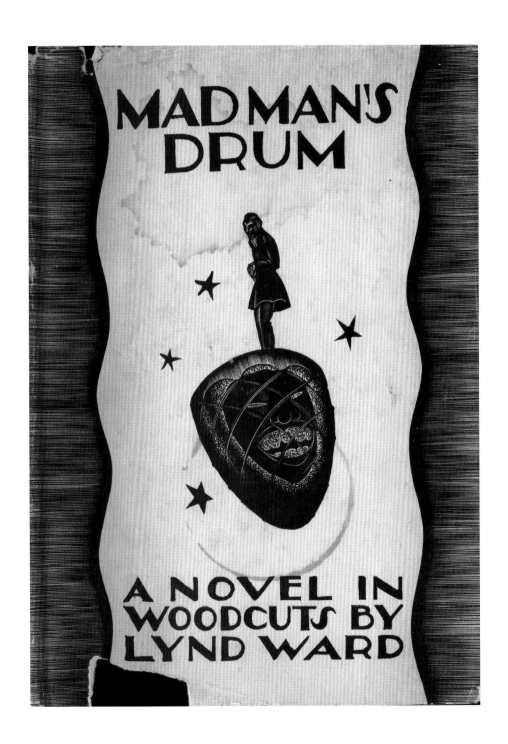

MAD MAN'S DRUM

A NOVEL IN
WOODCUTS BY
LYND WARD

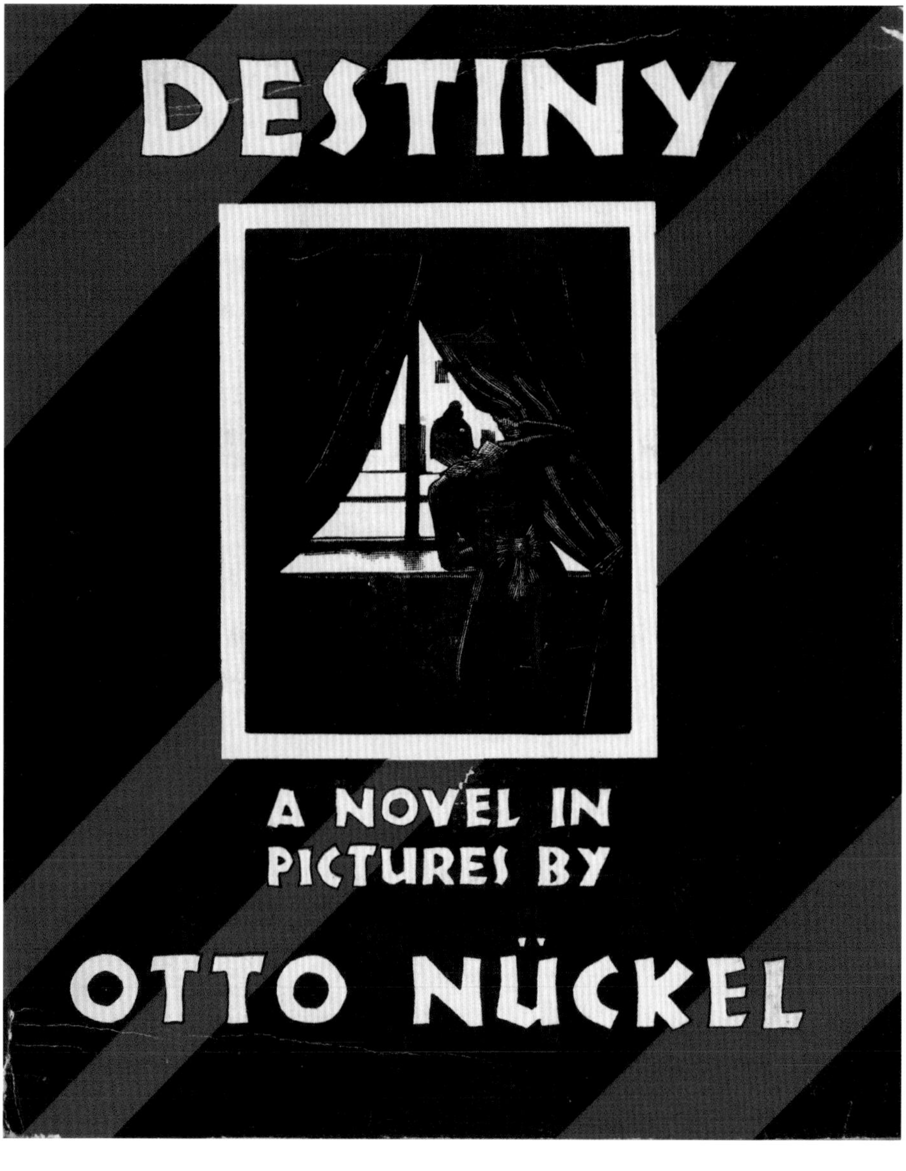
DESTINY
A NOVEL IN
PICTURES BY
OTTO NÜCKEL

CHILDHOOD

A. SWEMMER
LONDON, CHARING CROSS ROAD

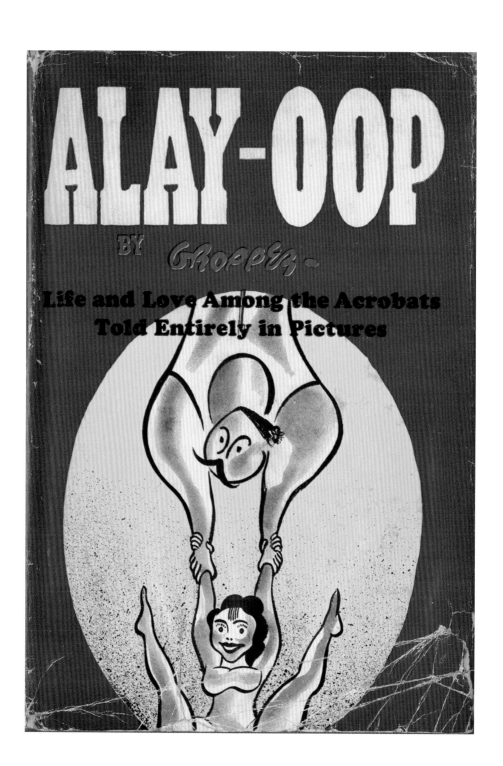

ALAY-OOP

BY GROPPER

Life and Love Among the Acrobats
Told Entirely in Pictures

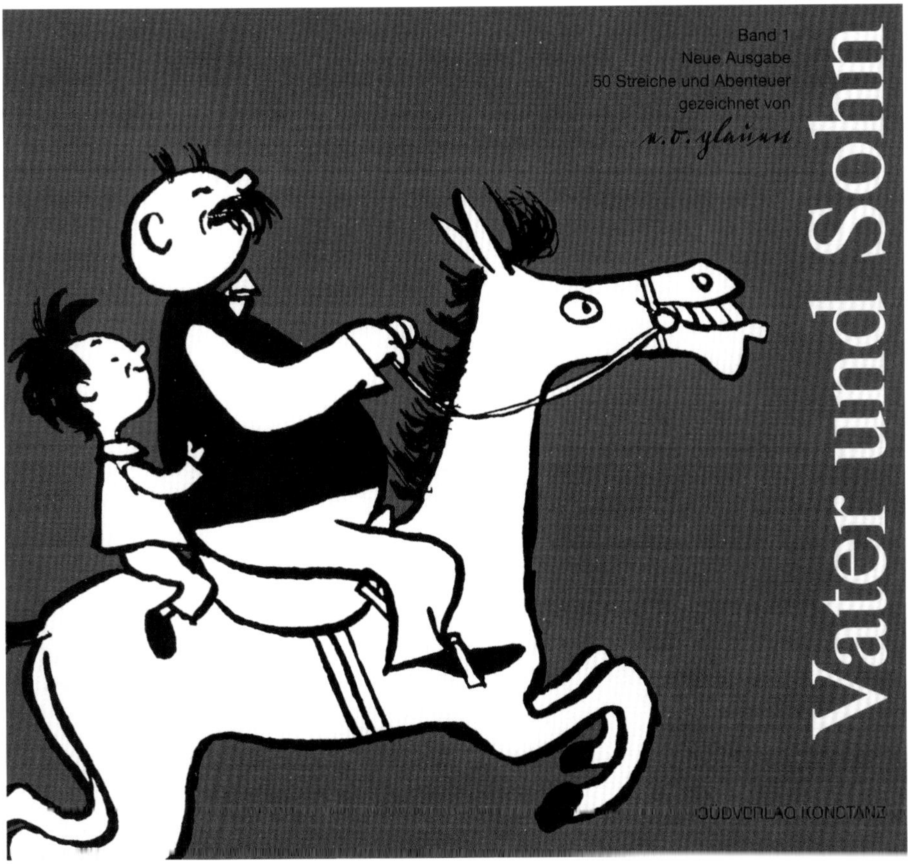
Band 1
Neue Ausgabe
50 Streiche und Abenteuer
gezeichnet von
Vater und Sohn
SÜDVERLAG KONSTANZ

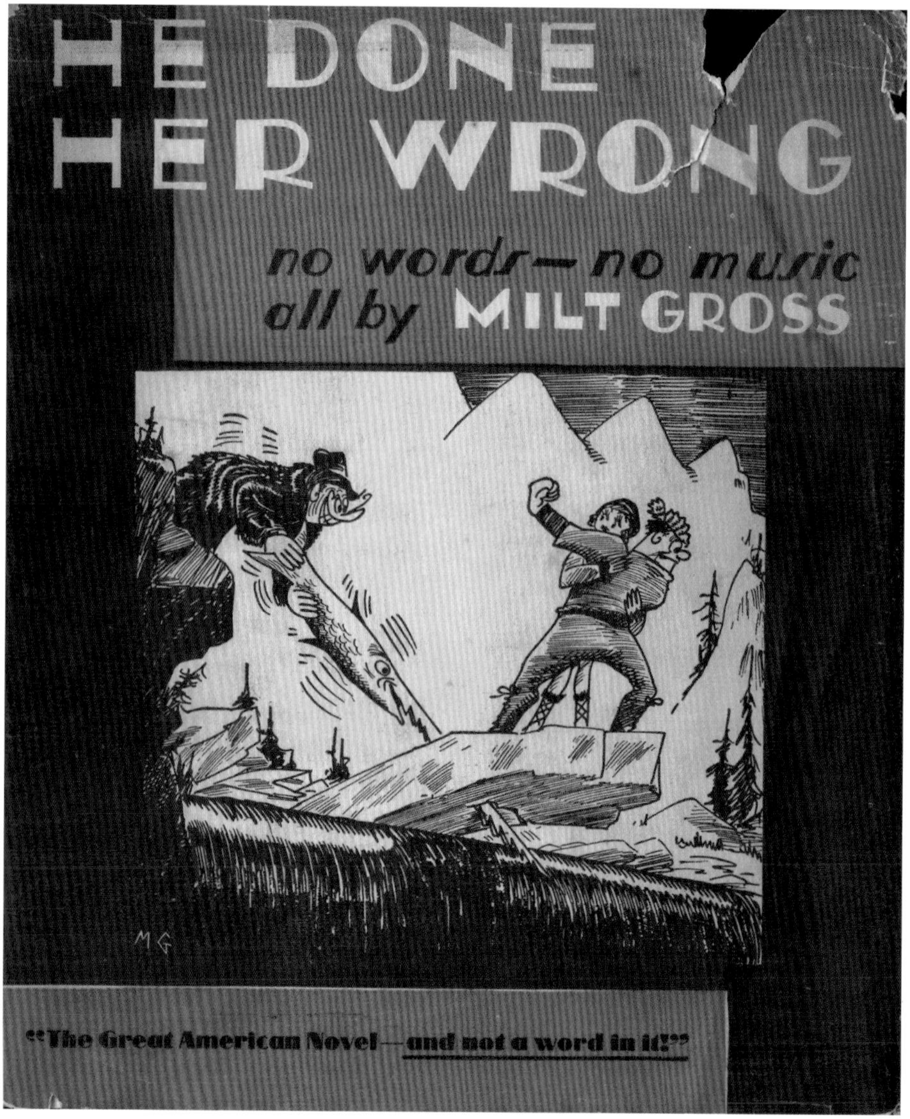
HE DONE
HER WRONG
no words—no music
all by MILT GROSS
MG
"The Great American Novel—and not a word in it!"

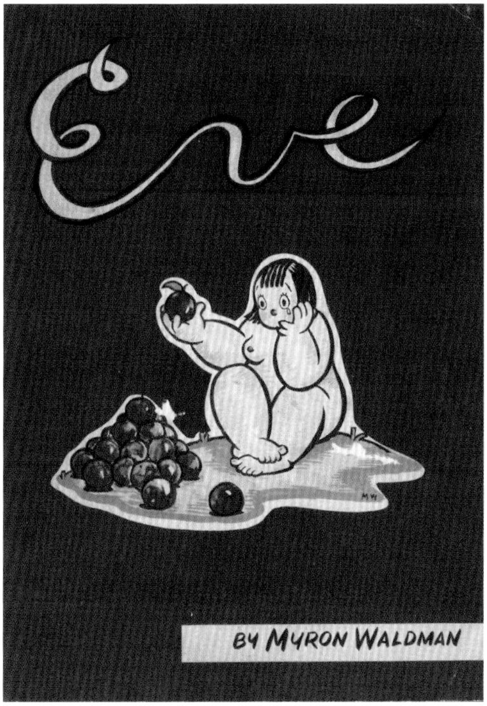
Eve
BY MYRON WALDMAN
MW

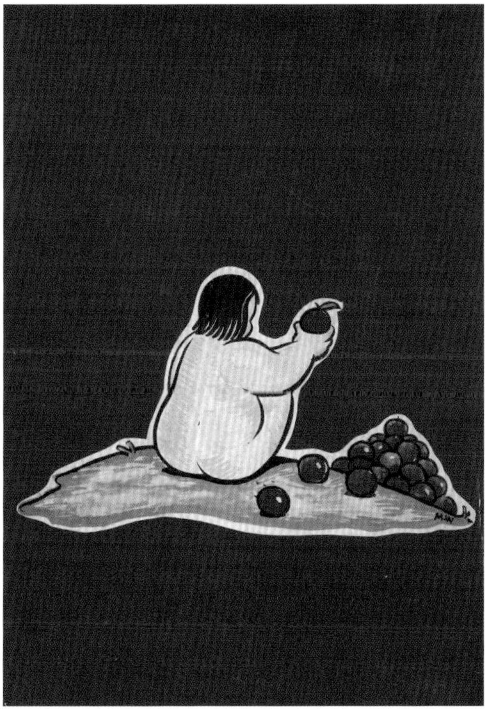
MW

MY WAR

by

SZEGEDI SZUTS

with an Introduction by
R. H. MOTTRAM

A sequence of 206 drawings which tell a story of youth and war.

A startling draughtsmanship—at once impressionistic and realistic—combines with a quick humanity to make this work of Szegedi Szuts emotionally disturbing and artistically fine.

AND PUBLISHED BY MORROW

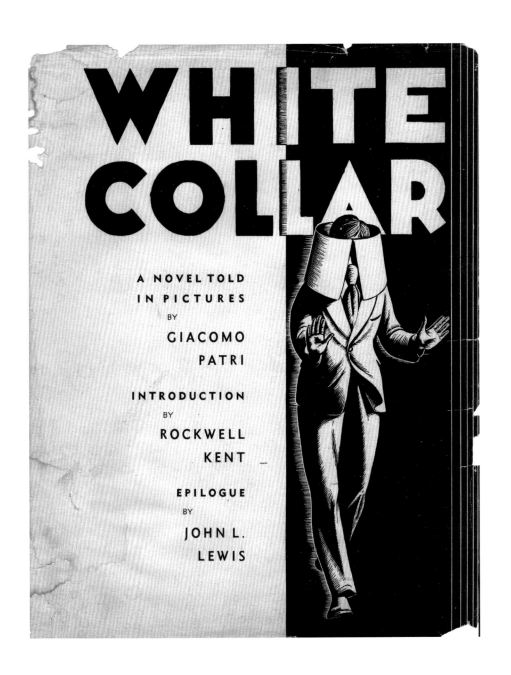

WHITE COLLAR

A NOVEL TOLD
IN PICTURES

BY

GIACOMO
PATRI

INTRODUCTION
BY

ROCKWELL
KENT

EPILOGUE
BY

JOHN L.
LEWIS

HYDE
SOUTHERN CROSS
WARD RITCHIE
PRESS

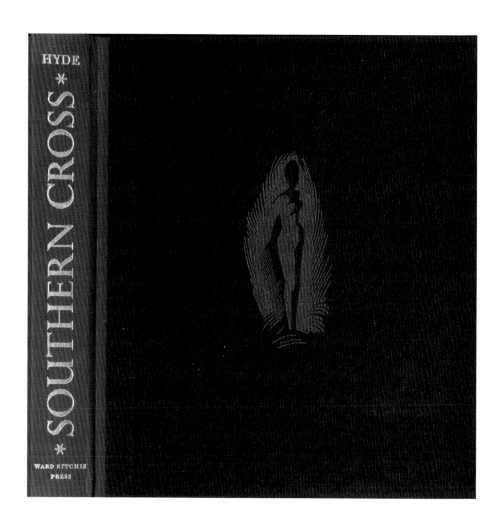

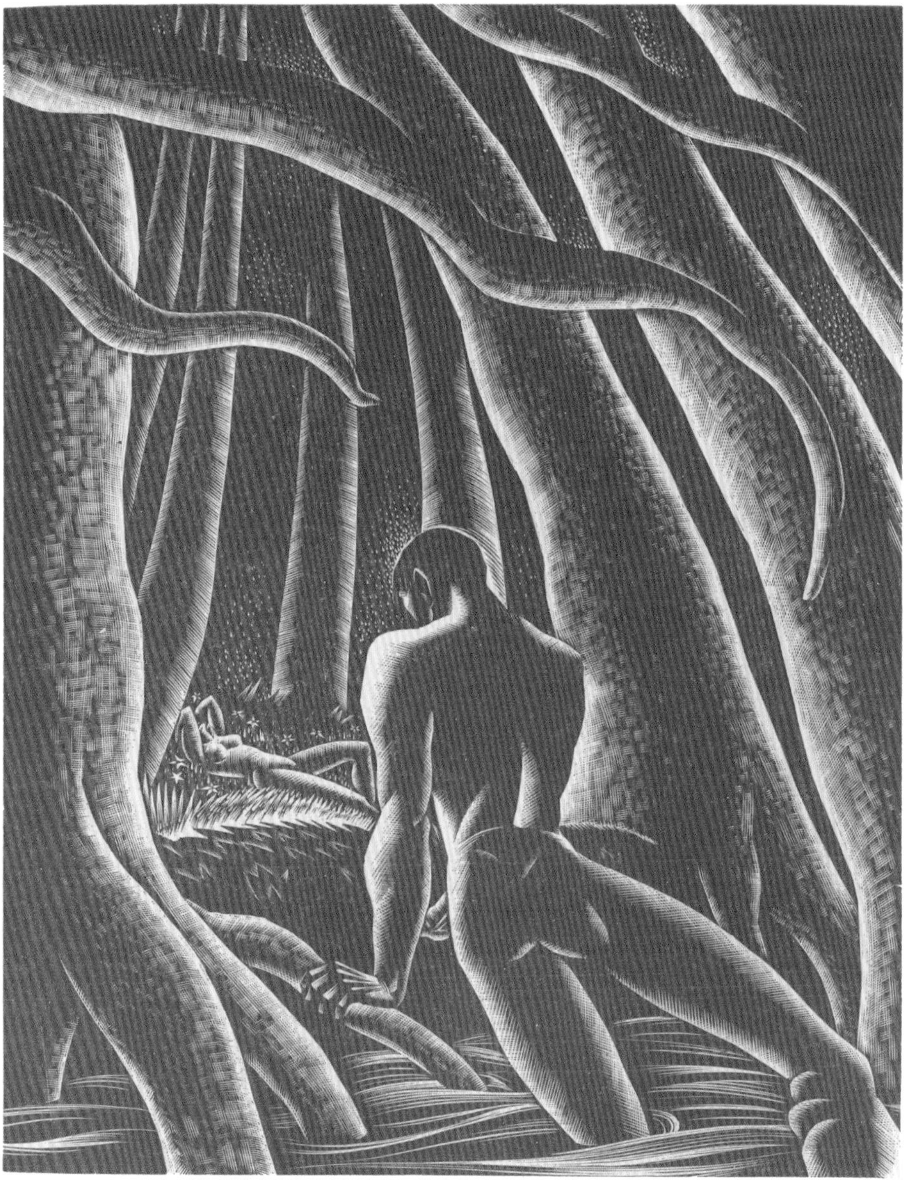

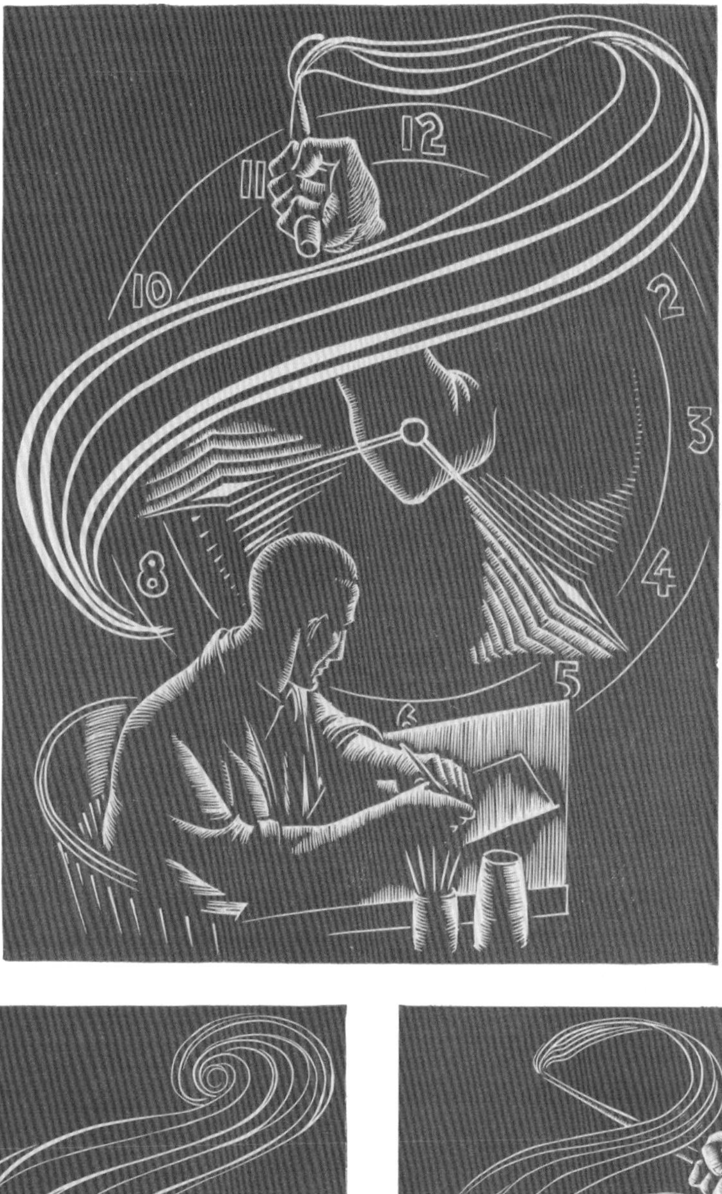
12
11
10
2
3
4
5
6
8

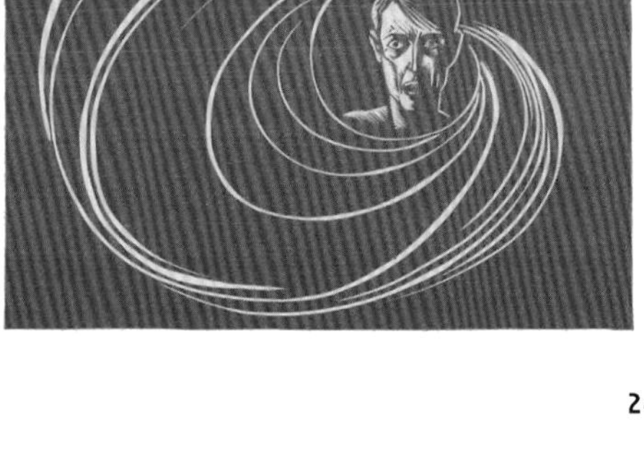

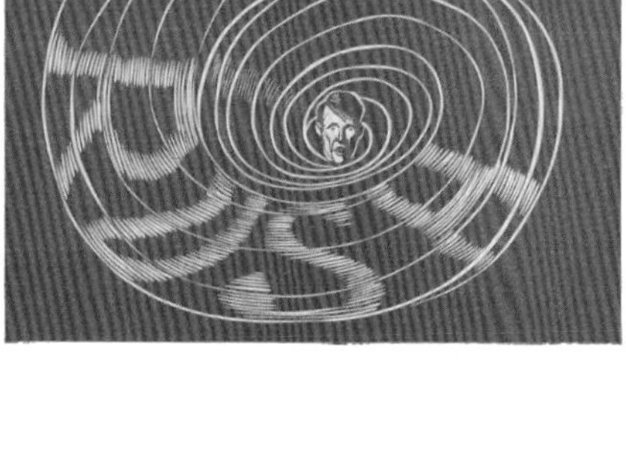

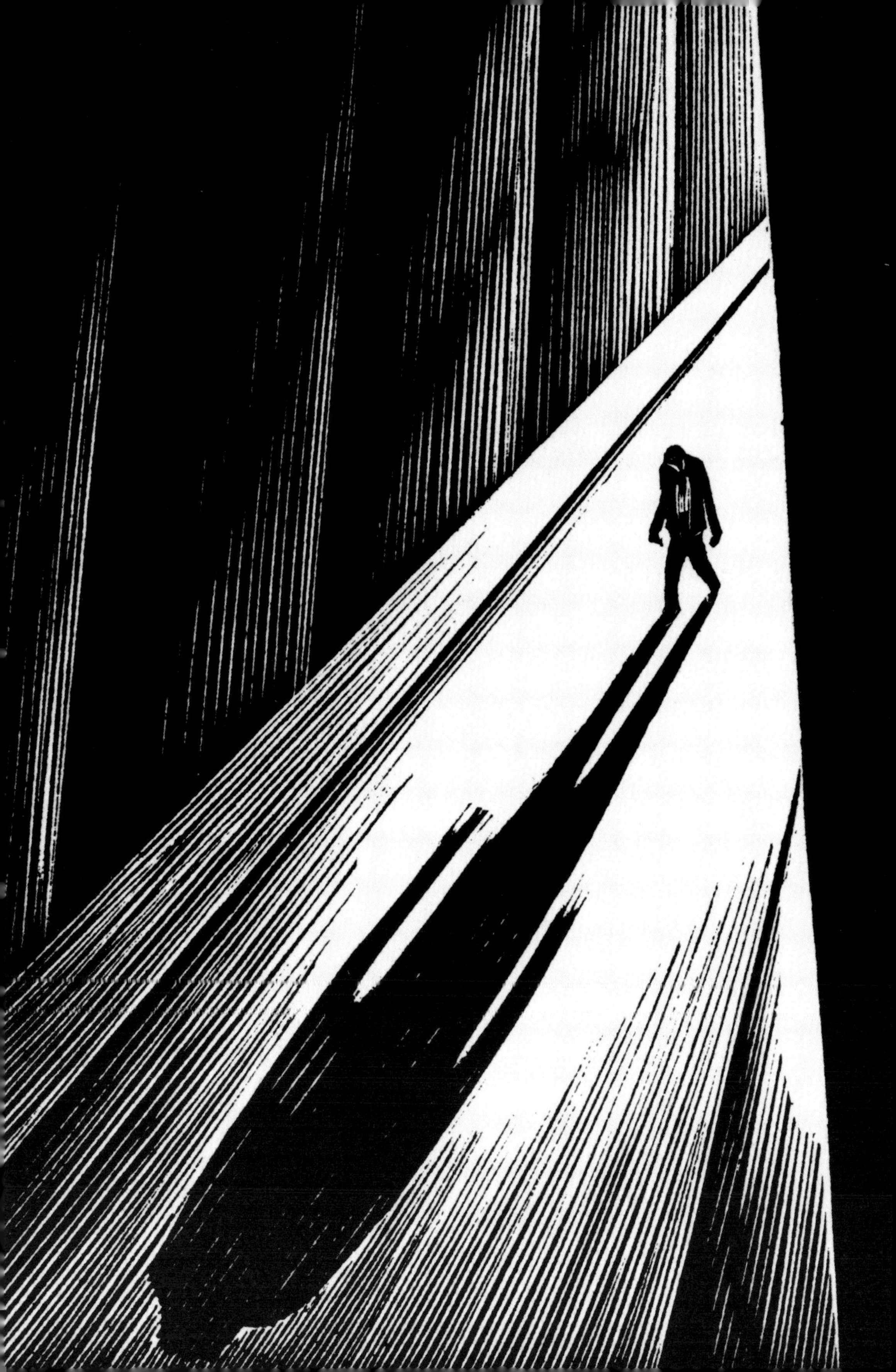

List of Works

MY BOOK
OF HOURS
167 DESIGNS ENGRAVED
ON WOOD BY
FRANS MASEREEL
Foreword by-ROMAIN ROLLAND

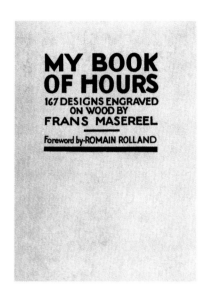

Frans Masereel

NOTE: For a complete list of the many editions of Frans Masereel's work, refer to either one of these two extensive bibliographies:

Avermaete, Roger. *Frans Masereel.* Bibliography and catalogue by Pierre Vorms and Hanns-Conon von der Gabelentz. New York: Rizzoli, 1977.

Ritter, Paul. *Frans Masereel: eine annotierte Bibliographie.* Munich: K.G. Saure, 1992.

For the works listed below, only the original edition is included, as well as the first edition published by Kurt Wolff, and subsequent English language editions.

25 Images de la Passion d'un Homme. Genève: Édité par Frans Masereel, 1918.

Die Passion eines Menschen. München: Kurt Wolff, 1921.

Graphic Witness: Four Wordless Graphic Novels by Frans Masereel, Lynd Ward, Giacomo Patri, and Laurence Hyde. Selected and introduced by George A. Walter. Richmond Hill, Ontario: Firefly Books, 2007.

Mon livre d'heures: 167 images dessinées et gravées sur bois. Genève: A. Kundig, 1919.

Mein Studenbuch: 167 Holzschnitte. München: K. Wolff, 1920.

My Book of Hours: 167 Designs Engraved in Wood. Paris: Se trouve chez l' auteur, 1922.

Passionate Journey: A Novel in 165 Woodcuts. New York: Lear, 1948.

Passionate Journey. New York: Dover Publications, 1971.

Passionate Journey: A Novel in 165 Woodcuts. New York: Penguin Books, 1988.

———. San Francisco: City Lights Books, 1988.

Le soleil: 63 images dessinées et gravées sur bois. Genève: Éditions du Sablier, 1919.
Die Sonne: 63 Holzschnitte. München: K. Wolff, 1920.
The Sun: a Novel Told in 63 Woodcuts. London: Redstone, 1990.

Histoire sans paroles. 60 images dessinées et gravées sur bois. Genève: Éditions du Sablier, 1920.
Geschichte ohne Worte: 60 Holzschnitte. München: K. Wolff, 1922.
The Idea and Story Without Words. Two Novels Told in Woodcuts. London: Redstone Press, 1986.

Idée, sa naissance, sa vie, sa mort: 83 images, dessinées et gravées sur bois. Paris. Édition Ollendorf, 1920.
Die Idee: 83 Holzschnitte. München: K. Wolff, 1924.
Story Without Words; and, The Idea: Two Novels Told in Woodcuts. London: Redstone Press, 1986.

La Ville: cent bois gravés. Paris: A. Morencé, 1925.
———. Paris: Pierre Vorms, 1928.
La Ville: cent gravures sur bois. Belvès: Pierre Vorms, 1961.
The City. New York, Dover Publications, 1972.
The City: 100 Woodcuts. London: Redstone Press, 1988.
The City. New York: Schocken Books, 1989.
The City: A Vision in Woodcuts. Mineola, New York: Dover Publications, 2006.

L'oeuvre: soixante bois gravés. Paris: Pierre Vorms, 1928.
Das Werk: 60 Holzschnitte von Frans Masereel. K. Wolff, 1928

GODS' MAN
A NOVEL IN WOODCUTS
BY
LYND WARD

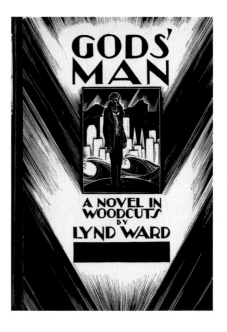

Lynd Ward

Gods' Man: A Novel in Woodcuts. New York: Jonathan Cape and Harrison Smith, 1929.

———. London: Jonathan Cape, 1930.

———. Cleveland: World Publishing Company, 1966.

———. New York: St. Martin's Press, 1978.

———. Toronto: Eric S. Rosen Publishing, 1997.

———. Mineola, New York: Dover Publication, Inc., 2004.

Madman's Drum: A Novel in Woodcuts. New York: Jonathan Cape and Harrison Smith, 1930.

———. London: Jonathan Cape, 1930.

———. Tokyo: Kokusho Kankokai, 2002.

———. New York: Dover Publications, 2005.

Wild Pilgrimage. New York: H. Smith & R. Haas, 1932.

———. Cleveland: World Publishing Company, 1960.

Graphic Witness: Four Wordless Graphic Novels by Frans Masereel, Lynd Ward, Giacomo Patri and Laurence Hyde. Selected and introduced by George A. Walker. Richmond Hill, Ontario: Firefly Books, 2007.

Prelude to a Million Years: A Book of Wood Engravings. New York: Equinox, 1933.

Song Without Words: A Book of Engravings on Wood. New York: Random House, 1936.

Vertigo. New York: Random House, 1937.

Storyteller Without Words: The Wood Engravings of Lynd Ward. New York: Harry N. Abrams, Inc., 1974.

Otto Nückel

Des Schicksal; eine Geschichte in Bildern. München: Delphin Verlag, [1928?].

Destiny: A Novel in Pictures. New York: Farrar & Rinehart, Inc., 1930.

Schicksal eine Geschichte in Bildern. Zürich: Limmat Verlag Genossenschaft, 1984.

Destin. Paris: IMHO, 2005.

Destiny: A Novel in Pictures. New York: Dover Publications, 2007.

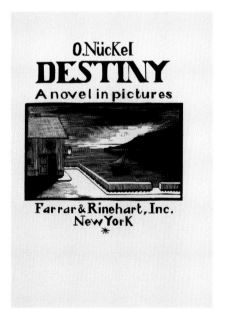

O.Nückel

DESTINY
A novel in pictures

Farrar & Rinehart, Inc.
New York
*

Helena Bochořáková-Dittrichová

Enfance. Gravures sur bois. Paris: Dorbon-aîné, 1930.

Childhood: A Cycle of Woodcuts. London: A. Zwemmer, 1931.

William Gropper

Alay-oop. New York: Coward-McCann, Inc., 1930.

e.o. plauen

Vater und Sohn. Berlin: Ullstein, 1936.

———. Konstanz Germany: Südverlag GmbH, 1949, 1962, 1993.

Milt Gross

He Done Her Wrong: The Great American Novel and Not a Word in It—No Music, Too. Garden City,
    New York: Doubleday, Doran & Company, 1930.

———. New York: Dell Publishing Company, Inc., 1963.

———. New York: Dover Publications, 1971.

Hearts of Gold: The Great American Novel and Not a Word in It—No Music, Too. New York: Abbeville
    Press, 1983.

He Done Her Wrong: The Great American Novel and Not a Word in It—No Music, Too. Seattle:
    Fantagraphics Press, 2005.

Myron Waldman

Eve. New York: Stephen Daye, 1943.

István Szegedi Szüts

My War. London: John Lane, 1931.

————. New York: W. Morrow & Co., 1932.

Giacomo Patri

White Collar: A Novel in Linocuts. San Francisco: Pisani Printing and Pub. Co., 1940.

————. Millbrook, CA: Celestial Arts, 1975.

Graphic Witness: Four Wordless Graphic Novels by Frans Masereel, Lynd Ward, Giacomo Patri, and Laurence Hyde. Selected and introduced by George A. Walker. Richmond Hill, Ontario: Firefly Books, 2007.

Laurence Hyde

Southern Cross: A Novel of the South Seas Told in Wood Engravings by Laurence Hyde. Los Angeles: Ward Ritchie Press, 1951.

————. Montreal: Drawn & Quarterly Books, 2007.

Graphic Witness: Four Wordless Graphic Novels by Frans Masereel, Lynd Ward, Giacomo Patri, and Laurence Hyde. Selected and introduced by George A. Walker. Richmond Hill, Ontario: Firefly Books, 2007.

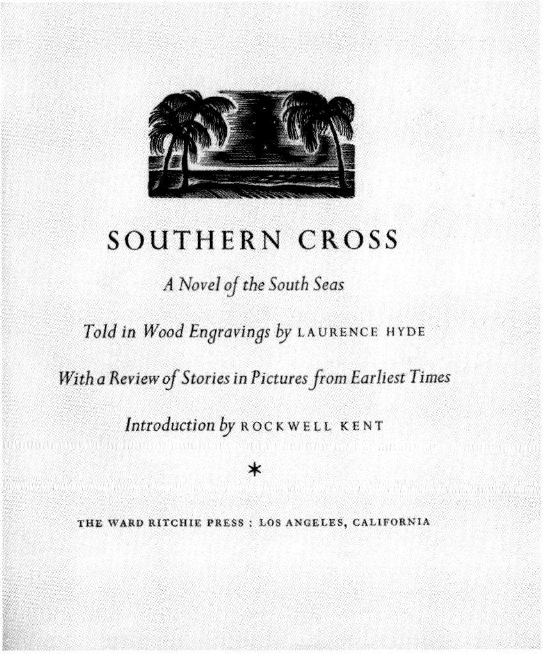

SOUTHERN CROSS

A Novel of the South Seas

Told in Wood Engravings by LAURENCE HYDE

With a Review of Stories in Pictures from Earliest Times

Introduction by ROCKWELL KENT

THE WARD RITCHIE PRESS : LOS ANGELES, CALIFORNIA

Permissions/Copyrights

Frans Masereel

Debout Les Morts (1917). Woodcut, 5 ¾ x 4 ¼ in.

25 Images de la Passion d'un Homme (1918). Woodcut, 4 ⅞ x 3 ¾ in.; 5 x 4 ⅛ in.; 5 x 4 ¼ in.; 5 ¼ x 4 ¼ in.; 5 ⅜ x 4 ⅛.

Passionate Journey (1919). Woodcut, 3 ½ x 2 ⅝ in.

The Sun (1919). Woodcut, 3 ⅞ x 3 ⅛ in.

Story Without Words (1920). Woodcut, 3 ½ x 2 ⅜ in.

The Idea (1920). Woodcut, 3 ½ x 2 ⅝ in.

The City (1925). Woodcut, 5 x 3 ⅜ in.

Das Werk (1928). Woodcut, 3 ⅝ x 2 ⅞ in.

Lynd Ward

Gods' Man (1929). Wood engraving, 4 x 3 in.; 4 ¾ x 3 in.; 5 x 3 in.; 5 x 3 ½ in.; 5 x 4 in.; 6 x 4 in.

Madman's Drum (1930). Wood engraving, 5 x 4 ½ in.; 5 ½ x 3 ¾ in.; 6 ½ x 4 ½ in.

Wild Pilgrimage (1932). Wood engraving, 5 x 4 ½ in.; 6 ½ x 4 ½ in.

Prelude to a Million Years (1933). Wood engraving, 5 x 3 in.; 5 ¼ x 3 ¼ in.

Song Without Words (1936). Wood engraving, 5 ⅝ x 3 ⅝ in.

Vertigo (1937). Wood engraving, 3 ½ x 2 in.; 3 ½ x 3 ½ in.; 5 x 3 ½ in.

Otto Nückel

Destiny: A Novel in Pictures (1930). Leadcut, 2 ¾ x 2 ¾ in.; 2 ¾ x 4 in.; 2 ¾ x 4 ¾ in.; 3 ½ x 2 ¾ in.; 3 ⅝ x 2 ⅞ in.; 4 x 2 ¾ in.; 4 ¾ x 2 ¾ in.; 4 ¾ x 4 in.

Helena Bochořáková-Dittrichová

Childhood: A Cycle of Woodcuts (1931). Woodcut, 3 ⅝ x 2 ¾ in.

William Gropper

Alay-oop (1930). Crayon, pen and ink, 7 ⅞ x 5 ⅜ in.; 7 ⅞ x 10 ¾ in.

e.o. plauen

Vater und Sohn in Gesamtausgabe. Erich Ohser © Südverlag GmbH, Konstanz, Germany, 2000.

  Vater und Sohn (1936). Pen and ink, 6 ¾ x 6 ⅝ in.

Milt Gross

© Milt Gross

  He Done Her Wrong: The Great American Novel and Not a Word in It—No Music, Too (1930).
  Pen and ink, 2 x 2 ¼ in.; 2 ½ x 3 in.; 2 ¾ x 4 ½ in.; 3 ½ x 3 ¼ in.; 3 ½ x 4 ½ in.; 4 x 4 in.;
  4 ¼ x 3 in.; 4 ½ x 3 ¾ in.; 5 x 4 ¼ in.; 5 x 5 in.; 5 ¼ x 4 in.; 5 ⅜ x 4 ¼ in.; 5 ⅝ x 3 in.;
  5 ⅝ x 4 ½ in.; 8 x 7 in.

Myron Waldman

© Myron Waldman

  Eve (1943). Pen and ink, 5 x 4 ½ in.; 10 ¾ x 8 in.

István Szegedi Szüts

© István Szegedi Szüts

  My War (1931). Pen and ink, 6 x 4 ½ in.

Giacomo Patri

© Giacomo Patri. Used by permission of Georges Rey, Trustee of the estates of Giacomo and Tamara Rey Patri.

  White Collar: A Novel in Linocuts (1940). Linocut, 2 ½ x 2 ¾ in.; 2 ½ x 4 ¼ in.; 3 ⅛ x 2 ⅝ in.;
  3 ¼ x 3 ¾ in.; 3 ½ x 2 ½ in.; 4 ¼ x 4 ⅝ in.; 4 ⅜ x 3 ¼ in.; 4 ⅜ x 4 ½ in.; 4 ¾ x 3 ½ in.;
  4 ¾ x 4 in.; 5 ⅛ x 3 ¾ in.; 5 ⅛ x 3 ⅞ in.; 5 ¼ x 3 ⅞ in.; 5 ¼ x 4 ⅛ in.; 5 ½ x 4 ½ in.;
  5 ½ x 4 ¾ in.; 5 ½ x 4 ¾ in.; 5 ¾ x 4 ½ in.; 5 ¾ x 4 ⅝ in.; 6 x 4 ¼ in.; 6 ⅛ x 4 ⅜ in.;
  6 ⅛ x 4 ½ in.; 6 ¼ x 4 ⅜ in.; 6 ¼ x 5 ⅛ in.; 6 ⅜ x 4 ⅝ in.; 6 ½ x 4 ⅞ in.; 6 ⅞ x 4 ½ in.

Laurence Hyde

© The Estate of Laurence Hyde

  Southern Cross: A Novel of the South Seas (1951). Wood engraving, 3 x 4 ⅛ in.

Sources

Chapter One

Eisner, Will. *Graphic Storytelling*. Tamarac, FL: Poorhouse Press, 1996. P. 1.

Ginsberg, Allen. *Howl: Original Draft Facsimile, Transcript & Variant Versions, Fully Annotated by Author, with Contemporaneous Correspondence, Account of First Public Reading, Legal Skirmishes, Precursor Texts & Bibliography*. Edited by Barry Mills. New York: Harper & Row Publishers, 1986. P. 139.

Harvey, R. C. *The Art of the Comic Book: An Aesthetic History*. Jackson: University Press of Mississippi, 1996. P. 68.

Lang, Lothar. *Expressionist Book Illustration in Germany 1907–1927*. Boston, MA: New York Graphic Society, 1976. P. 70.

McCloud, Scott. *Understanding Comics: The Invisible Eye*. Northampton, MA: Kitchen Sink Press, 1993. P. 18.

Chapter Two

Avermaete, Roger. *Frans Masereel*. London: Thames and Hudson, 1977. P. 26.

Lanier, Chris. "Frans Masereel: A Thousand Words." *The Comics Journal,* no. 208, (November 1998). P. 114.

Willett, Perry. *The Silent Shout: Frans Masereel, Lynd Ward, and the Novel in Woodcuts*. Bloomington: Indiana University Libraries, 1997. P. 20.

Chapter Three

McCurdy, Michael. Personal interview conducted on June 21, 1996.

Ward, Lynd. *Storyteller Without Words: The Wood Engravings of Lynd Ward*. New York: Harry N. Abrams, Inc., 1974. P. 22.

Chapter Four
Lehmann-Haupt, Dr. H. "The Picture Novel Arrives in America." *Publishers Weekly*. (February 1, 1930). P. 612.

Chapter Five
Novák, Arne. "Introduction," in Helena Bochořáková-Dittrichová, *Childhood; A Cycle of Woodcuts*. London: A. Zwemmer, 1931. P. [5].

Chapter Six
Lozowick, Louis, and William Gropper. *William Gropper*. Philadelphia: Art Alliance Press, 1983. P. 39.

Chapter Seven
Horn, Maurice (ed.). *The World Encyclopedia of Comics*. New York: Chelsea House Publishers, 1976. P. 526.

Chapter Eight
Mottram, R.H. Introduction to István Szegedi Szüts, *My War*. London: John Lane, 1931. P. [xi].

Chapter Nine
Kent, Rockwell. Introduction to *White Collar: A Novel in Linocuts* by Giacomo Patri. Millbrook, CA: Celestial Arts, 1975. P. 9.
Rey, Georges. "San Francisco's Cultural Cioppino." http://carnap.umd.edu/chps/Faculty/Rey.html (November 26, 2004).

Chapter Ten
Ainslie, Patricia. "Laurence Hyde: An Interview". *The Devil's Artisan: A Journal of the Printing Arts,* no. 21 (1987) and no. 22 (1988).
———. *The Wood Engravings of Laurence Hyde*. Calgary: Glenbow Museum, 1986.
Cohen, Martin. S. "The Novel in Woodcuts: A Handbook." *Journal of Modern Literature*. 6:2 (April 1977): 171–195.

Index

About the Author

David A. Beronä is a historian of woodcut novels and wordless comics who has published and presented papers widely on wordless books and is on the editorial board of the *International Journal of Comic Art*. He is also the director of Lamson Library at Plymouth State University, New Hampshire, and a visiting faculty member at the Center for Cartoon Studies, White River Junction, Vermont. David A. Beronä lives with his wife, Rose O'Brien, in Gilmanton, New Hampshire.

Acknowledgments

I wish to thank Father Alfred Drapp, David McDargh, Robert Heman, Calvin Vance, and Garth Walker, who encouraged me to see things differently from an early age; my friend since childhood, David Boyer from Enon, Ohio; and my dearest departed friend, Chris Handley, who taught me to live fully one day at a time.

My comics research would never have started without the support of the late art historian and a communications theorist, Professor Estelle Jussim from Simmons College, Boston. I want to thank John Lent, prolific author and managing editor of the *International Journal of Comic Art*, who opened the doors for my journal publications, and Lucy Caswell, curator of the Cartoon Research Library, Ohio State University, and former editor of *INKS: Cartoon and Comic Art Studies*, who published my first article on wordless books. I also wish to thank the support for my early research from Roberta Gray, Library Director, and Mary Ann Wallace, Curator of the Maine Women's Writers Collection, both from Westbrook College, Portland, Maine; and Claudia Morner, librarian at the University of New Hampshire.

Special thanks to Perry Willett, Chris Lanier, Kurt Brian Webb, Robert Young, Judith M. Friebert, George A. Walker, Patricia Ainslie, Arthur Jaffe, and Ed Ripp who have shared their knowledge and interest in woodcut novels during the last twenty years. A special note of thanks goes to Nanda Ward, Robin Ward Savage, Georges Rey, Anthony Hyde, and Gene Gropper for their support.

My personal thanks go out to James Sturm, artist and director of the Center for Cartoon Studies, who had faith in my book and introduced me to my agent Judy Hansen, who believed wholeheartedly in my book from the very start. Finally, I want to thank my editor Charles Kochman for his zeal and insight; his assistant Sofia Gutiérrez; Anet Sirna-Bruder in production; and book designer Robert McKee for his exciting visual ideas.

Editor: Charles Kochman
Editorial Assistant: Sofia Gutiérrez
Designer: Robert McKee
Production Manager: Anet Sirna-Bruder

Front cover: Giacomo Patri
Back cover: Frans Masereel

Library of Congress Cataloging-in-Publication Data

Beronä, David A.
    Wordless books : the original graphic novels / by
David A. Beronä ; introduction by Peter Kuper.
        p. cm.
    ISBN 978-0-8109-9469-0 (harry n. abrams)
    1. Wood-engraving—20th century. 2. Graphic
novels—History and criticism. I. Title.

    NE1095.B47 2008
    769.9'041—dc22
                        2007041336

Printed and bound in China
10 9 8 7 6 5 4 3 2 1

HNA
harry n. abrams, inc.
a subsidiary of La Martinière Groupe
115 West 18th Street
New York, NY 10011
www.hnabooks.com